THE LIVING WORD COMMENTARY

Editor
Everett Ferguson

The Letters of Paul to Timothy and Titus

The Letters of Paul to Timothy and Titus

Carl Spain

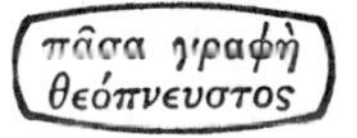

R. B. SWEET CO., INC.

Austin, Texas

Library of Congress Catalog Card Number: 75-133509

Standard Book Number: 8344-0006-5

PRINTED IN U.S.A.

Acknowledgment

This commentary is based on the text of the Revised Standard Version of the Bible, copyrighted 1946 and 1952 by the Division of Christian Education, National Council of Churches, and used by permission.

Writers in *The Living Word Commentary* series have been given freedom to develop their own understanding of the biblical text. As long as a fair statement is given to alternative interpretations, each writer has been permitted to state his own conclusions. Beyond the general editorial policies, the editors have sought no artificial uniformity, and differences are allowed free expression. A writer is responsible for his contribution alone, and the views expressed are not necessarily the views of the editors or publisher.

Contents

I

General Introduction

The Meaning of the Term "Pastoral"

As early as the thirteenth century Thomas Aquinas made a reference to 1 Timothy as a letter that provides something of a "pastoral rule." But it was probably Paul Anton's series of lectures on the three letters, delivered in 1726, which he entitled "The Pastoral Epistles," that established this terminology. The term has become a convenient abbreviation for all three letters as one corpus of writing. They do have much in common from the viewpoint of linguistic style. They also have a common historical setting.

On the other hand, it is misleading to group these letters under the one title, "Pastoral Epistles." The uniqueness of each letter is obscured when it is viewed as only part of a corpus of literature. Each letter was intended to be very personal. Even the greetings at the end of 2 Timothy and Titus are of this nature. To be sure, their contents are designed to influence and shape the outline and content of the public admonitions of these two preachers, and they have proved useful to the whole church. Nevertheless, from beginning to end each maintains its personal nature.

The word for "pastor" and the family of words to which it belongs (e.g., shepherd, flock, sheep) are completely missing from all three letters and are never used to designate the office or ministry of Timothy and Titus. If the term "pastoral" is used to describe the unique situation in which Timothy and Titus were involved, it must be with the significant nuance of meaning that depicts shepherds who are engaged in an agonizing struggle with "fierce wolves" (cf. Acts 20:28, 29). The church at Ephesus, as well as elsewhere, was under attack by powerful outside forces, and evil men had worked their way into the Christian fellowship. The prediction was that matters would get much worse and that Christians were moving toward more grievous times.

From Roman imprisonment Paul had written the church at Ephesus, where Timothy was stationed when Paul wrote these letters, urging them to put on "the whole armor of God" and to "keep alert with all perseverance" (Eph. 6:11, 18). Christians were involved in a confrontation with "the world rulers of this darkness," and "the evil day" when they would face "the flaming darts of the evil one" was at hand (see Eph. 6:10-20).

Paul's predictions had come to pass, and his language in 1 Timothy is the language of conflict: "Wage the good warfare" (1:18); "Fight the good fight" (6:12); "Guard that which is entrusted to you" (6:20). By the time he wrote 2 Timothy, the situation was even more critical with Paul's final imprisonment and impending execution: "Take your share of suffering for the gospel in the power of God" (1:8), "the gospel for which I am suffering and wearing chains" 2:8); "Take your share of suffering as a good soldier of Jesus Christ" (2:3); "The saying is sure, If we have died with him, we shall also live with him; if we endure, we shall also reign with him" (2:11, 12); "Indeed all who desire to live a godly life in Christ will be persecuted, while evil men and impostors will go from bad to worse, decievers and deceived" (3:12-13); "As for you, always be ready, endure suffering, do the work of an evangelist, fulfill your ministry" (4:5); and "I am already on the point of being sacrificed; the time of my departure has come. I have fought the good fight . . . I have kept the faith" (4:6, 7).

Authorship

History of the Debate

There was some dispute in the second century over these letters, but it was not until the nineteenth century that the problem of authorship was rendered acute. Eusebius (*circa* A.D. 325) referred to the letters as "manifest and certain" (*Church History* III, 3 and 25). The Muratorian Canon (A.D. 170) included them as the writings of Paul. Irenaeus (A.D. 178) repeatedly quoted by name all three epistles in his *Against Heresies.* Tertullian (A.D. 200) quoted several times from 1 and 2 Timothy in his *Prescription of Heretics.* Clement of Alexandria (A.D. 194) repeatedly quotes from all three epistles as by "the apostle" Paul (cf. *Exhortation* 9 and *Miscellanies* I. xiv; II. xi; III. vi; IV. viii). On the other side of the controversy, Basilides, an early second century Gnostic, rejected them. Marcion (*circa* A.D. 140) excluded them from his canon of scripture, and Tatian (A.D. 170) is supposed to have rejected them. Jerome (*circa* A.D. 400) in the preface of his Commentary on Titus said that these heretics rejected them because of their teaching against asceticism and not on genuinely critical grounds.

In more modern times the genuineness of 1 Timothy was denied by Schmidt in 1804. In 1807, Schleiermacher denied the authenticity of 1 Timothy on the basis of 75 words which he found nowhere in the New Testament outside of that epistle. This list of words was later expanded to include those from 2 Timothy and Titus, bringing the total to 175 words. In 1812, Eichorn launched his critical attack, and in 1834 Baur submitted his theory that they were written in the second century to counteract the heresies of Marcion and the Gnostics. In 1886, H. J. Holtzmann submitted what has been regarded as the classical statement against the Pauline authorship. The latest outstanding accretion to the anti-Pauline evidence was added by P. N. Harrison in his book, *The Problem of the Pastoral Epistles,* published in 1921. Many modern writers (e.g., William Barclay, C. K. Barrett) have accepted Harrison's basic assumptions and conclusions, whereas many others do not (e.g., Donald Guthrie, E. K. Simpson, J. N. D. Kelly, and R. C. H. Lenski). In 1962, Reginald H. Fuller predicted a growing acceptance of the deutero-Pauline character of these epistles. But in 1963 two able scholars, J. N. D. Kelly and C. K. Barrett, published commentaries that represent different conclusions, thus indicating that the matter is still very much open for consideration.

The Role of Luke as Paul's Scribe

The close relationship between the language of the letters to Timothy and Titus and that of Luke is a significant one. Luke was Paul's close companion for about fifteen years prior to the writing of these letters (Acts 16:11; 20:6; Col. 4:14). His history of the early church from Acts 7:58 on concentrates on "the gospel to the uncircumcised" (cf. Gal. 2:8) in which Paul played the leading role. Therefore, it seems reasonable to conclude that the language of Paul would have been familiar to Luke, and that of Luke familiar to Paul. We know that Paul did not write his letters in his own hand but used a scribe (e.g. Rom. 16:22; 1 Cor. 16:21; 2 Thess. 3:17; Gal. 6:11), which may have been due to some physical difficulty (see Gal. 4:12-15; 6:11) as well as the fact that he was so often in chains (cf. Col. 4:18). In light of this, Paul's words to Timothy are significant regarding Luke's role as Paul's scribe: "Luke alone is with me" (2 Tim. 4:11).

From the standpoint of the vocabulary of the letters to Timothy and Titus, it is significant that the 175 words listed as occurring only in the Pastorals sustain a closer relationship to Luke than any other New Testament writer other than Paul. In addition to these words, those who deny Paul's authorship have added another 131 words which they do not find in Paul's other writings, but which they do find elsewhere in the New Testament. Of these 131, there are 86 that are found in Luke. Outside of Luke the largest number is found in Hebrews, which has 39.

The Historical Setting

Two Roman Imprisonments?

The historical allusions in these letters have caused some to doubt their authenticity on the ground that they do not fit into the known life of Paul prior to his first Roman imprisonment. There is, however, no evidence that Paul was executed at the end of the two years mentioned in Acts 28:30, 31. It is altogether reasonable to conclude that he was released and his life extended to include the events mentioned in these letters (e.g. 1 Tim. 1:3; 2 Tim. 1:8, 16, 17; 4:13, 20; Tit. 1:5; 3:12).

In Romans 15:28 Paul expressed his desire and intent to go to Spain after visiting Rome. Those who deny the Pauline authorship of these letters on historical grounds usually attempt to discredit the tradition that Paul actually did reach Spain after his release from imprisonment. They also attempt to show that the book of Acts itself argues for Paul's execution rather than his release. If this was the case, then, of course, it is assumed that he could not have written these letters.

In reference to the visit to Spain, Clement of Rome, writing from Rome about A.D. 96, says that Paul did go "to the extremity of the west" (I *Clement* v.). The second century apocryphal *Acts of Peter* and the Muratorian Canon (1. 37) attest the journey to Spain. Jerome repeats the same testimony (*Lives of Illustrious Men* III.5). In the light of such tradition it is possible that Paul did go to Spain. But the case for the extension of his life beyond the years of his first Roman imprisonment does not rest on whether he did or did not reach Spain. Paul in his other letters, and Luke in Acts, gives clear evidence that things did not always work out as he planned them or according to his expressed intentions. In announcing his future plans Paul had a habit of implying "if the Lord will" (see 1 Cor. 4:18; Phil. 1:19-20). The fact that he said to the Ephesians elders, "you will see my face no more" (Acts 20:25, 38), is the strongest evidence that the book of Acts supplies for those who say that Luke is trying to tell his readers that Paul's conviction and execution at his first defense was certain. This statement to the elders does not mean that Paul never did see them again, and if he did, it would not discredit Luke as a historian in recording these words.

The important question, and the only one that has any bearing on whether the subsequent events recorded in the letters to Timothy and Titus are historical, is whether the book of Acts contains evidence that Paul was executed at the end of his trial. The note of optimism found in his prison epistles does not necessarily mean that Paul was actually freed to fulfill those hopes which he expressed in Philemon 22, Philippians 1:12-14, 19, 20. They do indicate that he was hopeful. In Philippians 1:24-26 he seems very confident that he will return to Philippi. Nothing in the book of Acts suggests pessimism on the matter of his deliverance. Luke puts in several statements pointing to the innocence of Paul and a favorable outcome of his case (Acts 23:29; 26:32; 28:21, 30, 31).

The Date of Writing

The three letters to Timothy and Titus, we conclude, were written during the period following Paul's release from "house arrest" in Rome (Acts 28:30), perhaps in the latter part of A.D. 62 or early in A.D. 63, and prior to his execution about A.D. 67. The last of these letters, 2 Timothy, was dictated to Luke during the final imprisonment that preceded the execution (see 2 Tim. 4:6-8). The other two letters were apparently written during a time of freedom a short time earlier. They could have been written from Macedonia or Greece. It is impossible to determine whether the events referred to in 1 Timothy and Titus occurred immediately following Paul's release from Rome and prior to his trip to Spain from Nicopolis, perhaps via Dalmatia and Gaul (2 Tim. 4:10), or the trip to Spain followed immediately upon Paul's release from house arrest in Rome and that the events mentioned in 1 Timothy came after the trip to Spain.

Some commentators insist that all three letters were written prior to A.D. 64, on the assumption that Paul was one of the victims of the persecution following the burning of Rome. Eusebius, however, in his fourth century *Chronicon*, gives the year 67 as the time of Paul's death.

Vocabulary and Style

The vocabulary and style of the Pastorals have entered into the debate surrounding the authorship of these letters. P. N. Harrison (see p. 9 above) based his denial of the Pauline authorship of the Pastorals on what are largely stylistic and linguistic considerations. He contended that all of the 175 words unique to the Pastorals "are as foreign to Luke as to Paul" (p. 53). To this group of words he added another 131 words which do occur elsewhere in the New Testament outside of Paul's other epistles, making a total of 306 out of the 848 (exclusive of proper names) which make up the vocabulary of the three letters. Harrison holds rigidly to a total of 2,177 words which he allows for Paul's vocabulary, based on the other letters of Paul.

Even though many words in Harrison's list sustain a close cognate relation to the language of Paul or Luke, or both, he insists that they are utterly foreign words. Yet when some of the words in his special list sustain a cognate relation to the writers of the second century, he says that "we feel justified in regarding them, in each case, as simply another form of the same word" (p. 82), and "they belong to one family, and formed a part of the same working vocabulary" (p. 84). For example, he permits the word *antidiatithēmai* ("to oppose," 2 Tim. 2:25) to be represented in the second century by *diatithēmai,* but he ignores Luke's use of *diatithēmai* (Luke 22:29; Acts 3:25). He connects *hedraiōma* ("foundation," 1 Tim. 3:15) with the language of Ignatius through the word *hedraios,* but ignores Paul's use of the same word (1 Cor. 7:37; 15:58). For the word *adēlotēs* ("uncertainty," 1 Tim. 6:17) he allows the cognate *adēlōs* in 1 Clement and Hermas but ignores Paul's use of *adēlōs* ("uncertain," 1 Cor. 9:26). *Ekzētēsis* ("useless speculations," 1 Tim. 1:4) is represented by Justin's *ekzēteō* and Lucian's *zētēsis,* but the use of these same words by Paul and Luke is overlooked (Rom. 3:11; Luke 11:50; Acts 25:20).

One of the strangest twists in Harrison's linguistic logic is in connection with Paul's use of the *alpha* privative. This is the prefix *a* or *an* which is equivalent to our English prefix *un,* as in unholy. Harrison permits *aphilagathos* ("no lover of good," 2 Tim. 3:3) to be represented in the second century by *philagathos* ("lover of good"), and *stomachos* ("the stomach," 1 Tim. 5:23) by the second century occurrence of *astomachos.* There are nine words in Harrison's list that have the same relation to the language of Paul. For example: "not ashamed" (2 Tim. 2:15), and "ashamed" (Rom. 1:16; Luke 9:26); "not condemned" (Tit. 2:8), and "to condemn" (Gal. 2:11); "unholy" (1 Tim. 1:9; 2 Tim. 3:2), and "holy" (Eph. 4:24; cf. Acts 2:27; 13:35; 1 Tim. 2:8; Tit. 1:8).

It is difficult to imagine that the educated apostle Paul might be familiar with the adverb and adjective forms of a word and be unfamiliar with the noun equivalent. Yet Harrison classifies the noun "purity" (*hagneia*, 1 Tim. 4:12) as not Pauline and disregards his use of "pure" (*hagnos*, 2 Cor. 11:2; Phil. 4:8), and "purely" (*hagnōs*, Phil. 1:27). Similarly, he lists "godly" (*eusebōs*, Tit. 2:12) as unknown to Luke and ignores Luke's use of the noun, verb, and adjective equivalents in Acts 3:12; 17:23; 10:2, 7.

A study of the words classified as foreign to Paul and Luke and the rest of the New Testament reveals that there are 112 that sustain a probable, or possible, relation to the language of Paul, and that 111 sustain such a relation to the language of Luke, and altogether 149 to both men. This leaves 26 words, of which 3 are found in the Septuagint. Several of these remaining words are words that would be familiar to Luke as a medical doctor: gangrene, stomach, to drink water, to beget or bear children, child-bearing, given to wine, to be sick, and abstaining from wine. Five words have cognate forms in other New Testament writers, and 12 are old words that were in common use in Paul's time. These remaining 26 words, therefore, do not deserve to be classified as necessarily foreign to Paul and the New Testament. Three of the words involve textual variations in which the variant is found elsewhere in the New Testament. And there were several words which Paul might not have had occasion to use in his other writings, such as the "cloak" he left behind, and the "parchments" which he wanted Timothy to bring with him.

Harrison's careless use of "foreign" is much like his use of "habitual" in his argument concerning the indeclinable words used in the Pastorals, which he regards as his strongest argument. He lists 112 of these (enclitics, particles, prepositions, pronouns) which he says Paul used habitually and are not found at all in the Pastorals. It is worthy of note that 35 occur in only one of Paul's epistles, 58 in only two, 70 in only three, and 84 in only four of the ten works which Harrison recognizes as Pauline. Harrison claims that "nothing to approach this list can be produced in the case of any Pauline epistle." To test Harrison's method and conclusion, J. W. Roberts has used the Thessalonian letters, since they are the first in the Pauline corpus and the Pastorals are last. They also are only slightly shorter in length and were separated from Paul's other letters by about the same amount of time. Roberts' study yielded precisely the same results. If one wishes to assume that Paul did not write the Thessalonian letters, he has 114 Pauline words which are absent to weigh against the Pauline authorship, or 2 more than Harrison has for his theory against the authorship of the Pastorals (see *Restoration Quarterly,* Vol. 8, No. 2, pp. 104-110).

Some scholars are impressed by the fact that many of Paul's favorite theological words are absent entirely from the Pastoral epistles. To illustrate, the words for "cross" and "to crucify" occur twenty-seven times in Paul's general letters but never in the Pastorals. It should be noted, however, that "cross" does not occur in Romans, and it is found in only five of the other ten Pauline letters. The words "son" and "adoption" are used forty-six times in Paul's other epistles but not once in the Pastorals. It should be noted that "adoption" is not used in seven of the other epistles and only once in Galatians, once in Ephesians, and three times in Romans. "Son" is also missing from two of Paul's other letters. The word for "freedom" and kindred words occurs twenty-nine times in the other epistles but never in the Pastorals. But Galatians uses them nine times, and four letters do not use it at all. Ephesians and Colossians use "freedom" once each, but in a different doctrinal context. Paul's great emphasis on "freedom" and "liberty" in Christ is confined to four of the other ten: Romans, Galatians, 1 and 2 Corinthians.

There are some great words and themes which are not touched on, much less developed, in these letters. Each of Paul's letters, however, was characterized by certain distinctive ideas, phrases and words. The absence of the word "blood" from the Pastorals must not be held as significant in view of the fact that it is also missing from Philippians, Philemon, 1 Thessalonians, 2 Thessalonians, and 2 Corinthians. "Spirit" and "spiritual" are found twenty-four times, but sixteen of these are in 1 Corinthians, and none occurs in 2 Corinthians and four other letters.

The Threat of Jewish Gnosticism

The gnostic aspect of the heresy which confronts Timothy and Titus is evidently an early manifestation of the Gnosticism that became rampant in the second century. This heresy in its ultimate development was characterized by two evil extremes. One extreme turned the grace of God into license. Its adherents were addicted to lust and greed and gross immorality (see 1 Tim. 6:3–5; 2 Tim. 3:1–9). The other extreme promoted a legalistic asceticism (cf. 1 Tim. 4:3). Legalistic Jews as early as the time of Paul and Timothy found that certain elements of Gnosticism (cf. *gnōsis,* "knowledge" in 1 Tim. 6:20) could be adapted for their own purpose and used in excluding the uncircumcised of other nations from the fellowship of the saved by basing salvation on a special kind of knowledge available only through their own special allegorical approach to the Old Testament. This strange Jewish Gnosticism was founded on an unlawful use of the law (cf. 1 Tim. 1:3–4, 6–11). It was a more subtle threat to the church because of a feigned faith in the Scriptures. Its promoters used the Old Testament to devise their fables and to formulate their demands. The Gnostics insisted that to climb the ladder to God a very special knowledge was necessary; a strict asceticism was essential to the good life. Certain Jews claimed that it was the Jewish law and the Jewish food regulations that provided the special knowledge and the necessary asceticism.

In fighting this heresy, Paul places great emphasis on salvation for all men (1 Tim. 2:3, 4, 7). This salvation comes through Jesus who as a man was manifested in the flesh (cf. 1 Tim. 2:5; 3:16). Those who were addicted to rigid asceticism denied the humanity of Jesus on the ground that he could not have been a flesh and blood being without at the same time being sinful, since to them all earthly matter was evil per se. The epistles to Timothy and Titus are not, however, to be viewed merely as a refutation of this heresy. They must also be studied as a healthful and positive affirmation of the good life in Christ which is the product of a sincere dedication to the faith and the good doctrine.

Selected Bibliography

Lexicons and Dictionaries

Arndt, William F., and F. Wilbur Gingrich. *A Greek-English Lexicon of the New Testament.* Chicago: The University of Chicago Press, 1957.

Kittel, Gerhard. Editor, *Theological Dictionary of the New Testament.* Translated by Geoffrey W. Bromiley. Grand Rapids: Wm. B. Eerdmans Publishing Co., 1964-.

Commentaries

Barclay, William. *The Letters to Timothy, Titus, and Philemon.* The Daily Study Bible. Edinburgh: The Saint Andrews Press, 1956.

Barrett, C. K. *The Pastoral Epistles.* The New Clarendon Bible. Oxford: The Clarendon Press, 1963.

Guthrie, Donald. *The Pastoral Epistles.* Grand Rapids: Wm. B. Eerdmans Publishing Co., 1957.

Hendriksen, William. *Exposition of the Pastoral Epistles.* Grand Rapids: Baker Book House, 1957.

Kelly, J. N. D. *The Pastoral Epistles.* Black's New Testament Commentaries. London: Adam and Charles Black, 1963.

Lenski, R. C. H. *The Interpretation of St. Paul's Epistles to the Colossians, to the Thessalonians, to Timothy, to Titus and to Philemon.* Minneapolis: Augsburg Publishing House, 1964 (A reprint of the 1937 edition).

Lock, Walter. *The Pastoral Epistles.* The International Critical Commentary. New York: Charles Scribner's Sons, 1925.

White, Newport J. D. "The Epistles to Timothy and Titus." *The Expositor's Greek Testament.* Ed. W. Robertson Nicoll. Vol. IV. Grand Rapids: Wm. B. Eerdmans Publishing Co., n.d.

Special Studies

BARRETT, C. K. *Luke the Historian in Recent Study.* London: The Epworth Press, 1961.

HARRISON, P. N. *The Problem of the Pastoral Epistles.* Oxford: Oxford University Press, 1921.

MOULE, C. F. D. "The Problem of the Pastoral Epistles," *Bulletin of the John Rylands Library,* Vol. 42, No. 2. March, 1965.

II

The First Letter of Paul to Timothy

Introduction

Paul, Timothy and Luke

Behind the writing of this letter there was a period of about fifteen years of vigorous evangelistic effort described in the book of Acts and Paul's other epistles. Paul was first introduced to Timothy when he came to Lystra and Derbe on the first missionary journey (Acts 14:1-7). A short time later, Paul came back to Lystra and enlisted Timothy as his missionary companion. Timothy's father was Greek and his mother Jewish, and Paul circumcised him because of the Jews (Acts 16:1-3). This was the beginning of an important father and son relationship. Timothy traveled with Paul through the cities, delivering to the churches the decrees of the apostles and elders in Jerusalem, which were designed to establish peace between the circumcised and the uncircumcised (Acts 16:4; cf. Acts 15:19-29). Through Phrygia and Galatia they traveled together until they came to Troas where the Macedonian call came (Acts 16:6, 9).

At Troas Luke joined them on the mission to Macedonia. Timothy accompanied Paul to Thessalonica, where the preaching of the gospel met with "great opposition" (1 Thess. 2:2). Timothy stood by when Paul went to Beroea (Acts 17:10). Again persecution arose and Paul left Timothy behind to continue the work, or perhaps to recover from one of his "frequent infirmities" (see 1 Tim. 5:23), with instructions to join Paul as soon as possible (Acts 17:15). Timothy soon joined Paul in Athens (1 Thess. 3:1). The young missionary's rapid growth in the faith is indicated by the responsible tasks given him in connection with the Thessalonian church (1 Thess. 1:1; 3:1-6; 2 Thess. 1:1; 2:1-5) while assisting Paul also at Corinth (Acts 18:1-11).

Timothy also assisted Paul in his vigorous ministry at Ephesus on the third missionary journey. Here he became familiar with the forces at work in that city where he was destined to serve later in a time of great crisis in the church. From Ephesus Paul sent Timothy ahead to Macedonia (Acts 19:21-22) with instructions to proceed to Corinth (1 Cor. 16:10). After some delay, Paul and Timothy joined Titus in Corinth, where Luke also was with them (cf. Acts 20:3-6; 2 Cor. 8:6; 12:18). Leaving Titus at Corinth, Timothy and others then went ahead of Paul and Luke and waited for them at Troas, where a busy week was climaxed by an all-night sermon by Paul. From Troas Luke and Timothy traveled together by ship to Assos, where Paul, traveling by land, joined them (Acts 20:3-16). At Miletus they met with the elders from Ephesus.

From Miletus Paul traveled with Luke and Timothy by ship to various ports on their way to Tyre (Acts 21:1-6). Then, they went by ship to Caesarea where they spent "some time" with Philip, and Paul made his decision to go to Jerusalem in spite of the prophetic warning concerning the persecution that awaited him there (see Acts 21:7-14). After two years imprisonment at Caesarea, Paul traveled under guard to Rome, accompanied by Luke (Acts 27:1), who was his personal physician and companion during the Roman imprisonment (cf. Col. 4:14). Timothy was also with them in Rome during the two years that Paul waited for his first hearing before Caesar (see letters written from Rome: Phil. 1:1; Col. 1:1; Phile. 22, 23). From Rome Paul sent word to Philippi saying he would send Timothy to them as soon as he learned what his own fate would be (Phil. 2:19-23).

Timothy was intimately associated with Paul's correspondence. He is mentioned by name in eight of his letters. He received two of the other letters of Paul, and whether or not Paul wrote Hebrews, Timothy is mentioned in a significant and affectionate note in Hebrews 13:23.

Date of Writing

In spite of some uncertainties as to the exact time and place of the writing of 1 Timothy it is likely that the letter was written late in the year A.D. 62 or early in 63. This is on the basis of the fact that Festus became governor in A.D. 60. Shortly afterward Paul made his appeal to Caesar and the voyage to Rome (Acts 25:11-12; Acts 27—28). His period of house arrest in Rome lasted two years. On the basis of his letter to Philemon and his request for a place of lodging (Phile. 22), it appears that he planned a trip to Asia before going to Spain (cf. Rom. 15:28-32). Paul's original plans had not worked out as he had wished; events shaped up to give the trip to Asia priority over that to Spain. If Paul did make the trip to Asia first, this would probably mean that the visit to Ephesus where he left Timothy took place on that same trip in the same year. On the basis of 1 Timothy 1:3, Macedonia was probably the place from which Paul wrote.

The City of Ephesus

Originally, the city of Ephesus was Asiatic, with a culture that was Oriental. Under Greek rule, the Hellenistic culture gradually supplanted the Oriental. The Asiatic goddess of the Temple was given the name of the Greek Artemis, and the city became a mixture of the Greek and Asiatic. In 190 B.C., Ephesus became a part of the Roman province of Asia. Roman religion and government centered in Pergamum, but Ephesus was the commercial center of the province. It was located on the Cayster river at the entrance of a valley that extends deep into Asia Minor (modern Turkey). Its artificial harbor could accommodate the largest ships. A good highway system connected it with the main cities of the province, making it one of the most accessible cities in Asia.

The main reason for the city's great wealth and prominence was the temple of Diana (Latin for Artemis), which was world famous as a place of worship, a bank, a museum, and a sanctuary for criminals who claimed refuge under a law that prohibited the molesting of any person within a certain distance of its walls. The temple priests were the bankers in charge of vast revenues from the various temple enterprises, including ownership of valuable lands and fisheries. They controlled a thriving industry that employed skilled artisans in the manufacture of images to Diana and shrines for sale to a host of visitors (cf. Acts 19:24).

The Church at Ephesus

Timothy's beloved father in the faith achieved great fame as a teacher in Ephesus. On the first recorded visit to the city, he impressed the Jews with his arguments, and they urged him to stay longer. He promised to return (Acts 18:19-21), and on his return he spent three years teaching in the synagogue, in the school of Tyrannus, and from house to house (Acts 19:8-10, 21-22; 20:31). During these years he launched the first really effective campaign against the pagan worship of Diana. His influence filled the city and extended throughout Asia.

The value of this letter to Timothy, and its meaning to the church, can be measured in terms of the great fame and respect Paul enjoyed throughout the province. Timothy's influence was greatly enhanced by his intimate association with Paul. Paul's high praise for and confidence in the younger Evangelist was a matter of common knowledge. Timothy was probably in his thirties when Paul gave him the difficult task with which this epistle deals.

Outline of 1 Timothy

- I. Part One, 1:1-20
  - A. Salutation, 1:1, 2
  - B. The Charge to Timothy, 1:3-5
  - C. Teachers Without Understanding, 1:6, 7
  - D. The Law and Gospel, 1:8-16
  - E. A Unique Doxology, 1:17
  - F. Commitment Against Apostasy, 1:18-20
- II. Part Two, 2:1—6:2
  - A. Sound Doctrine on Public Worship, 2:1-15

1. Public Prayer for "all men," 2:1-7
2. Proper Relationship of Men and Women in the Public Assembly, 2:8-15

B. Sound Doctrine for Overseers, 3:1-7
C. Sound Doctrine for Men and Women Servants, 3:8-13
D. Proper Behavior for Christians, 3:14-16
E. Doctrines of Demons, 4:1-5
F. A Twofold Charge to Timothy, 4:6-16
G. Specific Instructions to Timothy, 5:1—6:2a

1. Timothy's Example, 5:1, 2
2. Honor for Older Widows, 5:3-10
3. Younger Widows, 5:11-16
4. Double Honor for Elders, 5:17-20
5. A Special Encouragement to Timothy, 5:21-25
6. Honor for Masters, 6:1, 2

III. PART THREE, 6:3-21

A. A Description of the Enemy, 6:3-10
B. The Man of God, 6:11-19
C. A Final Charge to Timothy, 6:20, 21a
D. Benediction, 6:21b

Commentary

Part One, 1:1-20

The Salutation, 1:1, 2

[1] Paul's use of **apostle** in his opening words to Timothy is typical of the apostle's constant effort to remind himself and his hearers of the true nature of his office as a preacher of the gospel and an apostle of **Christ Jesus.** He was "sent" by Christ to preach the word of Christ.

Paul, like the Twelve, was specifically designated an **apostle of Christ.** He was personally chosen and commissioned by the Lord (Acts 26:16-18). As Jesus came preaching the word of the Father who sent him (John 3:34), so Paul was to preach the word of the Christ who sent him. All other abilities possessed by Paul and the Twelve were bestowed by the Spirit to confirm the proclamation: "And he appointed twelve, to be with him, and to be sent (*apostellō*) out to preach (*kerussō*), and have authority to heal diseases and to cast out demons" (Mark 3:14; cf. Luke 9:2; Matt. 10:5-8; Acts 1:26; 2:37; 5:29; 8:1; 15:2, 4, 6, 22f.). Peter defined the apostolic ministry as one of prayer and preaching the word (Acts 6:2-4). The office and authority of these special apostles was to make known the will of Christ and to insist on obedience to his command. It was, indeed, an office with authority, but the authority was in the word spoken. It was the word of him to whom all authority in heaven and on earth was given (Matt. 28:18-20). In referring to himself as an apostle of Christ Paul was not boasting of himself. His exercise of apostolic authority is magnificently illustrated in his words and ministry to the church at Corinth which both Timothy and Titus heard

[1] **Paul, an apostle of Christ Jesus by command of God our Savior and of Christ Jesus our hope,**

[2] **To Timothy, my true child in the faith:**

Grace, mercy, and peace from God the father and Christ Jesus our Lord.

---

and witnessed: (2 Cor. 1:24; 2:17; 3:2, 3; 4:5; 1 Cor. 3:5). Therefore, Paul's introduction of himself as an apostle of Christ is not a mere formality, nor is it an attempt to boast of himself. It is especially appropriate in writing to Timothy because Timothy's ministry as a gospel preacher shared features with Paul's ministry.

Paul's ministry as a preacher was by the **command** (*epitagē*) of God and Christ Jesus. His use of *epitagē* compares with his language in Romans 16:25-27, where the preaching of the good news (*euangellion*) is according to the command (*epitagē*) of God and is a revelation of the mystery (*mustērion*) which had been kept secret but was now made manifest through the prophetic scriptures (see also 1 Corinthians 7:25).

The expression **God our Savior** is used by Paul only in the letters to Timothy and Titus (cf. Tit. 1:3; 2:10), but it is found in Luke's writings (Luke 1:47). The phrase **Christ Jesus our hope** is also unique, but the idea is expressed elsewhere by Paul (Rom. 5:1-2; cf. Acts 28:20; Col. 1:27; 1 Cor. 15:19; 2 Tim. 1:1; Tit. 2:13). God is designated "our Savior" and "hope" in the Greek version of Psalm 65:5.

[2] The word **true** (*gnēsios*) in relation to "child" (*teknon*) means "legitimately born." It may also mean "genuine" as in "true yoke-fellow" (Phil. 4:3), and genuine love (2 Cor. 8:8). With reference to Timothy it suggests genuine obedience. In the Scriptures true childhood is synonymous with obedience (cf. 1 Cor. 4:15-17; Phile. 10-13). In his appraisal of Timothy to the Corinthians, Paul emphasized his loyalty and obedience and urged them emulate Timothy's childlikeness (1 Cor. 4:15-17; see also commentary on 2 Tim. 1:2).

The use of **grace, mercy, and peace** conforms to the epistolary practice which was current in Paul's day. Each word takes on new meaning, however, in the context of

[3] As I urged you when I was going to Macedonia, remain at Ephesus that you may charge certain persons not to teach any different doctrine,

---

the gospel of Christ. Elsewhere, Paul uses only "grace" and "peace" in his salutations, but he makes frequent use of "mercy" in his letters. His use of **mercy** in this instance may be due to the fact that in 1 Timothy 1:13-16 he dwells significantly on the fact that in his past life he had ignorantly blasphemed, persecuted, and insulted Jesus Christ and was the "foremost of sinners," and he echoes the thought, "I received mercy . . . I received mercy." This blends perfectly with Paul's great emphasis on salvation by grace, and calls to mind his humble confession, "by the grace of God I am what I am" (1 Cor. 15:10; cf. also Rom. 3:24; 5:1-2; 6:14; 2 Cor. 12:9; Eph. 2:5-8).

The word **peace** (*eirēnē*) describes the real nature of the salvation that man may enjoy as the result of the Lord's grace and mercy. It implies the deeper meaning of salvation, which is a sense of well-being and security rather than the usual Greek concept which was somewhat limited to the idea of not being at war. This peace is from God. The source of it and the blessing of it are enlarged upon by Paul in Philippians 4:4-7.

The Charge to Timothy, 1:3-5

[3] Paul's use of the word **urge** (*parakaleō*) suggests one of the most significant thoughts that motivated Paul and shaped the pattern of his apostolic service to the church. He also uses it later in the letter to convey to Timothy the way and manner in which he is to exercise his evangelistic authority. The word *parakaleō* means "to appeal to," or "to encourage," even "to beg." It is free of any suggestion of arrogance or the "puffed up" attitude of one who talks down to the one addressed. With this word Paul suggests the worth and dignity of the other person. He used it in his appeal to Philemon (Phile. 9). It describes the proper attitude of a father with his children (Eph. 6:4; Col. 3:21). *Parakaleō* is an encouraging, comforting and helpful word. Paul uses it several times in telling Timothy

how to instruct the brethren (2:1; 5:1; 6:2; cf. 2 Tim. 4:2; Tit. 2:6, 15). The language of 2 Timothy 2:24 describes the role of the evangelist as a gentle comforter and encourager, even in dealing with his opponents. The Spirit is described as the Comforter (*paraklētos*), and the ministry of a Spirit-filled preacher will be a comforting ministry (see John 14:16; 1 John 2:1; 2 Cor. 1:6).

One of the main reasons for Timothy to remain at Ephesus was in order that he might **charge certain persons not to teach any different doctrine.** The word **charge** (*parangellō*) means "to instruct," but it carries also a note of urgency. It suggests to "preach" or "insist on." The word was used for military orders, but its use here conforms to the style of leadership appropriate in God's family. It blends with the meaning of *parakaleō* in this same verse. The idea of command is implied, but the manner and spirit in which the command is given is also suggested, being grounded in the word **urged** on which it is dependent. It suggests "speaking for" God, but also "speaking with" those who are being charged (cf. 1:5; 4:11; 6:14; 6:17). For a fuller identification of the certain persons see comments on 1:6, 19, and compare 2 Timothy 2:17.

The serious problem which prompted Paul to leave Timothy in Ephesus pertained to the teaching of false doctrine. The word translated **to teach any different doctrine** is *heterodidaskaleō,* very typical of Paul who is the only New Testament writer who uses the prefix *hetero* in word formation (cf. 1 Cor. 14:21; 2 Cor. 6:14). Throughout his letters to Timothy and Titus Paul placed great emphasis on sound doctrine, the good doctrine, the truth, and the faith (cf. 1:10; 4:3, 6; 6:1, 3; Tit. 1:9; 2:1). This emphasis on orthodoxy has led some to contend that these letters represent a post-Pauline development. It is in the frequency of their use, however, that these letters differ from Paul's other writings rather than in a difference of thought or meaning. His emphasis on "the doctrine" (*hē didaskalia*) in reference to a body of doctrine and what is taught is found also in Ephesians 4:14 and Colossians 2:22. When the will of God lies behind *didaskalia* in the New Testament, the singular is always used, as in Romans 12:7

4 **nor to occupy themselves with myths and endless genealogies which promote speculations rather than the divine training [a] that is in faith;**

[a] Or *stewardship,* or *order*

---

and Ephesians 4:14, where it is given a strongly objective shade of meaning in relation to historical content (see Kittel, Vol. II, p. 161).

[4] These certain persons were occupied with false doctrine. That is, they were addicted to or given to this concern. The same word is used in 3:8 with reference to wine addiction and in 4:13-16 with reference to Timothy's dedication to the gospel ministry.

The word **myths** is defined as "legend" or "fable." Paul also warns against "Jewish fables" (Tit. 1:14; cf. 2 Peter 1:16). Among the Greeks prior to New Testament times, the word "myth" had meanings both good and bad. Eventually, however, even among the Greeks, **myths** (*muthos*) came to be the complete opposite of truth (*alētheia*).

The term **endless genealogies** has sometimes been interpreted to refer to the aeons of the Gnostics. The aeons were the series of descending emanations by which they claimed to bridge the gulf between the divine and the material. It may be a fair description of what they did, but there is no evidence that the Gnostics ever used the term genealogies in reference to aeons. It is more likely that these endless genealogies were the occupation of those who gave heed to Jewish myths (Tit. 1:14). These Jewish Gnostics used the Old Testament genealogies for their allegorical and legendary interpretations of the Scriptures. The word **speculations** is synonymous with "dispute over controversial questions" (cf. 6:4; Rom. 14:1; Acts 15: 1-2).

The alternate translations **divine training** (*oikodomēn*) or **stewardship** (*oikonomian*) involve variant readings in the manuscripts. If Paul used *oikodomēn,* reference is being made to divine edification, that which builds up. If he used *oikonomian,* he meant the divine plan, stewardship, or regulation. It might, therefore, be translated "divine edification in faith" (see Rom. 14:9) or God's plan of salvation (cf. also Eph. 3:2). Either word would fit the

5 whereas the aim of our charge is love that issues from a pure heart and a good conscience and sincere faith.

---

context here, although *oikonomian* has better manuscript support.

[5] For the meaning of **charge** see discussion of 1:3. The **aim** of the teaching which divinely edifies in faith is threefold: love out of a pure heart, a good conscience, and sincere faith.

Paul's word for **love** is *agapē. Agapē* has been defined as divine rather than human, an intellectual and unemotional virtue. *Philē* (friendship love) has been defined as human and mundane. Such definitions are an oversimplification that might serve Gnostic purposes better than Christian. In Romans 12:9-13, where Paul urges "Let love (*agapē*) be genuine," he proceeds to describe genuine love by using *philē* in three word formations—"brotherly love," "brotherly affection" and "hospitality."

Paul emphasizes love out of a **pure heart.** He and Timothy were contending with heretics who placed emphasis on ceremonial purity and ceremonial defilement, with an outward definition of "clean," "pure," and "holy" (4:1-5, and cf. Col. 2:20-23). Paul calls for inward purity. The word **heart** suggests that which is "within" and places the emphasis where Jesus placed it in Matthew 15:18-20. For a fuller treatment of the "clean" and the "unclean" by Paul, read Romans 14:13-23, and compare Titus 1:15.

In addition, the aim of the charge is **a good conscience.** In 1 Timothy and elsewhere (1 Cor. 8:1-13; 10:25-29; 1 Tim. 1:19), Paul uses "conscience" in close association with what one "knows" on the basis of what he has been taught and what he is accustomed to. A **good conscience** is one that is strong in the knowledge of the truth. Ignorance is associated with the weak conscience. For this reason, Paul goes on immediately to an emphasis on "sound doctrine" or healthful teaching.

The aim of Paul's charge calls for **sincere faith** (cf. 2 Tim. 1:5). The word **sincere** means "without hypocrisy" (see Rom. 12:9 and 2 Cor. 6:6). In his threefold analysis of the aim of Christian teaching, Paul has combined love and faith and conscience just as he did in Romans 14, 1

[6] Certain persons by swerving from these have wandered away into vain discussion, [7] desiring to be teachers of the law, without understanding either what they are saying or the things about which they make assertions.

[8] Now we know that the law is good, if any one uses it lawfully,

---

Corinthians 8 and 10. And here, as elsewhere, he is concerned about that which makes for peace and the upbuilding of the church.

Teachers without Understanding, 1:6, 7

[6] These **certain persons** boasted of their knowledge of the Law, but they were ignorant of its true purpose and were using it for their own unholy and unlawful purpose. Paul describes their teaching as **vain discussion** (*mataiologia*). The same word is translated "idle talk" (Tit. 1:10). Their discussions were empty, futile, and useless. They claimed to be the true teachers of the holy scriptures, but their teaching "missed the mark" (*astochēsantes,* which is translated **swerving**—cf. 6:21; 2 Tim. 2:18). They have **wandered away** (cf. 2 Tim. 4:4).

[7] Paul was an educated man, having been trained in the rabbinical school. He achieved fame as a teacher (Acts 22:3; 26:4, 5; 19:9, 10), and he was acquainted with the futile dialogue and empty discussions of men who coveted a reputation for scholarship. These men of "knowledge" had missed the main point and purpose of the law. Timothy's task was to convince them that their use of the law was contrary to sound doctrine and out of harmony with the glorious gospel (see 1:11, and 6:3-4).

The Law and the Gospel, 1:8-16

[8] Here Paul is speaking of the law of God contained in the Old Testament. The terms that Paul uses in appraising the law are "holy," and "spiritual," and "just," and "good" (Rom. 7:12-14). His description of the law as "the old written code" (Rom. 7:6) implies no disrespect. He delights in the fact that God "has qualified us to be ministers of a new covenant" (2 Cor. 3:6), and even though he

[9] understanding this, that the law is not laid down for the just but for the lawless and disobedient, for the ungodly and sinners, for the unholy and profane, for the murderers of fathers and murderers of mothers, for manslayers, [10] immoral persons, sodomites, kidnapers, liars, perjurers, and whatever else is contrary to sound doctrine,

---

says "now that faith is come we are no longer under a custodian" (Gal. 3:23-26), he still regards the Old Testament as "the holy scriptures" (Rom. 1:2). The sacred writings of the Old Testament lead to salvation in Christ (2 Tim. 3:15-17). Paul appeals to these scriptures in his own teaching (1 Tim. 5:18; Rom. 15:4; Gal. 4:30).

But there were certain things the law could not do. It could not offer perfect remission of sins, nor could it offer eternal life through obedience to its commands. It was "the law of sin and death" (Rom. 8:2). The law itself was not evil (Rom. 7:7). The good news that Timothy proclaimed was that in Christ is perfect remission of sins and eternal life, which could not be found under the law.

By the proper use of the law Timothy was to condemn the sins listed in 1 Timothy 1:9, 10 and "whatever else is contrary to sound doctrine" (1:11). In this way he could bring men to a knowledge of, or a conscience of, sin (Rom. 3:20; 7:7, 14, 23; 5:13, 20). He could use it to make men know that the wages of sin is death (Rom. 7:11, 13; 5:12; 6:23; 2 Cor. 3:6). He could use it to bring men to Christ for the remission of sins (Gal. 3:22; Heb. 10: 3, 4, 17-22).

[9, 10] In the phrase **understanding this,** Paul proceeds to point out in specific terms what it was about the law that "certain persons" (1:3, 6) did not understand. These words should not be construed to mean that the law is only for certain people who are lawless, and that people who are good and just do not need law. Paul includes every man in his description of the lawlessness which prompted God to give the law. Paul even includes himself by his use of the word sinners (cf. 1:15, 16). And it was Paul who declared that "none is just" and "Christ died for the ungodly" (Rom. 3:9, 10; 5:6, 8). It was also Paul who said of the law and of himself, "we know that the law is spiritual, but

[11] in accordance with the glorious gospel of the blessed God with which I have been entrusted.

I am carnal, sold under sin" (Rom. 7:14). Neither does Paul imply that good people do not need civil law. He deals with the matter of civil obedience and the duty of the Christian under civil law in Romans 13:1-7 (cf. also Tit. 3:1, 2). In this verse Paul is referring to the law of God set forth in the Old Testament. The point being made by such a listing of types of sinners is essentially the same as that which Paul stresses at greater length in his letter to the Romans (Rom. 1:18—2:16). It serves to demonstrate in very specific terms how the law was given to expose man's unrighteousness.

The expression **sound doctrine** is emphasized by Paul in the letters to Timothy and Titus. His metaphorical use of **sound,** meaning healthy, is found only in these letters (see also 6:3; 2 Tim. 1:13; 4:3; Tit. 1:9; 2:1, 8). Paul's beloved physician, Luke, makes frequent use of the word in reference to physical health or soundness (Luke 5:31; 6:10; 7:10; 15:27; Acts 4:10). This metaphorical use of terms for "health" in reference to spiritual matters, sin and salvation, finds a parallel in Jesus' use of "to be restored to health," in reference to restoring spiritual health (Matt. 13:15; Luke 4:18). It was also used in this way by Luke in recording Paul's language in Acts 28:27. Both Jesus and Paul were quoting from Isaiah. The use of terms for health in referring to spiritual matters finds clear illustration in the word for "to save" (*sōzō*), which means to heal, to save or free from disease, or to save from death. It is a term that Luke uses frequently in regard to physical health and safety (e.g., Luke 23:25; Acts 27:20, quoting Paul; 8:48; Acts 14:9). Both Luke and Paul use the term figuratively in reference to spiritual health and safety (e.g., 1 Cor. 1:21; Luke 19:10; 2 Tim. 1:9; Tit. 3:5). Therefore, the use of **sound,** meaning healthy or saving, is not unusual, even though this figurative usage is found only in the words addressed to Timothy and Titus.

[11] Another rendering of this verse, instead of **the glorious gospel of the blessed God,** may be "the gospel of the glory of the blessed God," which may be a more ac-

[12] I thank him who has given me strength for this, Christ Jesus our Lord, because he judged me faithful by appointing me to his service. [13] though I formerly blasphemed and persecuted and insulted him; but I received mercy because I had acted ignorantly in unbelief,

---

curate translation. In either case, the **glorious gospel** was essential to man's salvation (cf. Rom. 1:16, 17), and there was a body of sound, healthy doctrine, based on the sound words of Jesus (cf. 6:3), which was in harmony or accord with this glorious gospel. There is an essential relationship between the gospel (*kērugma*) and the doctrine (*didachē*) of the Christian faith.

Paul had been **entrusted** (*pisteuō*) with the gospel and the doctrine. His use of *pisteuō* implies that God had confidence in Paul in bestowing this trust upon him. In the next verse he expresses gratitude for the Lord's kindness in judging him faithful and trustworthy (1:12).

[12] Paul was humbly aware of the fact that the one who had appointed him to his ministry had also given him the **strength** to accomplish the task (cf. Phil. 4:13). The word **appointing** is the same as the "arranging" in 1 Corinthians 12:18 (see also 1 Cor. 12:28).

[13] Paul could, by the grace of God, endure insults and persecutions, because he himself had once insulted and persecuted the Lord, yet the Lord had loved him and been gracious toward him. This is the key to Paul's remarkable strength and ability in manifesting love and grace toward those whom he served, even though they often insulted and persecuted him (see Rom. 8:37-39; 2 Cor. 11:23-29; 12:14, 15).

In this verse Paul reviews his life prior to his conversion (see Acts 7:58 to 8:3; 9:1-4). As a Pharisee he had not been aware of his need of mercy (compare the Pharisee of Luke 18:9-14 and Luke 7:30-47). What Paul is saying to Timothy is discussed more fully in Philippians 3:4-12 where he reviewed his life without Christ, when he had such confidence in his own righteousness through the law. Now his trust is in a righteousness not his own, a righteousness from God by faith in Christ Jesus.

Ignorance was the circumstance in which his forgive-

[14] and the grace of our Lord overflowed for me with the faith and love that are in Christ Jesus. [15] The saying is sure and worthy of full acceptance, that Christ Jesus came into the world to save sinners. And I am the foremost of sinners;

---

ness took place. It was not the procuring cause of the forgiveness.

[14] The word **overflowed** (*huperpleonazō*) means "to be exceedingly abundant." Paul delighted in the use of superlatives, especially in describing the grace of God (cf. Eph. 3:20). The word used here is in exactly the same linguistic style as that which Paul uses in Romans 5:20: "where sin abounded (*pleonazō*) grace abounded all the more" (*huperperisseuō*).

Paul's use of **grace** as a source of power and strength, rather than a gift, leads some to think that a new concept of grace has emerged that differs from Paul's doctrine of grace in his other writings. Here **grace** overflows with the faith and love that are in Christ. The preposition **with** (*meta*) indicates a very close connection between the Lord's grace and the other two virtues. But Paul does elsewhere use grace in the sense of a source of power, rather than as a gift itself (2 Thess. 2:16; 1 Cor. 15:10; 2 Cor. 12:9). It may be that in his words to Timothy Paul has both concepts in mind. He received God's grace as a gift, and the virtues of faith and love are the result also of this grace (see 2 Tim. 2:1).

[15] The expression **the saying is sure** is found only in the letters to Timothy and Titus (3:1; 4:9; 2 Tim. 2:11; Tit. 3:8). It suggests the idea of a truth that can be trusted. It certainly is most appropriate in contrast to the false, untrue, and unreliable teaching of the "certain persons" mentioned in 1:3, 5, 19. It may be used here because the heresies condemned are Jewish, and the heretics were familiar with the Septuagint and the service of the Synagogue. The expression was very familiar to Synagogue worshipers who used it regularly in the prayer that followed the Shema. It was commonly used to introduce or to follow a citation. The language of Psalm 93:5 suggests the same idea: "Thy

testimonies are sure." Psalm 19:7b has the same force: "The testimony of the Lord is sure, making wise the simple." Paul's words here are *pistos ho logos,* which means "faithful is the word." The apostle John combined *pistos* and *logos* with "truth" (*alēthinos*) in Revelation 21:5 (see also Rev. 19:9; 22:6; John 19:35). The phrase possibly became a part of the language of the church as it worshiped and taught in the context of a growing body of traditions, many of them false, concerning the true teaching of Christ and the true gospel of Christ (see comments on 2:11). Paul's use of it here may be somewhat unique, but it certainly is not a strange or new thought.

The word **full** (*pasēs*) is the key word in the expression **worthy of full acceptance** (see also 4:9). Without it Paul's vital point would be blunted. It signifies "the greatest," "the highest," or "the very best." The thing that deserves the very best acceptance and approval is the truth that **Jesus Christ came into the world to save sinners.** Such a great truth deserves more than a halfhearted approval. It deserves a wholehearted proclamation—anything less would be equal to its denial (see Matt. 9:13).

Paul goes on to show that he himself has fully accepted the fact that Jesus came to save sinners by including himself as not one whit behind the worst of sinners and using himself as an illustration. His use of the present tense **I am,** rather than the past "I was," is significant. Paul was totally committed to the fact that a sinner cannot save himself. Not one good thing that he himself might accomplish could save him. In an earlier letter Paul had freely admitted that he was created for good works and that he should walk in them (Eph. 2:10), but he denied their value in saving him from his own sins (Eph. 2:8, 9; cf. Tit. 3:4, 5). Only Christ could save. He is the righteous one (see 1 John 2:1, 2). Does this mean that Paul could continue in sin that grace might abound? He would answer, "God forbid" (Rom. 6:1, 2)! In being justified, or made righteous in Christ, we find ourselves to be sinners, and it is no longer we that live, but Christ who lives in us (Gal. 2:17-20). Paul shows his full acceptance of this fact in his thankful words, "By the grace of God I am what I am, and

16 but I received mercy for this reason, that in me, as the foremost, Jesus Christ might display his perfect patience for an example to those who were to believe in him for eternal life. 17 To the king of ages, immortal, invisible, the only God, be honor and glory for ever and ever.[b] Amen.

[b] Greek *to the ages of ages*

---

his grace toward me was not in vain. On the contrary I worked harder . . . though it was not I, but the grace of God which is in me" (1 Cor. 15:9, 10).

[16] Paul looks beyond himself and his own salvation to a reason much greater than himself. He had received grace that it might, through him, be extended to more and more people. Paul believed that if God's grace did not flow through him it would cease to flow into him. If he does not save others, he himself is unsaved (1 Cor. 9:16, 17). His words **for an example** are significant in the context of his message to Timothy. The true minister of the word will be an example of what a sinner can be by the grace of God.

A *Unique Doxology, 1:17*

[17] The insertion of a doxology here is typical of Paul (cf. Eph. 3:20-21; Gal. 1:5; Phil. 4:20; Rom. 16:27). The reference to God as King compares with Paul's frequent reference to the Kingdom of God (Eph. 5:5; Col. 4:11; Phil. 2:6). The kingship of both the Father and the Son is recognized in Paul's writings (e.g., Col. 1:13). But the dominant idea throughout Paul's writings is that Jesus, as Lord, is ruling by the power of God the Father (see 1. Cor. 15:24, 25; see also comments on 6:16 for a discussion of the word **immortal** as used here; cf. 2 Tim. 1:10).

Paul always uses **glory** (*doxa*) in his doxologies, but his insertion of the word **honor** (*timē*) is unique and is found only in this letter, here and in 6:16 (see Rev. 5:13). It may be that Paul's use of it here is intended to underscore his emphasis on **honor** which permeates this letter. One honors God by honoring others in the various relationships which Paul discusses in chapters 2 through 6 (cf. 5:2, 17; 6:1). In 1 Timothy Paul places great emphasis on the respect and honor shown by women for men, wives for husbands, younger for older, children for parents, congregation for

**18 This charge I commit to you, Timothy, my son, in
accordance with the prophetic utterances which pointed
to you, that inspired by them you may wage the good
warfare, 19 holding faith and a good conscience. By rejecting conscience, certain persons have made shipwreck of
their faith,**

---

elders, servants for masters. These instructions are preceded (1:17) and followed (6:15, 16) by the unique use of honor in ascribing glory to God.

Commitment Against Apostasy, 1:18-20

[18] The word **charge** (*parangelia*) is the same as in 1:3, 5. All that Paul has said concerning the false teachers and the wrong use of the law in justifying oneself (vss. 6-16) was inserted to emphasize the true nature of Timothy's charge as a minister of the gospel of Christ. The word **charge** means "instruction," and it is given to inspire Timothy. Paul had known discouragement in the face of great odds, and he knew the value of an encouraging word.

Timothy's charge was **in accordance with the prophetic utterances.** The word **with** (*kata*), as in 1:11, means "according to," or "in agreement with." The **prophetic utterances** that **pointed to** Timothy may have been like those that pointed to Barnabas and Paul (Saul) in Acts 13:1-3. It was probably in a similar situation that Timothy had been appointed and set apart for the work to which the Lord had called him (cf. 4:14).

The words used here, **wage** (*strateuō*) **the good warfare** (*strateia*) are almost uniquely Pauline in the New Testament (see 2 Cor. 10:3-5). No words could better describe the meaning and purpose of Paul's charge to Timothy and the nature of the fight in which Timothy is engaged (cf. Eph. 6:10-20; 1 Cor. 9:7; James 4:1, 1 Peter 2:11).

[19] In this verse Paul deals with two of the three things included in the charge of 1:5: **faith,** and **good conscience.** Here he says that **rejecting conscience** causes the shipwreck of one's faith. It seems likely, in the context of 1 Timothy, that Paul is using the term **good conscience** in reference to the mind or heart that has learned the truth

[20] among them Hymenaeus and Alexander, whom I have delivered to Satan that they may learn not to blaspheme.

---

and possesses knowledge that is true. As in 1 Corinthians 8:1-3, Paul equates the belief of error with the weak conscience. If a person has been mistaught, his conscience is defiled (1 Cor. 8:1-13). If he refuses to be taught better and persists in his misknowledge or misunderstanding, he is an opinionated heretic (Tit. 3:10). If he reaches a point where he is no longer sensitive to the truth, his conscience is seared (1 Tim. 4:2). One must not miss the force of the relationship between "sound doctrine" and "good conscience" in 1 Timothy which accords with what Paul teaches elsewhere. The root cause of all the trouble is false teaching. In 1 Corinthians 8, as in 1 Timothy, Paul's discussion links conscience (*suneidēsis*) with true knowledge (*gnōsis*). In the fight against Gnosticism, one fact stands out: the good conscience is equal to a knowledge of the truth and a love of the truth. In Ephesians 4:17-19, Paul emphasizes the character and the cause of the immoral and irreligious lives of the Gentiles. In contrast, the good life of Christian faith is based on the good conscience. And basic to it all is learning Christ and being taught the truth as it is in Christ (Eph. 4:17-21; cf. 1 Tim. 2:11; 3:1-9, 14, 15; 1 Cor. 4:6; 14:31, 35; John 6:45; Matt. 13:15).

Paul's sudden change of metaphor from the military to the nautical may be a play on words to suggest that the Christian must also be a good sailor. Paul certainly had experienced shipwreck on his voyage to Rome. But it is possible that this change of analogies is no more significant than his rapid-fire change of metaphor from the soldier, to the athlete, to the farmer in 2 Timothy 2:3-5 (cf. "babes," "field," and "building" 1 Cor. 3:1-3, 5-9, 9-19).

[20] **Hymenaeus and Alexander,** and certain others (cf. 1:3, 6) had rejected conscience, and in so doing had shipwrecked their faith. These persons Paul had **delivered to Satan.** Because of the serious state of these men and the threat they presented to the health of the church, Paul pronounced upon them his "anathema" (for the purpose of such action cf. 1 Cor. 5:5; Rom. 9:3; 1 Cor. 16:22; 1 Thess. 3:14, 15). For the Christian, the anathema (curse) of de-

1 First of all, then, I urge that supplications, prayers,
intercessions, and thanksgivings be made for all men,
2 for kings and all who are in high positions, that we may
lead a quiet and peaceable life, godly and respectful in
every way.

---

livering a brother to Satan is not an end in itself. It is the means to an end that accords with the one goal of saving every man. Paul's expression, **that they may learn not to blaspheme,** signifies that the experience of discipline is designed to teach them. It was to be corrective discipline performed in love (cf. 1 Cor. 5:2; 16:14; 2 Cor. 2:6-11).

PART TWO, 2:1—6:2

Sound Doctrine on Public Worship, 2:1-15

[1] Paul indicates by the words **first of all, then, I urge,** that he is beginning an important series of vital truths. For the meaning of **I urge** see comments on 1:3 above. The word **supplications** (*deēsis*) means "requests," or "entreaties" (cf. Phil. 4:6; Matt. 9:38). It is like the word "beg," and is much like saying a fervent "please." **Prayers** (*proseuchē*) is a word always used of requests addressed to God (cf. Rom. 15:30). **Intercessions** (*enteuxis*) combines two great ideas: the verb form means "to have an intimate talk with someone"; the noun was also used of petitions submitted to a king or governor. Thus it signifies to the Christian the high privilege of having an intimate talk with the ruler of the universe. **Thanksgiving** (*eucharistia*) means "gratitude." The phrase **for all men** suggests that gratitude, as well as supplications, prayers, and intercessions, should be expressed for all men. There were some in the church who did not have this feeling for all men, especially for the uncircumcised Gentiles.

[2] Paul urges that **kings** be included in the public prayers of God's family. The word king (*basileus*) is also translated "ruler" or "sovereign." In 6:15 Paul uses the word Sovereign (*dunastēs*) along with king (*basileus*) in reference to God. God is, therefore, King of kings, Lord of lords, and Christians are urged to invoke his divine power

[3] This is good, and it is acceptable in the sight of God our Savior,

---

and sovereignty on behalf of those who govern the lives of all men.

The word **quiet** (*hēsuchia*) is used also in 2:11 urging women to be **quiet** and submissive in their relation to men in the public services of the church. It is descriptive of the Christian's life under the rulers of civil affairs (cf. 1 Pet. 2:13-17; 1 Thess. 3:12; 4:11). Luke uses it more than anyone else, especially in Acts where Paul's ministry is disturbed by noisy riots and confusion stirred up by those who opposed the truth. The word **peaceful** (*ēremos*) suggests tranquility and contentment. Paul's favorite synonym is *eirēnē* (see 1:2), which defines peace in terms of concord and unity (cf. Rom. 14:19; 1 Cor. 14:33; Eph. 4:3).

The word **godly** (*eusebeia*) may be translated "piety," "religion," or "godliness." Luke used it in describing Cornelius (Acts 10:7). Peter used it in the speech recorded by Luke (Acts 3:12) and in 2 Peter 1:3, 6f; 2:9; 3:11. Paul used it in the speech at Athens (Acts 17:23). It is an important word in 1 Timothy: "religion" (3:16; cf. 2 Tim. 3:5), "religious duty" (5:4), "godliness" (4:7, 8; 6:3, 5, 6, 11; cf. Tit. 1:1).

Respectful (*semnotēs*) implies reverence, dignity, holiness, and seriousness. Those who say that this word is foreign to Paul fail to recognize that Paul is the only New Testament writer who uses a cognate form (*semnos*) to describe things venerable, or honorable (Phil. 4: 8; cf. 1 Tim. 3:8, 11; Tit. 2:2, 7). Both *semnos* and *semnotēs* are derived from *sebomai,* meaning to venerate, to reverence, or to worship, which Paul uses elsewhere (Rom. 1:25; 2 Thess. 2:4).

[3] The language here is almost identical with Paul's words in 2 Corinthians 8:21, where **good** (*kalon*) is translated "honorable." And the word translated **sight** is the same in both instances. The word **acceptable** (*apodektos*), as well as *apodochē* in 1:15 and 4:9, is considered by some as un-Pauline. Both terms are derived from *apodechomai* which is a word peculiar to Luke in the New Testament.

4 who desires all men to be saved and to come to the knowledge of the truth.

Paul himself often uses *dektos* and *dechomai.* The use of the prefix *apo* is very Pauline. Different prefixes are used with *dechomai* in Romans 15:16 where the offering of the Gentiles is **very acceptable** to God, and in 2 Corinthians 6:17, 18 where God promises to **accept** those whose lives conform to his will.

[4] God's plan for all men consists of two parts: (1) to be saved, and (2) to come to know the truth. The order in which Paul arranges these two parts is significant, and his words in verses 4-7 are essential to an understanding of his purpose in the remaining portion of this epistle. A close parallel is found in Titus 2:11 (cf. Phil. 1:27). The parenthesis found in verses 4-7 is, therefore, germane. It explains why the evangelists must not only save the lost but also teach and exhort the saved. In verse 8 Paul resumes what he started in verses 1, 2.

The frequent occurrence of **the truth** (*hē alētheia*) in this letter does not mean, as some contend, that a new concept has been introduced. Paul uses **the truth** frequently in this letter (2:7, 3:15; 4:3; 6:5; cf. 2 Tim. 2:15; 3:8; Tit. 1:1), but it carries the same meaning as it does in his use of it elsewhere. Compare "the truth of the gospel" (Gal. 2:5, 14); "obeying the truth" (Gal. 5:7); "God's word . . . the truth" (2 Cor. 4:2); "they refused to love the truth" (2 Thess. 2:10); wicked men "suppress the truth" (Rom. 1:18). See also comments on "the faith" (4:1) and "the teaching" (1:3; 3:2). What Paul is contending for here is the same as "the word of the truth, the gospel" (Col. 1:5; Eph. 1:13). Compare 3:15. The word **knowledge** (*epignōsis*) is almost a technical word in the Pastorals for conversion. The closest parallel elsewhere is in Colossians 2:2, 3, addressed to a church with a problem much like the one Timothy confronts in Ephesus, where Paul expresses hope "that their hearts may be encouraged [*parakaleō*, exhorted, cf. 1 Tim. 2:1; 5:1] as they are knit together in love, to have all the riches of assured understanding [*sunesis*, cf. 2 Tim. 2:7] and the knowledge [*epignōsis*] of God's mystery of Christ."

[5] For there is one God, and there is one mediator between God and men, the man Christ Jesus,

---

[5] There is **one God** for all men, who wants all men saved. The salvation of all men is through one **man,** Christ Jesus (cf. 2 Cor. 5:18). In Galatians 3:20 Paul emphasizes the oneness of God in connection with the person of Christ as **mediator** (*mesitēs*).

The mystery of Jesus' perfect humanity and his perfect divinity is the great mystery of the Christian faith (3:16). Paul affirmed the deity of Christ (Phil. 2:5-11; Col. 1:15-20; Tit. 2:13), but here he emphasizes that the intermediary between God and man is himself a **man.** It is worthy of notice that Paul usually employs the term "God" in reference to the Father, and the term "Lord" is used of Jesus as "the Christ." According to Paul, God wants "every tongue to confess that Jesus Christ is Lord, to the glory of God the Father" (Phil. 2:11). But the main point is that Jesus Christ is the exalted Lord because of his having become perfectly human and obedient (Phil. 2:5-11). It is through Jesus as a human being that man's salvation and encouragement is accomplished. So, to Timothy Paul says that **the man, Christ Jesus,** "gave himself as a ransom for all" (2:6), or that, as in Philippians 2:7, 8, it was as a man that the Lord humbled himself in obedience. It is through the obedience of this one man that all are made righteous, just as by one man's disobedience all became sinners (Rom. 5:18-21). In fighting the heresy which certain Jewish Gnostics were propagating, the emphasis on Jesus as a man who was manifested in the flesh (cf. comments on 3:16) is most important. Those who were given to rigid asceticism denied the humanity of Jesus on the grounds that he could not have been flesh without at the same time being sinful, since to them all earthly matter was evil. What Paul is saying to them is consistent with the emphasis of the book of Hebrews, which is a full treatise on the subject that is so briefly discussed here. Hebrews 1:2, 3 recognizes the deity of the Lord, but the rest of the book emphasizes his humanity. For a portrayal of Jesus as the man who gave himself a ransom for all, see Hebrews 5:7 (read also Ps. 22:1; 22:4, 5, 7, 8, 11, 14-19; cf. Matt. 27:29, 30, 35, 43, 46-49). When Jesus died, man died. This

6 who gave himself as a ransom for all, the testimony to
which was borne at the proper time. 7 For this I was ap-
pointed a preacher and apostle (I am telling the truth, I am not lying), a teacher of the Gentiles in faith and truth.

---

is the truth that Paul heralds in Romans 6:6, 8 (cf. Rom. 6:3, 11; 1 Cor. 15:1-3; 2 Cor. 5:14).

[6] The word **ransom** (*antilutron*) is not used by Paul elsewhere. It means to give one's life for, or instead of, someone else. Here it is followed by the preposition *huper,* meaning on behalf of. *Huper,* of course, is very Pauline. The terminology here signifies that Jesus gave himself "instead of," and "on behalf of," all men. The use of *anti* with the word for ransom (*lutroō*) is found in Mark 10:45 and Matthew 20:28, meaning to give oneself for someone else. The meaning is certainly not foreign to the New Testament. Even though Paul usually uses *apolutroō,* he uses *lutroō apo* in Titus 2:14, "to redeem from" (see 1 Peter 1:18). The complete New Testament idea is to redeem from, to die instead of, on behalf of, and also to redeem some one for or unto something better (Tit. 2:14)

The phrase **at the proper time** (*kairois idiois*) has been given various interpretations, Some interpret it to mean that the apostles gave their witness in their own time or season. Others take it to mean that Jesus gave himself as a ransom at the appointed time in the unfolding of God's plan. The latter seems to accord with 6:15, where the same phrase is used (cf. Gal. 4:4).

[7] For a discussion of Paul's appointment as an ***apostle*** see comments on 1:1. Concerning his use of **preacher** (*kērux*) it is worthy of notice that this is the only place where the term is used in this epistle. The same pattern is also characteristic of the letter to Titus, where *kērugma* ("preaching") is used only once (Tit. 1:3). In both instances Paul is referring to himself. The verb "to preach" (*kerussō*) is used once in 1 Timothy concerning Jesus' being preached among the nations (3:16). This peculiar linguistic style in writing to two preachers does not mean that Timothy and Titus were not preachers or proclaimers (*kērux*), but Paul uses other terms for preaching in describing the unique ministry of those two men as depicted in 1 Timothy

and Titus. In 2 Timothy, a letter different in purpose and content, Paul uses the family of words to which *kērux* belongs in speaking of Timothy's task (see comments on 2 Tim. 4:2-5). There are several different words which were used in the early church to describe the ministry of preaching. The key words used in 1 Timothy and Titus to define their ministry in Ephesus and on Crete are: "to charge or instruct" (*parangellō,* see comments on 1 Tim. 1:3, 5; cf. 4:11; 6:17); "to teach or instruct" (*didaskō,* see comments on 1 Tim. 1:3; 2:4; cf. 4:11, 13, 16); "to exhort, urge, admonish" (*parakaleō,* see discussion of 1 Tim. 1:3; cf. 2:1; 4:13; 5:1; 6:3); "to command" (*epitassō,* see discussion of 1 Tim. 1:1; cf. 1 Cor. 7:25; Tit. 2:15); "to convict or convince" (*elengchō,* 1 Tim. 5:20; cf. 2 Tim. 3:16; 4:2; Tit. 1:9; 2:15). Paul's emphasis, as indicated by his use of the above terms, is on the teaching and exhorting aspects of preaching. This accords with the fact that both evangelists are charged with the task of entrusting the truth to faithful men who can "give instruction in sound doctrine" (Tit. 1:9; 1 Tim. 3:2; 2 Tim. 2:2). This linguistic peculiarity actually serves to underscore the fact that the preacher (*kērux*) of the gospel must give some attention to instructing and exhorting those who have been saved.

It is also interesting to notice that Luke, in Acts, never refers to Paul as a **preacher** (*kērux*), perhaps because in the Greek world the word was technical for a particular kind of "herald." He does record the fact that the Athenians called Paul "a preacher," using *katangeleus* (Acts 17:18), which also means one who heralds or proclaims. The related verb form, *katangellō,* meaning to herald or proclaim, is used by Luke to describe Paul's preaching. This word is often used where *kērussō* might have been used. And what is true of *kērussō* is true of *katangellō* in the fact that the content of the proclamation is revealed in the context. For example: preaching the word of God (Acts 13:5; 15:36); preaching the God whom the Athenians worshipped in ignorance (17:23); preaching in Jesus the resurrection from the dead (4:2); proclaiming light to the Gentiles (26:23). The same rule applies to *kērux,* preacher, and *kērussō,* to proclaim. The proclamation, or message, is *kērugma,* but the content of the message must be determined by the context

8 **I desire then that in every place the men should pray, lifting holy hands without anger or quarreling;**

---

in which the word is used. Paul himself offers several examples: preach the word of faith (Rom. 10:8); preach against stealing (Rom. 2:11); preach circumcision (Gal. 5:11); preach the gospel (Gal. 2:2; 1 Cor. 9:14; Mark 16:15, 20); preach the word (2 Tim. 4:2); preach Jesus (1 Tim. 3:16; cf. Acts 8:35); preach another Jesus (2 Cor. 11:4); foolishness of preaching Christ crucified (1 Cor. 1:21-23); preach Christ as risen (1 Cor. 15:12).

Paul's third term used to describe his ministry is perhaps the key to understanding his particular and peculiar purpose in writing to Timothy and in interpreting the rest of the text of 1 Timothy. Paul describes himself also as **a teacher of the Gentiles in faith and truth.** His use of **teacher** (*didaskalos*) serves to bring us back immediately to the teaching (*hē didaskalia*) to which the rest of the book is devoted. And his specific reference to his special ministry to **Gentiles** also accords with the fact that he and Timothy are contending with Jewish Gnostics who have contempt for Paul's ministry to "all men" and who would exclude the uncircumcised from the Christian fellowship. Paul had just affirmed that God wants all men to be saved and to come to know the truth. Also note "ransom for all" (2:6). His own ministry was primarily to Gentiles, and he had dedicated himself to teaching those among them who were saved by his proclamation of the gospel. Paul is saying, therefore, that what he is teaching and what he is instructing Timothy to teach is not for Jews only but for all men, and it is designed to edify a fellowship made up of all men, both Jew and Gentile (cf. Col. 3:11; Gal. 2:8-16; 3:7-14).

[8] The subject of discussion in verse 8 is what Paul introduced in verse 1. The word for **desire** (*boulomai*) means a wish or intention. It is much like the word *thelō* which is used to express God's desire in verse 4. Both *boulomai* and *thelō* suggest not only desire but also a desire that directs one's energies and shapes his decisions. Jesus used both words with much the same meaning (Matt. 6:10; Luke 22:44).

Paul's use of **the men** is emphatic in contrast to **women,**

[9] **also that women should adorn themselves modestly and sensibly in seemly apparel, not with braided hair or gold or pearls or costly attire**

---

and this emphasis continues through verse 15. All men could pray in the assembly, as in the synagogue. The phrase **in every place** probably signifies the public gatherings of the church (cf. 1 Cor. 1:2). The expression **lifting up holy hands** is most appropriate in conjunction with the word for **pray** (*proseuchomai,* see comments on 2:1). It was also a common gesture for prayer in the ancient world as shown by Christian art and sculpture. It dates back to Hebrew usage (cf. Ps. 141:2; 63:4; 28:2). Men are to plead, beg, and entreat. The hands lifted toward God suggests the hands of a dependent child lifted toward a father who has the power to grant what the child needs and desires. These lifted hands must be **holy hands.** The word **holy** (*hosios*) means "devoted" and "pleasing to God" (cf. James 4:8, Ps. 24:3, 4). They must also be helping hands (Eph. 4:28). The man who gives the back of his hand to his brother cannot open palms of requesting hands to the heavenly Father.

The word **anger** (*orgē*) suggests violent emotions or wrath (compare Titus 1:7). The word **quarreling** (*dialogismos*) has been translated by some to mean "doubt," suggesting that one who prays should not do so with doubt in his heart. But it seems that **quarreling** or "disputing" goes better with **anger.** In Romans 14:1 it is translated "disputes over opinions." The word is used in the New Testament with a bad connotation. It is derived from *dialegomai,* which is often used with a good meaning in reference to Paul's "arguing" in the synagogues (Acts 18:4; 19:8; 20:9). It is also used often to describe the kind of doubt and questioning that the Scribes and Pharisees engaged in as they argued with Jesus.

[9] In verses 9 and 10 Paul tells God's woman how to make herself attractive and beautiful. The word **adorn** (*kosmeō*) pertains to making something or someone attractive, such as a house (Luke 11:25), the doctrine of God (Tit. 2:10), those who oversee God's family (1 Tim. 3:2). It is used to describe the beauty and attractiveness of the

bride of Christ adorned for her husband (Rev. 21:2, 19). In this connection, the reference to Adam and Eve in verses 13 through 15 may also be a suggestion to the woman that, in making herself attractive, her desire should be to her husband (see Gen. 3:16).

The word **seemly** (*kosmios*) is the adverb form of **adorn.** Those who classify the word as foreign to the New Testament seem to ignore the use of *kosmeō* (Luke 11:25; 21:5) and *kosmos* (1 Peter 3:3, 5) where the meaning is the same as here. The word translated **apparel** (*katastolē*) is derived from a word which Luke used in Acts 19:35, 36, meaning "to arrange in order" (see comments on 3:2). A *stolē* is a long robe (Luke 15:22; cf. Luke 20:46; Rev. 6:11; 7:9, 14). *Katastolē* was used in the wider sense of demeanor. It suggests clothing that accords with the honorable character of the wearer.

The word **modestly** (*aidōs*) suggests an attitude of respect and reverence toward others in a sociological sense. Or, without excluding this, it may also signify the reverence (*aidōs*) of Hebrews 12:28. Reverence and respect in deportment toward others is an essential part of reverence and respect for God. The use of *aidōs* here is to signify the Greek concept of the modest demeanor of the wife, and the linking of this term with **sensibly** (*sōphrosunē*, "discreetly") is also in line with Greek usage. The term modesty suggests simplicity and reverence. In modern usage, immodest apparel suggests clothing that is designed to expose the body to the view of others. Such an exposure would have been considered disgraceful and disrespectful, and the word apparel suggests a garment that covers the nakedness of the body. But it should be noted that Paul's use of modest in this passage is in reference to clothing that is expensive and extravagant. One sign of worldiness (*kosmikos*, Tit. 2:12) is the devotion of excessive time and money to the outward adornment of the body. **Braided hair or gold or pearls or costly attire** is descriptive of a worldly woman who spends much energy and money in the effort to make herself physically attractive. Greek art shows elaborately adorned hairdos. She is without shame or modesty. Just as a gold ring is not proper in a swine's snout (Prov. 11:22), so extravagance and vanity in adorning the body and in pro-

[10] but by good deeds, as befits women who profess religion.

viding for things temporal is not proper for one who professes reverence for God and the hope of the life that is eternal. In 1 Corinthians 11:1-16, Paul indicates, as he does here, the vital importance of the hair and of wearing apparel in the relationship of men and women.

[10] Women who **profess religion** will adorn themselves with **good deeds.** The word translated **religion** is *theosebeia,* a combination of two words, *theos* (God) and *sebomai* (worship or reverence). The latter is distinctively Pauline and Lukan in the New Testament, with the exception of one occurrence in a quotation from Isaiah in Matthew 15:9 (see Mark 7:7). Those who classify *theosebeia* as foreign to the New Testament fail to recognize the significant use of *theosebēs* in John 9:31. The use of the term **religion** in translating this word is subject to question, especially if it is construed to mean the ceremonial rather than the ethical or moral aspects of one's service to God. In John 9:31 it is translated "a worshiper of God." The substantive form used here carries the same meaning. *Theosebēs,* meaning "God-fearer," was commonly used to describe the reverence of Jews for Jehovah. But it was also a term commonly applied to Gentiles who accepted the ethical aspects of the Law of Moses and expressed their reverence for God through the **good deeds** of the Law while rejecting the ceremonial and sacrificial demands of the Law. Paul himself used the phrase **good deeds** to describe Gentiles who were not under the Law yet practiced the good deeds of the Law (cf. Rom. 2:7, 10, 22-24; Eph. 2:10), and the point he is making here to Timothy concerning women is that one who is a God-fearer will manifest this respect by living a life of good deeds. Luke's history of Paul in Acts uses the two words that make up in the compound form *theosebomai* in the phrase *sebomai ton theon,* translated "worshipper of God." It is used with a very special reference to people other than Jews (e.g., Acts 18:7, 13; 16:14). Luke's use of *sebomai* is also descriptive of those among the Gentiles who were worshipers of God such as in Acts 13:43, 50; 14:2. It seems that every time Luke uses *sebomai,* with or without

[11] Let a woman learn in silence with all submissiveness.
[12] I permit no woman to teach or to have authority over men; she is to keep silent.

---

theos, he is referring to God-fearers among the Gentiles who had accepted the ethical demands of God's law. As an apostle to the Gentiles, Paul was no doubt cognizant of the special meaning of this terminology among them. And his use of it here puts the emphasis on an ethical life that is common to both Jew and Gentile (cf. also Rom. 1:25). The use of good deeds as a description of the proper adornment for women is in line with the language of 1 Peter 3:16.

The word translated **profess** signifies a promise, and is the word so translated in 2 Timothy 1:1 and Titus 1:2 in reference to the promises of God. Women who profess the service of God have made a sacred promise, and they should behave themselves in light of their promise to God.

[11] The word Paul uses for **silence** (*hēsuchia*) suggests quietness. The same word is used in 2:2 to describe the quiet and peaceful life. Paul used it also in urging Christians to work in quietness (2 Thess. 3:12). It is not to be confused with the word in 1 Corinthians 14:28 translated "not to speak," which Paul used in admonishing women to keep silent in the congregational meeting (cf. also 1 Cor. 14:34, 35). Not only the women but also the men were admonished not to speak under certain circumstances (1 Cor. 14:28, 30). The language to Timothy urges women not to create confusion by insubordinate conduct toward men who are charged with the responsibility of leading and teaching the congregation.

The word **submissive** (*hupotagē*) means to be in subjection. It is used in 3:4 with reference to the children of elders. It may also be translated "obedient" (2 Cor. 9:13). Paul uses it to describe the husband-wife relationship (Eph. 5:21-23).

[12] The word **silent** in this verse is the same as in verse 11. Paul states emphatically that he does not permit any woman **to teach** or exercise **authority** over men in the public worship. His use of *epitrepō* may suggest that he does not appoint a woman to such a position in the church. It is the

[13] For Adam was formed first, then Eve; [14] and Adam was not deceived, but the woman was deceived and became a transgressor.

---

same word he used in 1 Corinthians 14:34. The word **to have authority** (*authenteō*) describes the role of one who is master (*authentēs*).

[13] Paul uses Adam and Eve to illustrate the abiding principle of authority and submission, just as he used Abraham and David to establish the principle of justification by faith (Rom. 4:1 to 5:1). Compare also his use of Adam and Eve in 1 Corinthians 11:1-16.

The fact that **Adam was formed first** gave man priority (1 Cor. 11:8). In the very nature of things woman is created to be "the glory of man" (1 Cor. 11:7). And here, as elsewhere, woman is to give visible proof of her reverence for God and her respect for man's priority by the way she acts and the way she dresses in public (cf. 1 Cor. 11:5, 6, 10, 13, 15). Man is to give visible proof of his own high calling by the way he acts and the way he dresses in his public reverence for God and his exercise of authority over woman (cf. 1 Cor. 11:4, 7, 14).

[14] Paul is not arguing that Adam was less sinful than Eve. Elsewhere he speaks of the transgression of Adam and affirms that sin came into the world through one man and death through sin (Rom. 5:12-14; 1 Cor. 15:22). What Paul is saying here is in exact accord with Genesis 3:1-7 which puts emphasis on the subtlety of the serpent in deceiving Eve. Some suggest that Paul's instructions here are purely temporary and were based on the expediencies of that day, and that the permanent truth is "neither male nor female" (Gal. 3:28). It seems, however, that the subject under consideration in Galatians 3:28 is the same as in Colossians 3:11 and concerns unity in Christ. Just as the oneness of the Father and Son is not threatened by the Son's subjection to the Father, so the unity of man and woman, husband and wife, is not threatened by her subjection to him. Paul does not imply by "neither male nor female" that difference of place and function within the church had been abolished. Women who conducted themselves in harmony with Paul's instructions to the churches in Corinth (1 Cor. 11:14) and

15 **Yet woman will be saved through bearing children,[c] if she contines [d] in faith and love and holiness, with modesty.**

[c] Or *by the birth of the child*
[d] Greek *they continue*

Ephesus (1 Tim. 2:1-15) did enjoy places of prestige and honor. Woman's subjection to man is a permanent truth. It is based on the creative act of God (Gen. 1:26-28; 2:7-8, 18-24), and on God's covenant with them (Gen. 3:16-19). The dignity and honor of woman is not threatened by this divine rule of submission (see Tit. 2:5). In this capacity she is ruler in an all-important sphere (see 5:14; Tit. 2:5). In some respects the husband-wife relationship calls for a mutual submissiveness based on love and honor (see 1 Cor. 7:3-5, 12-14, 16; 11:11; Eph. 5:21-33).

[15] The word **woman** does not actually occur in the original text. Literally, *sōthēsetai* (**will be saved**) is the third person singular and should be rendered "she shall be saved." But **woman** is used because of the likelihood that "she" is a generic in reference to all women, as in verses 9-12, rather than a specific reference to Eve herself. Paul's use of the aorist (past) tense in referring to Eve in 13, 14 and his switch to the future tense in verse 15 is interpreted as a return to his discussion of women in general.

The word **woman** in this context (see vs. 14) is *gunē*, and it may be used to refer to any adult female, married or unmarried, or it may be translated "wife." Paul is not implying that all adult females must marry and bear a child in order to be saved. In his first letter to Corinth he expressed a fervent wish that the unmarried women and the widows would remain unmarried. At the same time he made it clear that he was neither commanding celibacy nor recommending free love and childbirth outside the marital state (see 1 Cor. 7:8-10; 25-26). His language to Timothy is to be interpreted in light of his concern about a distressing moral problem in Ephesus rather than in light of the "impending distress" which he had in mind when he wrote 1 Corinthians. His advice to Timothy is to urge the younger widows to marry, bear children, rule their household, and give the enemy no occasion to revile (5:14). The context here is the heresy at Ephesus where there obviously was a low view of marriage (1 Tim. 4:2ff.). In opposition the family structure is highlighted in the Pastorals. Paul may seem to contradict himself. But, even in his words to the Corinthians he also recognized that in some situations marriage is advisable (1 Cor. 7:2). It was advisable in the situation in Ephesus.

The word for **bearing children** (*teknogonias*) means more than merely giving birth to a child. It implies also the rearing of the child. The salvation of the wife involves her love for her husband and for her children (cf. 5:14; and Tit. 2:4, 5). She must be anxious about pleasing her husband just as he must be anxious about pleasing his wife (1 Cor. 7:32-35).

The phrase **if she continues** presents a problem. The verb translated **continues** is in the form of the third person plural, and the literal translation would require "if they continue." This tends to make **children** the antecedent of **they.** But the word *teknogonias,* translated **bearing children,** may also mean "the birth of the child" (see RSV footnote) and does not necessarily suggest a plurality of children for each mother. The probability is that the reference to woman and child, whether expressed with the singular or the plural, is generic. Woman's salvation is the matter under discussion rather than the salvation of her children. It should be kept in mind that Paul's instructions to Timothy in this section pertain to the second phase or aspect of man's salvation, i. e., the acknowledgment of the truth in matters pertaining to the ethical demands of the good life that is worthy of the gospel of Christ (see discussion of 2:4). In light of this fact, the salvation of woman in 2:15 pertains to her acknowledgment of sound doctrine in her ministry as a wife and mother. Her hope is not in usurping the authority of men as public teachers in the general assembly nor in disregarding the divinely given priority of men in directing the public affairs of the church.

There is another view of woman's salvation by childbearing that is based on the reference in Genesis 3:15 to "the seed of woman." This view places emphasis on the use of the definite article in "the childbearing," and connects this with "the seed of woman," making it refer to the single act of the Virgin Mary in giving birth to Jesus. Thus all women are represented ideally in the person of Mary. If

[1] The saying is sure: If any one aspires to the office of bishop, he desires a noble task.

---

this is the case, then, the "woman" in verse 15 cannot be the "she" of the same verse. This interpretation seems most strained.

Another view is that all women join in suffering for the sin of Eve by giving birth to children. But this is hard to accept in view of the fact that childbirth was a phenomenon of Paradise and had nothing to do with sin (cf. Gen. 1:27, 28). Childbirth was not a curse. The element of a curse is found in the word "pain" (Gen. 3:16), just as work was not a curse (Gen. 2:15), although the aspect of toil and sweat and hardship was (Gen. 3:17-19).

Sound Doctrine for Overseers, 3:1-7

[1] Concerning the introductory formula, **the saying is sure,** see comments on 1:15. The word **aspires** (*oregetai*) means to reach after or stretch oneself toward. Paul uses it in 6:10 in reference to those who "crave" or reach after wealth. The word **desire** (*epithumei*) means to long for or eagerly desire. Such desire and aspiration is commendable when it issues from a heart filled with love for Christ and his church.

Paul's use of **task** (*ergon*) is consistent with the New Testament concept of office as a service or work. Compare "work" or "function" (*praxis*) in Romans 12:4, which is synonymous with the "work" or "service" (*ergon*) described in 1 Corinthians 12:4-6. Compare also Paul's use of *diakonia* (ministry, office) as an apostle (Rom. 11:13).

The nature of a bishop's task is significant in determining his qualifications for this ministry. And Paul is not content with a mere listing of the qualifications. They are given in the context of an epistle which devotes much attention to the task itself. The work of the eldership may be summed up in four verbs of action: to pastor or shepherd a flock (*poimainō*), to teach or instruct (*didaskaleō*), to exhort or admonish (*parakaleō*), and to visit, guard, or oversee (*episkopeō*). The pastoral, or shepherding, terminology is not found in these "Pastoral Epistles." However, the word "pastoral" is a perfect description of those portions of 1

Timothy and Titus that pertain to the episcopal ministry.

The synonymous relation between **bishop** (*episkopos*), elder, and pastor (*poimēn*) deserves attention. In Acts 14:23, Paul ordained elders in every church. In Philippians 1:1 he called such men bishops. The word *episkopeō* (to oversee) means to visit, to see to, or provide for (James 1:27; Acts 15:36; Matt. 25:36, 43; Luke 1:68; Acts 7:23-25). The office of the elders was described by James as a ministry of visitation on behalf of those who were physically and spiritually sick (James 5:14-16). The twelve apostles expressed pastoral concern when they admonished the body of the disciples in Jerusalem to look after and provide for (*episkopeō,* Acts 6:3) the Grecian widows by appointing seven men "full of the Holy Spirit and of wisdom," to visit them just as the Jewish widows had been visited or looked after. The need was not a purely physical one, and the ministry (*diakonia,* Acts 6:1, 2) was a spiritual one that required spiritual men, full of faith and wisdom. The pastoral connotation of the word *episkopos* is also conspicuous in Hebrews 12:15: "See to it (*episkopeō*) that no one fail to obtain the grace of God," and the language of the context is filled with pastoral concern for healing the lame, lifting drooping hands, strengthening weak knees, and providing the grace of God in an environment of peace and purity. The perfect identity of the ministry of a bishop with that of a pastor is clearly seen in Acts 20:28, 29, where the elders (*presbuteroi*) are called bishops (*episkopoi*), not pastors (*poimenes*) but, significantly, their task as bishops is described as taking heed to the flock (*poimnion*) and tending the flock (*poimainō;* see also 1 Peter 5:1-5 where the same association of words is found).

The pastoral terminology is not used in 1 Timothy and Titus because the church is discussed in the figure of a family rather than a flock. Keeping in mind the synonymous relation between bishop and pastor, 1 Timothy may be interpreted in light of Ephesians 4:11 where the elders are designated "pastors and teachers."

The task of the bishops was fourfold: (1) caring for or looking after God's family, (2) managing God's household, (3) teaching and admonishing God's children, and (4) guarding or protecting them against enemies without and

[2] Now a bishop must be above reproach, the husband of one wife, temperate, sensible, dignified, hospitable, an apt teacher,

---

within (see 3:2, 4-5; 5:17; cf. 1 Thess. 5:12,13; Tit. 1:9-11; Heb. 13:17; Acts 20:28-29).

[2] It is imperative, which is what the word **must** signifies, that one who aspires to the task of a bishop prove himself in certain aspects of character and in certain important human relationships, as well as in matters pertaining to the faith and the truth. Paul in the word **must** uses the key word in ethics (*dei,* meaning "ought") which appears frequently in his writings (3:7, 15; 2 Tim. 2:24; Tit. 1:11). The word is opposite in meaning from *luō,* meaning "to loose," i.e., not binding or necessary. *Dei* signifies that a thing is obligatory, proper and fitting. In chapters 3 through 6 Paul is dealing with certain aspects of Christian ethics relevant to the gospel (see comments on 1:10,11; cf. also Paul's use of *dei,* "must," in 2 Cor. 5:10; 11:30; 1 Thess. 4:1; Rom. 8:26; Acts 21:22).

A bishop must be **above reproach** or blameless. The word used here is *anepilēmpton,* which is also used concerning widows and her relations in 5:7 and concerning Timothy in 6:14. The word translated blameless in 3:10, concerning deacons, is *anegklētos,* but no significance can be attached to this use of two different words in reference to the two different ministries, because the word used of deacons is the same word Paul uses two times in reference to the elders in Titus 1:6, 7. Each time it is used in Titus it is followed by a list of characteristics, or qualifications. If **blameless** is one of the qualifications, Paul would have no reason to list it two times in describing the elders in Titus 1:6, 7. It seems that Paul is rather saying that it is imperative that a bishop be above reproach in respect to the specific traits of character and rules of conduct which follow (cf. 3:10 where deacons must also prove themselves "blameless" in certain respects). Of course, it should be understood that no person can be absolutely without fault in every respect. If one allows the term "blameless" and **above reproach** to be defined in terms of the things specified, this will make allowance for some degree of imperfection. Paul uses two different words for blameless which seem to be synonymous. One, *anepilēmpton,* is not used outside of 1 Timothy (3:2; 5:7; 6:14), but the other *anegklētos* (3:10; Tit. 1:6,7), is found elsewhere in Paul's epistles. It is derived from *egkaleō* which means to accuse or to bring charges against someone. It is also used in Romans 8:33 concerning accusations against God's elect, and in Acts 23:29 and 26:2 concerning accusations brought against Paul himself. Even though it does not imply guilt or innocence, Christian ethics would demand that the charges be proved and that the accused be judged guilty or innocent through a lawful and just procedure. Paul demands this in 5:19 concerning accusations (*katēgorian*) brought against an elder.

A bishop must be **the husband of one wife.** The language here seems to have the same force as that used of the widows in 5:9, "the wife of one husband." Various interpretations have been offered: (1) He must not be a polygamist, i.e., not presently living with a plurality of wives. (2) He must not be a digamist, i.e., married for the second time. Some would define digamy as any second marriage regardless of whether the first wife died or was put away for fornication. Others would define digamy as a second marriage following divorce for some other reason than fornication. (3) He must be a married man.

If Paul had polygamy in mind, some serious problems still remain involving the popular practice of digamy, which was a much more serious threat to the Christian community than polygamy was. It was generally believed among Christians that polygamy was wrong. Many later felt the same way about any second marriage, in spite of 1 Corinthians 7:39. Paul's use of the word **one** indicates that his primary concern in this qualification is not so much that an elder must be married but that his marriage must not be a second marriage that violates God's will. And this would apply to all Christians, especially to those who were appointed to be teachers and examples to other members of God's family. This would not imply that God's standard for a bishop is higher than for other Christians. But it does suggest that the officially ordained teachers of the church must not only teach but also exemplify the "sound words of our Lord

Jesus Christ and the teaching which accords with godliness" (see 6:3).

Concerning the third interpretation above, that a bishop must be a married man, it is probably safer to base the necessity of his being a family man on the other qualifications that follow rather than on the requirement that he be the husband of one wife, for it seems that the question of second marriages is the foremost consideration here (for Jesus' teaching about second marriages, see Matt. 5:31, 32; 19:3-9; cf. 1 Cor. 7:8-16, 39, 40). Paul does sanction a second marriage following the death of one's spouse (1 Cor. 7:39, 40; cf. Rom. 7:2-3). He also sanctions separations without remarriage in some cases, but he warns about the temptations that go with such a separation. The question of a second marriage following divorce must be answered in light of Matthew 5:32; 19:9; and Romans 7:3. For a discussion of second marriages for widows, see comments on 5:9.

The word translated **temperate** (*nēphalios*) means "temperate in the use of wine." But it is derived from *nēphō* which is frequently used figuratively. Since addiction to wine (*paroinon*, "given to wine") is listed in 3:3, it is likely that *nēphalios* (temperate) is used figuratively in reference to every form of mental and spiritual drunkenness, excess, passion, and confusion. To be temperate, or sober, means to be well-balanced, self-controlled (cf. Paul's use of *nēpho* in 1 Thess. 5:6-9; 2 Tim. 4:5; also 1 Peter 1:13; 4:7; 5:8; 1 Corinthians 15:34).

The word translated **sensible** (*sōphrōn*) signifies discreet, humbleminded, and modest. The same word is used of women in Titus 2:5, of elders in Titus 1:8, of older men in Titus 2:2, and of younger women in Titus 2:5. Those who classify this word as foreign to Paul and the New Testament also add three other words to their list: *sōphronōs* (soberly, discreetly, sensibly, Tit. 2:12), *sōphronismos* (sound mind, soberness, 2 Tim. 1:7), and *sōphronizō* (to make one sensible or discreet, Tit. 2:4). They ignore Paul's use of *sōphroneō* (to be of sound mind, to be sensible and discreet, 2 Cor. 5:13; Rom. 12:3; Tit. 2:6; cf. Luke 8:35), and Luke's use of *sōphrosunē* (discreetly, sensibly, Acts 26:25; cf. 1 Tim. 2:9, 15).

[3] no drunkard, not violent but gentle, not quarrelsome, and no lover of money.

The word **dignified** (*kosmion*) is the same as **seemly** in 2.9 and suggests well-ordered and decorous, or well-adorned behavior. It is used metaphorically here as in 1 Peter 3:3,5 (see comments on 2:9). **Hospitable** is a translation of a word composed of *philo* (love) and *xenon* (stranger or guest). Paul also uses it in Romans 12:13 in his discussion of genuine love. The verb (*xenizō*), meaning to be a host or to receive a guest, is used of entertaining angels (Heb. 13:2) and in Paul's request to Philemon to prepare a guest room for him (Phile. 22). The noun *xenos* is used of Gaius in Romans 16:23: "Gaius, who is host to me and to the whole church." The worthy widow of 1 Timothy 5:10 is one who has received or hosted strangers or guests (*xenodocheō*) in her home (see also Matt. 25:35; Rom. 16:5,23). It is most likely that one serving as a pastor of the flock of God would have many occasions to do good to all men, especially to those of the household of faith, by offering the hospitality of his home. No doubt his house would also be a frequent meeting place for God's people (cf. Acts 10:5, 6; 21:8-10; Rom. 16:1, 2; Acts 10:23; 28:7).

A bishop must be **an apt teacher** (*didaktikon;* cf. 2 Tim. 2:2, 24; Tit. 1:9). The word **apt** means qualified.

The letters to Timothy and Titus are unique in the New Testament in the use of the term *didaskalia* to refer to both the act of teaching and that which is taught. It occurs some twenty-six times in the New Testament. All but two of these are in Paul, and twenty of the occurrences are in the letters to Timothy and Titus (elsewhere in Paul see Col. 2:22; Eph. 4:14; Rom. 12:7; 15:4). In light of the great emphasis on teaching, one cannot treat lightly the requirement that an elder be a qualified teacher (for the use of *didaskalia* as the act of teaching, see 1 Tim. 4:13, 16; 2 Tim. 3:16; cf. Rom. 15:4; for the use of *didaskalia* in reference to what is taught, see 1 Tim. 1:10; 4:6; 6:3; 5:17; 6:1; 2 Tim. 3:10; 4:3; Tit. 1:9; 2:1, 7, 10; cf. Col. 2:22; Eph. 4:14).

[3] The word for **drunkard** is *paroinon.* The same word is found in Titus 1:7. It describes one who is addicted to wine and keeps it close at hand (see 3:8; Titus 2:3). For a

[4] He must manage his own household well, keeping his children submissive and respectful in every way; [5] for if a man does not know how to manage his own household, how can he care for God's church?

---

fuller discussion of Paul's teaching on the use of wine, see comments on 5:23.

A bishop must not be **violent** (see Titus 1:7). The word for **violent**, *plēktēn*, is kin to the word *plēsso*, meaning to strike, and suggests a pugnacious man who is inclined to settle arguments with his fists. He must be **gentle** (*epieikē*). The same word is translated forbearance, or gentleness (Phil. 4:5; Col. 3:13) kindness or graciousness (Acts 24:4), the gentleness of Christ (2 Cor. 10:1), gentleness in a master's treatment of his servant (1 Peter 2:18), and gentleness in reference to the conduct of all Christians (Tit. 3:2; cf. 2 Tim. 2:24, 25; 1 Thess. 2:7).

A bishop must not be **quarrelsome** (*amachon*). Kindred words are found in John 6:52, where *machomai* describes disputes among the Jews, and in 2 Corinthians 7:5 with reference to fightings or contentions. An interesting parallel is found in Paul's *logomachias*, disputes or quarrels about words (6:4). Compare also fighting among the brethren (James 4:2), quarrels over the law (Tit. 3:9), and the proper conduct of the Lord's servant (2 Tim. 2:24). This kind of fighting or contention is not to be confused with the noble fighting or contending suggested by the word *agōnizomai* (to fight or contend) in 6:12, 2 Timothy 4:7, Jude 3, and 1 Thessalonians 2:2.

A bishop must not be a **lover of money** (*aphilarguron*). Compare Paul's use of the same language in 6:10 and 2 Timothy 3:2. It is synonymous with the greed for base gain in Titus 1:7. The same terminology is found in Hebrews 13:5 and Luke 16:14 (see comments on 6:10). This reference to love of money is especially appropriate for elders, who might be tempted into office by the promise of the double honor and the wages mentioned in 5:17, 18. Certain false teachers imagined that godliness is a means of gain, and their love of money is rebuked in 1 Timothy 6:5 10.

[4, 5] An elder must **manage** (*proistēmi*) **his own household.** This same word is used in reference to deacons man-

aging their families (3:12) and again with reference to the elders ruling God's family, the church (5:17). This is the word Paul used in 1 Thessalonians 5:12, but the meaning is broader than ruling. Service and not position is emphasized in Romans 12:8; 16:2. Its association with the next word is significant here. Paul's word for **care for** in verse five is *epimeleomai* which, in relation to household (*oikōs*), suggests the responsibility of a steward whose task is to take care of God's family. In a closely related pasage (Tit. 1:7), a bishop, or elder, is described as God's "steward." Later in this chapter Paul refers to the church as the household of God (see comments on 3:15).

A Christian man's family is God's proving ground, a place of testing to see whether he should be entrusted to serve as a steward or ruler of God's family. God's plan for a mature congregation was a plurality of such men in every church (Acts 14:23; cf. Tit. 1:5; Phil. 1:1). His ability to keep his children **submissive** and **respectful** would inspire confidence in his ability to keep the members of God's family also submissive and respectful of the rule of God in their relationship to each other (see comments on 5:1-2).

The word for **submissive** (*hupotassō*) implies subordination. It is used in reference to the wife's submission to her husband (Tit. 2:5) and to the woman's submissiveness to man in the public worship and teaching of the church (2:12). It is used to describe Jesus' obedience to his parents (Luke 2:51). In this context it is significant that Paul had earlier written to the church at Ephesus, where Timothy is now serving, admonishing children to obey their parents in the Lord, and admonishing fathers to bring their children up in the discipline and instruction of the Lord (Eph. 6:1-4).

The term **respectful** (*semnotēs*) was used earlier by Paul to describe the life of every Christian in relation to kings and those in high positions, "a quiet and peaceful life, godly and respectful in every way" (2:2). The child's first school of training for such conduct is the home itself. If he does not learn it at home he will not likely demonstrate it in relation to the leaders of the church or of the state. If a man's children are "open to the charge of being profligate and insubordinate" (Tit. 1:6) it is a discredit to his ability

6 He must not be a recent convert, or he may be puffed up with conceit and fall into the condemnation of the devil; [f]

[f] Or *slanderer*

---

to teach and exemplify and rule his own family. An alternate translation applies the term **respectful** to the father himself, indicating that he must be a man of high principles and worthy of respect (see Lenski and Barrett). The application of the term **respectful** to the elder himself would agree with Paul's use of a cognate adjective (*semnos*), translated **serious** in reference to deacons (3:8), which means worthy of respect and honor, or dignified. It is a virtue which is emphasized in a special way in the letters to Timothy and Titus, and is urged upon all the members of God's family, both young and old. In addition to the passages already suggested, see also its use with reference to women being "serious" (3:11), to Titus showing "gravity" in his teaching (Tit. 2:7), and of older men being "serious" (Tit. 2:2).

[6] In urging that an elder must not be a **recent convert** Paul makes a figurative use of a term (*neophuton*) which literally means "newly planted." The word is used in early Christian inscriptions with the meaning "recently baptized." There is no other instance where the term is so used in the New Testament, but it does find striking parallels in Paul's metaphorical language in 1 Corinthians 3:6-9, where the church is likened to God's field, and the figure of planting, watering and growing is used with reference to the conversion and nurture of the children of God. It also occurs in Ephesians 3:17 where Paul prays that Christians may be "rooted and grounded in love" as well as Colossians 2:7.

If an elder is not well-rooted in faith and love, he may easily become **puffed up**, or conceited. In 1 Corinthians Paul had much to say about the conceit and carnality that hindered the Corinthians in their progress toward spiritual maturity. They were **puffed up** (see 1 Cor. 4:6, 19; 5:2; 8:1; 13:4; cf. also 1 Tim. 6:4 and 2 Tim. 3:4). Paul is calling for elders who have reached the spiritual growth and maturity which he describes in 1 Corinthians 13, where he says "love is not puffed up." Knowledge puffs up, but love builds up (1 Cor. 8:1). This compares with Paul's words to the Ephe-

[7] **moreover he must be well thought of by outsiders, or he may fall into reproach and the snare of the devil.**[f]

[8] **Deacons likewise must be serious, not doubled-tongued, not addicted to much wine, not greedy for gain;**

[f] Or *slanderer*

---

sian elders that their task as pastors and teachers is to speak the truth in love that all might grow up in every way into Christ (Eph. 4:11-16).

The expression **fall into the condemnation of the devil** is synonymous with the expression in verse seven, "fall into reproach and the snare of the devil." Both may be compared with Paul's language in 6:9 (cf. also 2 Tim. 2:26; Rom. 11:9). It seems that the condemnation is the act of God rather than the devil, and those caught in the devil's temptation, unless freed, are doomed to share the condemnation and ruin which has been appointed for the Tempter himself (see Matt. 25:41). Paul's word for **condemnation** here is *krima* (for other uses of this term by Paul see 5:12, Gal. 5:10, 1 Cor. 11:29, 34; cf. Rev. 17:1; 2 Peter 2:3).

[7] An elder must **be well thought of by outsiders.** The word **outsiders** (*exōthen*) refers to those who are not members of the body of Christ, who "do not belong" to the Christian fellowship. Compare Jesus' reference to those "outside" (*exō*) the circle of his disciples (Mark 4:11). Not only the elders, but also all Christians are urged to conduct themselves in such a way as to have a good reputation among those outside and to exert a saving influence upon them by their very manner of life (see 1 Cor. 5:1, 9-13; cf. 1 Peter 2:12-16; see also 1 Cor. 7:16; cf. 1 Peter 3:1). A good reputation is essential to an effective proclamation of the gospel and the salvation of those outside; it is also essential to effective leadership inside the fellowship (see 3:4, 5). Paul's own zeal in this matter is reflected in 1 Corinthians 9:19-23 (cf. Rom. 14:13, 19, 21; 15:1, 2). And he gave a special word to preachers of the gospel regarding their conduct and reputation (2 Tim. 2:22-26).

Sound Doctrine for Men and Women Servants, 3:8-13

[8] The term **deacons** (servant, minister) in the New Testament has both a specific and a general connotation.

The same is true of other terms such as elder and apostle. In a specific sense they refer to certain persons with certain specified qualifications and duties. In a general sense the word deacon (*diakonos*) is used by Jesus in reference to the true servant (Matt. 20:26-28; cf. John 12:26), and in a more specific sense it is used in reference to the minister of the gospel, or one who serves in the ministry of preaching the gospel (Col. 1:23, 25; Eph. 3:7; 2 Cor. 3:6; 1 Thess. 3:2; Col. 1:7; 1 Tim. 4:6; Col. 4:7). Paul uses it in reference to his special ministry to the uncircumcised (Rom. 15:8), a ministry (*diakonia*) which he magnified (Rom. 11:13). In 1 Tim. 1:12 he rejoiced that God had appointed him to his service (*diakonia*). The word is also used in a specific sense with reference to certain persons appointed to serve the congregation under the oversight of the bishops, as in these instructions to Timothy. Compare the reference to "the bishops and deacons" (Phil. 1:1), and the reference to Phoebe, a deaconess (female servant) of the church at Cenchreae (Rom. 16:1; cf. comments below on vs. 11). The specific use of the term deacon is sometimes described as an official use to designate one who has been appointed to an "office" in the church, but see comments on verse 11.

Paul has made very clear what the duties of the bishops were in the exercise of their office. But he is not so specific in describing the duties of deacons. Some light is thrown on the matter of specific duties by the appointment of certain men in the Jerusalem church to serve (*diakoneō*) in the daily ministration (*diakonia*) or service of the needs of the Grecian widows (Acts 6:1-6). This was a special appointment to a specific task which may have been a temporary rather than a permanent assignment. Some objection has been raised to the use of Acts 6 in describing the office of deacon on the ground that no reference is found to the existence of an eldership in the Jerusalem church prior to Acts 6. Elders are mentioned in Acts 11:30 and 15:2, 6, 22. This may be a moot question in light of the fact that the Jerusalem church was predominantly Jewish, and the Jewish communities were very accustomed to the oversight of the elders of each community. They were also accustomed to the appointment of special servants of the synagogue or congregation.

On the other hand it is not necessary to establish perfect identity between the deacons of Acts 6 and the men of 1 Timothy 3, since the principle of differentiation between oversight and assistance is present in both cases. One assigned to a task was given an office, whether it be temporary or permanent, and the permanence of the office depended on whether the person continued to be qualified and continued to serve. This would be true of any office, whether it be that of elder, deacon, or evangelist. Ideally, it seems that God did intend for the offices of elder, deacon and evangelist to be lasting ones (cf. Phil. 1:1; 2 Tim. 4:5; Eph. 4:11, 12). This would not exclude the possibility that some tasks might also be assigned on a temporary basis, depending on the emergency of the moment. As the church matured it was possible to be so organized that every emergency could be handled by persons already appointed by the church.

It seems safe to conclude that the work of **deacons** could involve any service to the congregation or community which they performed under the oversight of and as assistants to the elders. The special assignment given to the men in Acts 6:1-6 is described as "serving tables," but this need not be taken as a complete or exhaustive definition of the deacon's task. And it is probably an oversimplification of the ministries of the elders and deacons to say that the task of one pertains purely to spiritual matters and the task of the other to matters purely economic or material.

Paul continues his use of **must** (*dei*) in his instructions concerning the character and conduct of the deacons (see comments on 3:2). The term **likewise** connects with what has been said concerning bishops, just as the same word in verse 11 connects the instructions to the women with what is being said to deacons.

A deacon must be **serious** (*semnos*) or respectful and dignified (see importance of this virtue in the discussion of "respectful" in 2:2; cf. 3:4 and 3:11), and he must not be **double-tongued** (*dilogos*), or insincere. This implies that he must not be deceitful in his words, speaking one thing and meaning another. He must not be **addicted to much wine.** The word translated **addicted** (*prosechō*) means to turn one's mind to or to be occupied with. The same word

[9] they must hold the mystery of the faith with a clear conscience. [10] And let them also be tested first; then if they prove themselves blameless let them serve as deacons.

---

is used in 1:4 concerning those who "occupy themselves" with myths (cf. Tit. 1:14). Paul used it also in admonishing Timothy to "attend" (or give heed to) to his duties (4:13).

Deacons must not be **greedy for gain.** The same terminology is used in Titus 1:7 concerning elders (cf. 1 Peter 5:2). It is a compound word composed of *aischros,* meaning base, and *kerdēs,* meaning gain. The same two words, not in compound form, are used in Titus 1:11. This word for base, meaning evil, foul, obscene, shameful, ugly, dishonest, is peculiar to Paul in the New Testament. He uses it with reference to speech (Col. 3:8) women's hair (1 Cor. 11:6), women speaking in church (1 Cor. 14:35), filthiness (Eph. 5:4, 12). The translation "filthy lucre" (KJV) means dishonest gain.

[9] The word **mystery** (*mustērion*) is used again in 3:16. It may also be translated "secret," as in Mark 4:11 where Jesus speaks of the "secret of the kingdom" which had been given to the twelve apostles (cf. Matt. 13:11; Luke 8:10). Paul uses the word twenty-one times (e.g., Rom. 16:25; 2 Thess. 2:7; 1 Cor. 15:51; 4:1; Eph. 1:9; cf. also Eph. 3:3, 4, 9; 5:32; 6:19; Col. 1:26; 2:2; 4:3). Here Paul urges that the deacons at Ephesus must be loyal to the **mystery of the faith.** In Ephesians Paul spoke of this mystery and defined it as "the unsearchable riches of Christ," and he wanted "to make all men [cf. 1 Tim. 2:1, 4] to see what is the plan of the mystery hidden for ages in God who created all things, that through the church the manifold wisdom of God might now be made known. . ." (Eph. 3:8-10, 5:32). Since the church is God's divine agency for revealing this great secret to the world for the salvation of all men, it behooves every one who serves and represents the church to hold loyally to faith and a **clear conscience** (see comments on 1:5 and 1:19 and Paul's claim for himself in 2 Tim. 1:3). For a discussion of the term **the faith** see discussion of 4:1.

[10] As in the case of the elders, the deacons must also **be tested** before they are appointed. The word **tested**

[11] **The women likewise must be serious, no slanderers, but temperate, faithful in all things.**

(*dokimazō*) means examined. It suggests that their character must be proved. The same word is used in 2 Corinthians 13:5: "Test yourselves." It also suggests that one is qualified and accredited (1 Cor. 16:3). It is closely related to the word *dokimē*, meaning character or worth, which is used concerning the brother "whom we have often tested and found earnest" (2 Cor. 8:22), and also of Timothy's worth or character which was generally known and attested (Phil. 2:22). Just as Paul had "been approved [*dokimazō*] by God to be entrusted with the gospel" (1 Thess. 2:4), so deacons must first be approved, tested (*dokimazō*) before they are entrusted with their ministry. For the meaning of **blameless** see 3:2.

[11] What Paul has to say to **the women** is essentially the same as what he has said to the deacons, with the exception of the requirements regarding base gain and the ruling of the household. The expression **women likewise** (*gunaikas hōsautōs*) is the same form as that used in 2:9, where instructions were given to the men and the women concerning behavior in the public assembly for worship. Here it is in the context of Paul's instructions to certain men concerning their character and conduct as special appointees of the church. And in verse 12 Paul returns to his instructions to these men. This means that **the women** of verse 11 sustain a special relationship to the men called deacons, either as their wives or as special female servants, deaconesses, appointed by the church. If they are being especially instructed because they are the wives of the deacons, why does Paul fail to say a special word to the wives of elders in 3:2-7? In Titus 2:3-5 Paul has special advice for older women and for younger women, but it had nothing to do with whether or not their husbands were elders or deacons. The term **likewise** in verses 8 and 11 suggests that Paul is concerned with three special offices or ministries, one of which pertained to women. The office of oversight did not involve women, who were specifically forbidden to teach or exercise authority over men (see comments on 2:12).

The office of deacon did not involve oversight and authority over the church, so the appointment of certain women as special servants of the church introduces no contradiction with 2:9-15. The objection that no woman could be given an office in the church because this would imply giving her authority is without ground because the idea of office in the New Testament does not necessarily imply authority. The term "rule" is limited to the office of elder and is not used to describe the office of deacon (cf. 3:13 and 5:17). Paul does associate command and authority with the office of the evangelist in his ministry (see Tit. 2:15; cf. 2 Tim. 4:2; 1 Tim. 5:19-22). The woman Phoebe was introduced to the church in Rome as a deaconess of the church (a servant of the congregation) at Cenchreae (Rom. 16:1), which suggests that she had been appointed by the church to represent the congregation in some special service appropriate for a woman to perform. It seems more in harmony with the immediate context and with the general context of the Scriptures to translate verse 11 **women,** rather than "wives" of the deacons. The term deaconess (*diakonissa*) is not used in the New Testament and may not have come into use at the time Paul is writing, but Paul does use the word deacon in a feminine sense in his reference to Phoebe.

According to the above reasoning, we may proceed with Paul's instructions to the women who were appointed to serve the congregation. They were to be **serious,** which is synonymous with "respectful" (see comments on 3:4). They were to refrain from **slander** (*diabolos*). Compare Ephesians 5:25-27 where Paul, urging Christians to put away falsehood and to speak the truth with his neighbor, said "give no opportunity to the devil" (*diabolos*). Compare also the language of James 3:6-10 concerning the tongue as a restless evil (see James 4:7; cf. John 8:44).

Paul also urged the women to be **temperate** (*nēphalios*). On the meaning of this term see comments on 3:2 in reference to the elders. And they were to be **faithful,** or trustworthy, in all things. See comments on Titus 1:6 concerning "faithful" or "believing" children. Compare Paul's use of "faithful" to characterize himself (1:12), Timothy (1 Cor. 4:17), God (2 Thess. 3:3), and Christ (Heb. 2:17).

**12 Let deacons be the husband of one wife, and let them
manage their children and their households well; 13 for
those who serve well as deacons gain a good standing
for themselves and also great confidence in the faith which
is in Christ Jesus.**
**14 I hope to come to you soon, but I am writing these
instructions to you so that,**

---

[12] In this verse Paul turns his attention back to the men and continues what he began in verse 8. A deacon, like an elder, must **be the husband of one wife,** and he should **manage his household well** (see comments on 3:2-4).

[13] Deacons who **serve well** are promised certain rewards: not the "double honor" of elders (see 5:17), nor a promotion to the rank of elder (even though such might come to a deacon who serves well and who otherwise qualifies himself for the office of a bishop), nor financial gain for a job well done. Paul promises so much more: **good standing for themselves and great confidence** (or hope) **in the faith.** This would seem to be reward enough. Just as the satisfaction of being "a good minister" was reason enough for Timothy to be faithful in teaching (4:6), the rewards promised to the deacons who serve well are a great source of happiness, and joy to one whose first desire is to be of service to Christ and his church (cf. Matt. 20:26-28; 1 Peter 5:5, 6).

The phrase **good standing** (*bathmos*) means a "step," "degree," "grade," or "rank." It is not found elsewhere in the New Testament. The mystery religions did use the term for the various ranks and steps of promotion in the soul's journey heavenward, and philosophers used it in reference to the gradual attainment of wisdom (see Arndt and Gingrich). Paul lifts the term out of this context and gives it a Christian frame of reference, as the honorable standing or place gained in the esteem of believers. **Great confidence** may refer to speaking openly to others about **the faith** or to a free and confident approach to God.

Proper Behavior, 3:14-16

[14] Paul had reason to believe that his journey to Ephesus would be **soon** or quickly (*tacheōs*) made, without

15 **if I am delayed, you may know how one ought to behave in the household of God, which is the church of the living God, the pillar and bulwark of the truth.**

---

delay or difficulty. But, on the basis of much experience in traveling, he was aware of the possibility of being delayed by the unexpected interruption of plans.

It is unimportant whether the expression **these instructions** should refer to what he has said in 2:1—3:13 or to what follows in 4:1—6:20 (cf. 4:6, 11). It seems altogether possible that the expression here is related to the entire epistle which is concerned from beginning to end with proper behavior in the church.

[15] Once again Paul uses **ought** (*dei,* must), indicating that what he is writing pertains to divine commands regarding Christian ethics (see comments on **must** in 3:2).

In line with the general terminology of this epistle, Paul describes **the church** (*ekklēsia*) as God's **household** (*oikos*) or family. He employs the language of the family fellowship again and again (cf. 1:2, 18; 2:13-15; 3:2, 4, 5, 13; 4:6; 5:1-9, 14-16; 6:2). It is the church of **the living God** (see comments on 4:10 below). Paul turns from the family imagery to the building use of *oikos* (house). The church is the pillar (*stulos,* "column") and **bulwark** (*hedraiōma,* "support" or "base") of **the truth.** Compare the use of **pillar** in Revelation 3:12 and Galatians 2:9. The word for **bulwark** occurs only here in the New Testament, but it is a cognate form of the word *hedraiōs,* meaning steadfast, used by Paul (e.g., 1 Cor. 15:58; Col. 1:23).

The injection of these words is a pause in the context of his instructions which is characteristic of Paul, and it compares with his letter to the church at Ephesus concerning the place of the church in making known to the world the manifold wisdom of God. His instructions on proper conduct in the church deserve primary attention because of the great mission of the church (see 3:4, 5, 9-11, 14-21). The literary pattern highlights the theological and practical importance of the church: church structure (chapter 3), creed (3:16), heresy (4:1ff.)—compare the same elements in Ephesians 4.

16 Great indeed, we confess, is the mystery of our religion:
He[a] was manifested in the flesh,
vindicated[t] in the Spirit,
seen by angels,
preached among the nations,
believed on in the world,
taken up in glory.

[a] Greek *Who;* other ancient authorities read *God;* others *Which*
[t] Or *justified.*

---

[16] **Great indeed** is a translation of *mega,* which has many shades of meaning in the New Testament. Here it carries the idea of sublime, very important, unusual and extraordinary. Paul uses it as a superlative in lifting love above faith and hope (1 Cor. 13:13) and in describing the unusual opportunity or "wide" door for effective work which had opened to him in Ephesus (1 Cor. 16:8, 9).

The expression **we confess** is a translation of the adverb (*homologoumenōs*) meaning "confessedly," or "without controversy." It is much the same in meaning as the expression "The saying is sure and worthy of full acceptance" (1:15). The use of the word **religion** here as a translation of *eusebeia* (godliness, piety) is subject to the same question and discussion as was its use in 2:10 as a translation of *theosebeia* (reverence for God, piety toward God). Some translators prefer the expression "the mystery of godliness." See comments on the unique importance of the word "godly" (*eusebeia*) in connection with 2:2.

Paul's reference to the **mystery,** or revealed secret, which turns out to be Christ, should be compared with Colossians 1:25-27 and Romans 16:25, 26. See also the comments on 3:9. He now proceeds to give a sixfold analysis of the great truth which the church supports. The poetry of the verse is much like a hymn, and there does seem to be a deliberate assonance in the rhythmic diction and parallelism of the stanzas (cf. the parallelism of 2 Tim. 2:11-13). Paul may or may not be stressing historical sequence in the events heralded in this poetic utterance. If lines two and three are references to the resurrection and appearance that followed, and line six is a reference to the ascension, then items four and five present a problem with reference to the historical sequence. It would seem, from this viewpoint, that line six should precede lines four and five. If, on the other hand, other interpretations are granted of lines two, three, and four, it is possible that Paul is arranging the events in order of occurrence. The following comments on the six lines are suggestive of such a possibility.

1. **He was manifested in the flesh.** He refers to Christ as a manifestation of "the living God" (John 1:1, 14). The word for **flesh** (*sarx*) is the same in John. The word **manifested** (*phaneroō*) is translated "appeared" in 1 John 3:5, 8. In 2 Timothy 1:10 Paul speaks of the grace that was "manifested through the appearing of our Savior Christ Jesus" (cf. also Tit. 1:3).

Paul's use of **flesh** agrees with Romans 1:3 where he speaks of "the gospel concerning his Son, who was descended from David according to the flesh." As in Galatians 4:13 it has a "bodily" connotation, and is synonymous with "body" (*sōma*) in Romans 7:4 where the body of Christ is the same as his flesh (*sarx*) in Ephesians 2:15. Both terms are used in Colossians 1:22, "his body (*sōma*) of flesh (*sarx*)." The Hebrew letter gives special emphasis to the manifestation of God, through Jesus, in human flesh (Heb. 2:14; 5:7; 4:15; 2:17f.). God sent "his own Son in the likeness of sinful flesh and for sin, he condemned sin in the flesh" (Rom. 8:3; cf. also 8:5-8).

2. He was **vindicated in the Spirit.** The word **vindicated** means "justified" or declared righteous and just. God's supreme act in vindicating Jesus according to the Spirit of holiness was by his resurrection from the dead (Rom. 1:4). But even during his ministry in the flesh Jesus did not walk according to the flesh but, sinlessly according to the Spirit. Jesus is called "the righteous one" (Acts 7:52). For Paul's use of the terms "manifestation" and "righteousness" in connection with God's redemptive love through Christ, read Romans 3:21-26 (cf. also Rom. 1:16, 17).

3. He was **seen by angels.** The word for **seen** (*horaō*) has more than one meaning. It may mean to catch sight of, to witness with the eyes. It may also mean to take care of, to see to and watch after something or someone. In the latter sense it is used in Matthew 27:4, "See to it yourselves" (cf. also Matt. 8:4; 9:30; 18:10; 27:24; Acts 18:15;

1 Thess. 5:15). If being seen by angels means that angels saw him, there were many occasions when such happened, before his incarnation, during his earthly ministry, and in connection with his resurrection and ascension (Eph. 1:20ff.; 1 Peter 3:18-22 especially suggest this last). There is another possible interpretation other than Jesus being visible to angels, and that is that Jesus was cared for, seen to, or ministered to by angels during his manifestation in the flesh (Matt. 4:11; John 20:12). If this latter interpretation be what Paul means, **seen by angels** would suggest a visitation for the purpose of ministering to and being of assistance to someone.

4. He was **preached among the nations.** The term **nations** is synonymous with Gentiles. Some interpret this to refer to the execution of the Great Commission (Matt. 28:18-20) and apply it to the proclamation of the gospel beginning with the day of Pentecost in Acts 2 (cf. Eph. 3:7ff.). However, the word **nations** (*ethnos*), meaning Gentiles, is also used in reference to the great Galilean ministry of Jesus which fulfilled Isaiah's prophecy (Matt. 4:12-17; cf. Luke 2:30-32; Matt. 15:21-28).

5. He was **believed on in the world.** The word **world** (*kosmos*) has different connotations in various contexts. Here it refers to mankind in general. Jesus so used it in John 3:16-19 (cf. John 8:12; 9:5; 10:36), when he spoke of men believing in him. Compare also Mark 14:9; 16:15, and Romans 1:8.

6. He was **taken up into glory.** This is an obvious reference to the Lord's ascension. The word for **taken up** (*analēmpsis*) is translated "received up" in Luke 9:51 in reference to Jesus approaching ascent to the Father. Following his resurrection appearances, Jesus was "taken up into heaven" (Mark 16:19; cf. Acts 1:2; 11, and 22). He was taken up into **glory** (*doxa*). Following his resurrection Jesus said, "Was it not necessary that the Christ should suffer these things and enter into his glory" (Luke 24:26). Peter speaks of "the sufferings of Christ and his subsequent glory" (1 Peter 1:11). It was a glory which Jesus had with the Father before the world was made (John 17:5). It was also into a special dispensation of glory at the Father's right hand in heavenly places, far above all rule, authority,

1 Now the Spirit expressly says that in later times some will depart from the faith by giving heed to deceitful spirits and doctrines of demons,

---

power and dominion, and as head over all things for the church (see Eph. 1:19-23). Paul promises that all who have died with Christ and have been raised with Christ, who live their lives in Christ, will also "appear with him in glory" (see Col. 3:1-4).

Doctrines of Demons, 4:1-5

[1] The use of **now** as a translation of *de,* rather than "but," suggests the resumption of an interrupted discourse, but this has been a matter of debate. In view of Acts 20:28ff. it is natural for Paul to move from church order to doctrinal matters. The translation "but," would not do violence to the meaning, since what Paul says here about the doctrines of demons is certainly in contrast to the gospel.

By his use of the words **the Spirit expressly says,** Paul suggests that what he is saying is an inspired prophetic utterance. The saying is in keeping with the apocalyptic expectation of apostasy in the endtime (cf. 2 Thess. 2). This is the only instance of the use of the adverb **expressly** (*rhētōs*) with the verb *legō* (to speak), but the language compares with Matthew 1:22: "what the Lord had spoken by the prophet" (*rhēthen . . legontes*).

The expression **later times** (*husterois kairois*) is not the same as that used by Peter in Acts 2:17 concerning "the last days" (*eschatais hēmerais*), which Paul also uses in 2 Timothy 3:1. If Paul is using **later** (*husterois*) in a comparative sense, it simply means at some time in the future from the time of the prophetic utterance. The language here is very much like that to the church of the Thessalonians (2 Thess. 2:3-11), where the "apostasy" of verse three is the same as the departure here in 4:1. Both words are from *aphistēmi,* meaning to abandon, to rebel, to desert. It is translated "forsake" (Acts 21:21), and "fall away from" (Heb. 3:12). Paul describes this apostasy again in 2 Timothy 4:3, 4: "The time is coming when people will not endure sound teaching . . . but will turn away from listening to the truth and wander into myths" (cf. 1 Tim. 1:3, 4).

2 through the pretensions of liars whose consciences are seared,

---

Paul's use of the term **the faith** (*hē pistis*) here and elsewhere in 1 Timothy, is interpreted by some to mean that a new concept, an unPauline one, of the faith objectively stated, rather than faith as the subjective response of trustful acceptance (as in Rom. 10), is being introduced (cf. 3:9; 4:6; 6:10; 2 Tim. 2:18; 4:7). Paul's use of **the faith** and "the truth" in relation to "the gospel" is the same to Timothy as "the faith of the gospel" (Phil. 1:27), "belief in the truth" (2 Thess. 2:13), and "preaching the faith" (Gal. 1:23) which is synonymous with faith in the person of Christ (Gal. 3:23-26). In 2 Thessalonians "belief in the truth" (2:13, 15) is synonymous with "hold to the traditions which you were taught" (2:15). Paul does emphasize faith in the person of Christ (Phil. 3:9), but he also emphasizes fidelity to Christ in heeding "the sound words of our Lord Jesus Christ and the teaching which accords with godliness" (6:3; cf. Jesus in Matt. 7:24, 26, and Matt. 28:20).

The word for **giving heed to** is translated "addicted" in 3:8, "attend" in 4:13, "agree" in 6:3. The **deceitful spirits** are probably the same as the "evil men and imposters, . . . deceivers and deceived" (2 Tim. 3:13; cf. 2 Cor. 6:8; 2 John 7; Matt. 27:63). The word **deceitful** (*planois*) is a cognate form of the word for error (*planē*). In Ephesians 4:14 Paul speaks of the doctrines of cunning men who by their craftiness propagate "deceitful wiles" (cf. Rom. 16:17ff.), which may be translated the "wiles of error" and implies a systematizing of falsehood. The deceitful spirits are representatives of "the prince of the power of the air, the spirit that is now at work in the sons of disobedience" (Eph. 2:2).

Paul's use of the genitive of source indicates that the doctrines proceeded from demons rather than being doctrines about demons. Teaching about demons or devils is found elsewhere in the New Testament (e.g., Matt. 10:8; 12:28; Mark 1:34; 7:26f.; 16:9, 17; 1 Cor. 10:20f.).

[2] The deceitful spirits lure people away from the faith into demonic doctrines by using **liars whose con-**

3 who forbid marriage and enjoin abstinence from foods which God created to be received with thanksgiving by those who believe and know the truth.[4] For everything created by God is good, and nothing is to be rejected if it is received with thanksgiving; [5] for then it is consecrated by the word of God and prayer.

---

sciences are seared, who deceive through their **pretensions.** The word **seared** (*kautēriazō,* meaning cauterized) occurs only here in the New Testament, but the thought expressed concerning the conscience is paralleled by Paul's reference to those who are "darkened in their understanding, alienated from the life of God because of the ignorance that is in them, due to their hardness of heart; they have become callous . . ." (Eph. 4:18, 19a). Compare the comments on **conscience** in 1:5 and 1:19.

[3-5] Paul mentions two particular doctrines which would be featured by the false asceticism which would lure some into the predicted apostasy: (1) They will **forbid marriage,** and (2) they will **enjoin abstinence from foods.** The word **enjoin** is added to remove the elipsis in Paul's statement. So Paul is saying that these liars would make it a binding obligation to abstain from foods and not to marry. These practices may have been based on the belief that they were now living the resurrection life (2 Tim. 2:18; cf. Mark 12:25). For another instance of heretical asceticism, see Colossians 2:20ff. **For everything created by God is good** (cf. Gen. 1:11-13; 9:2-4). Even the food laws that existed under the Law were no longer binding upon those in Christ (see Col. 2:16). Not only food but also marriage is according to the creation ordinance of God (see Gen. 1:27, 28; 2:21-25; cf. Eph. 5:21-25, 28, 29, 33; 1 Peter 3:1-7). Both foods and marriage are **consecrated** (*hagiazō*), or "made holy," **by the word of God** and **by prayer,** and neither should be regarded as unclean. Compare Paul's use of **consecrated,** or "sanctified," elsewhere (e.g. 1 Cor. 7:14; Rom. 15:16; 2 Tim. 2:21). The **word of God** would be God's declaration of the goodness of creation in Genesis 1. The **prayer** of thanksgiving consecrates creation to man's use. Good conscience is synonymous with the knowledge of the truth, and the weak conscience is

[6] **If you put these instructions before the brethren, you will be a good minister of Christ Jesus, nourished on the words of the faith and of the good doctrine which you have followed.**

---

synonymous with ignorance of the truth (cf. 1 Tim. 1:19; 1 Cor. 8:7-13; 10:25-29; for a discussion of **the truth** see comments on 2:4).

A Twofold Charge to Timothy, 4:6-16

[6] The word **minister** (*diakonos*) is used here in the same sense that it is used in Colossians 1:23 (cf. also 2 Cor. 3:6; 6:4; 1 Thess. 3:2; 1 Cor. 3:5). A striking contrast, using the same word, is found in Paul's description of false teachers as servants, or ministers (*diakonos*) of Satan rather than servants of Christ (2 Cor. 11:13, 14, 23). For a discussion of the specific and general meanings associated with the word *diakonos*, see comments on the deacons in 3:8. Paul's word for **nourished** (*entrephō*) means to be reared or brought up. The use of *trephō* in compound forms is peculiar to Paul and Luke in the New Testament. Compare "brought up" (*anatrephō*, Luke 4:16; Acts 7:20), "nourished" (*ektrephō*, Eph. 5:29; 6:4). Compare also "nourishment" (*trophē*, Acts 9:19; Heb. 5:12). The idea of being **nourished,** or fed, on the words of the faith finds a close parallel in Hebrews 5:12-14. The association of **words to the faith** also finds parallels in Paul's use of "utterance" or spoken words in connection with proclaiming the mystery of the gospel (Eph. 6:19, 20) and the imparting "in words" the thoughts of God taught by the Spirit (1 Cor. 2:13; cf. 1 Thess. 1:5; 2 Thess. 2:15; 1 Cor. 14:1-6; 1 Tim. 1:13). Timothy had **followed** the words of the faith and good doctrine. **Followed** (*parakoloutheō*), in the sense in which it is used here, is found only here and in Luke 1:3 and 2 Timothy 3:10. It means "to follow closely," or "to investigate," and "to trace out thoroughly with the mind." It is also translated "observed" (2 Tim. 3:10). For a discussion of the significance of **the faith** see comments on 4:1; and for a discussion of **doctrine** see comments on 1:3 (cf. 1:10 and 4:1). Faith and teaching are often related in these letters.

[7] Have nothing to do with godless and silly myths. Train yourself in godliness; [8] for while bodily training is of some value, godliness is of value in every way, as it holds promise for the present life and also for the life to come.

---

[7] Timothy is urged to **have nothing to do with** (*peraiteomai*) **godless and silly myths,** which means to refuse, to reject or dismiss (cf. 5:11; Heb. 12:25; Tit. 3:10). The use of **godless** (*bebēlos*), meaning unholy and profane, is in contrast to **godliness** (*eusebeia* or piety; see comments on 2:2 and 3:16). It is translated "profane" in 1:9 (cf. 6:20; 2 Tim. 2:16; Heb. 12:16; Matt. 12:5; Acts 24:6). The word **silly** (*graōdeis*), found here only in the New Testament, means "old wives," or "old womanish." In a similar context Paul uses "stupid" and "senseless" (2 Tim. 2:23). For the meaning of **myths** as it is used in the New Testament, see the discussion of 1:4. On the contrary, or in opposition to the godless myths, Timothy is urged to **train** himself **in godliness.** The word **train** (*gumnazō*) means "to exercise." The same word is used concerning having our senses trained or exercised to discern good and evil (Heb. 5:14), and concerning those whose hearts are trained in greed (2 Peter 2:14). Paul is urging Timothy to discipline himself (see Heb. 12:11).

[8] Paul continues with a positive word on the value of **godliness.** He uses two words in this verse which some classify as foreign to Paul and the New Testament elsewhere: **training** (*gumnasia*) and **of value** (*ōphelimos,* "profitable"). On the contrary, cognate forms do appear elsewhere: "value" (*ōpheleia,* "profit," Rom. 3:1), and "to be of value" (*ōpheleō,* "to profit," Rom. 2:25; 1 Cor. 14:6; Gal. 5:2; Luke 9:25; Heb. 4:2), and the word "to train" (*gumnazō,* Heb. 5:14; 12:11; 2 Peter 2:14). **Bodily training,** says Paul, does have **some value.** Paul may be sounding a warning to Timothy concerning the danger of a false asceticism pertaining to the discipline of the body. Here, however, he does recognize that such training may be profitable for this life. In Colossians 2:23 he emphatically denies that "rigor of devotion and self-abasement and severity to the body" has any value at all in "checking the indulgence of the flesh." It takes **training in godliness**

[9] **The saying is sure and worthy of full acceptance.** [10] **For to this end we toil and strive,**[j] **because we have our hope set on the living God, who is the Savior of all men, especially of those who believe.**

[j] Other ancient authorities read *suffer reproach*

---

to check such indulgence and to develop the spiritual maturity essential to living victoriously in the **present life** and in the **life to come** (cf. Col. 3:1-4).

[9, 10] Compare comments above on 1:15 and 3:1 concerning the expression, **The saying is sure,** which in this case probably relates to what follows in verse 10. The toiling and striving which Paul refers to here is suggested by the word **training** in verse 7. The word **toil** signifies a weariness and exhaustion which accompanies suffering for righteousness. The word **strive** signifies suffering. Compare the "labor of love and steadfastness of hope in our Lord Jesus Christ" (1 Thess. 1:3). Using the same word, Paul said, "I worked harder" (1 Cor. 15:10), and "I labored over you" (Gal. 4:11). He uses the same word in 5:17 concerning the "labor" of elders (cf. 1 Thess. 5:12; Rom. 16:12).

Paul also established the goal of such discipline and toiling which challenges them to press on toward the mark: **we have our hope set on the living God.** Christian preaching to Gentiles had for its theme **the living God** (Acts 14:15; 1 Thess. 1:9). God is the ground of life and gives the life which is to come. The power of **hope** as an essential factor in encouraging and motivating Christians to steadfast endurance is underscored by Paul in Philippians 3:7-16. God is **the Savior of all men.** This does not suggest that all men will be saved. God does desire "all men to be saved" (2:4), and Jesus "gave himself as a ransom for all" (2:6), but this salvation is **especially for those who believe.** The word **especially** does not imply that all will be saved and that believers will be saved in a special way. The word *malista* is translated "particularly" (5:17) and "above all" (2 Tim. 4:13), and "especially" (Tit. 1:10; Phil. 4:22; Phile. 16). In this context it suggests that salvation is promised to believers in particular; they are the ones for whom it is specifically intended. Jesus was very specific on this matter (see John 3:15-18; Mark 16:15, 16). **A be-**

[11] **Command and teach these things.** [12] **Let no one despise your youth, but set the believers an example in speech and conduct, in love, in faith, in purity.**

---

liever is one who is obedient (see Matt. 7:21, 24-27; cf. 1 Peter 4:15-19; 2 Thess. 1:8; Heb. 5:9). The force of this verse may be a thrust against Gnostic exclusiveness which confined salvation to an elite.

[11] On this verse compare "charge" and "teach" in 1:3, where the word for "charge" is the same as **command** (*parangellō*) here. Compare also the role of the evangelist in teaching in the discussion of 2:7 and the duties of Timothy that are set forth in 4:13.

[12] The word **despise** means to treat with contempt or to esteem lightly and disrespect (1 Cor. 16:10f.). It is translated "disrespect" in 6:2. The word **youth** (*neotēs*) is not to be confused with "boy" or "teenager," for Timothy was probably in his thirties. Compare Acts 26:4, 5, where Paul's youth refers to the beginning of his responsible years as a young Pharisee. Compare also "younger widows" (5:11). Hellenistic authors used the word for men up to forty. Timothy was not to be intimidated by the disrespect some might have for him because of his being younger, and he was to conduct himself in such a manner that **youth** would not be put in a bad light (cf. 5:1). He was to **set the believers an example** (*tupos,* meaning pattern). Paul himself adhered faithfully to this spiritual strategy in helping brethren to understand the meaning of his words (cf. 2 Thess. 3:9). He urged Titus to do the same (Tit. 2:7), just as Peter also instructed the elders (1 Peter 5:3).

Specifically, Timothy was to set a pattern: (1) In **speech** (*logos*), both in daily conversation and in preaching. He was to "follow the pattern of sound words" which he had heard from Paul (2 Tim. 1:13). (2) In **conduct** (*anastrophē*), meaning behavior (3:15), or manner of life (Eph. 4:22). Compare Peter's language (2 Pet. 3:11), and Paul's words to the Philippians (Phil. 1:27; 3:20). (3) In **love** (*agapē*). See comments on the charge given to Timothy in 1:5. (4) In **faith** (*pistis*), of faithfulness, trustworthiness. Compare "true fidelity" in Titus 2:10. (5) In **purity** (*hagneia*), meaning chastity and propriety (cf. 5:2).

[13] **Till I come, attend to the public reading of scripture, to preaching, to teaching.**

---

[13] Pending Paul's arrival, hopefully soon and quickly (cf. 3:14), Timothy is to **attend** (*proechō*) to or occupy himself with three main duties (contrast those who occupied themselves with myths, 1:4), which were his principal concerns as an evangelist. Each of these duties is preceded by the definite article **the** (*tē*). Even though Paul does not use the technical language of synagogue worship, he does speak of three things here which were recognized items of worship in both Jewish and Christian assemblies.

(1) **The public reading of scripture.** The word **reading** (*anaginōskō*) means to read aloud. It is used in Acts 8:28-32, where Philip heard the Eunuch reading (see also Acts 13:15; 2 Cor. 3:14, 15). Copies of the holy scriptures were costly because of materials and the labor of scribes. People gathered to hear the word of God read (cf. Neh. 8:1-8). The preacher, with his gift for public proclamation (*kērux*), is urged to read God's word to the people. False teachers were leading many astray by the public misuse of the Old Testament scriptures. Timothy, by public reading, preaching, and exhortation, could convict men of the truth (see comments on 2 Tim. 3:15, 16).

(2) The **preaching.** The word for **preaching** (*parakaleō*) means to urge or exhort. Timothy was not only to read the Scriptures publicly, he was also to base his urgent exhortation on the Scriptures read (cf. Acts 13:15; Rom. 15:4). For a discussion of **preaching,** or exhortation, see comments on 1:3 (cf. 2:1; 5:1; 6:3).

(3) The **teaching.** This was a very significant part of Timothy's ministry as an evangelist, or missionary (see comments on 2:7). Teaching was a most important function in dealing with the problem caused by false teachers in Ephesus (see comments on 1:3). **The teaching** (*tē didaskalia*) may refer to the act of teaching or to that which is taught, the body of doctrine itself (see comments on the qualification of an elder as an "apt teacher," 3:2; cf. 2 Tim. 4:2 and Titus 1:9). In his teaching, Timothy was to occupy himself with the business of teaching, and he was to be faithful to sound doctrine which accords with

14 Do not neglect the gift you have, which was given you
by prophetic utterance when the elders laid their hands
upon you. 15 Practice these duties, devote yourself to them,
so that all may see your progress. 16 Take heed to yourself
and to your teaching: hold to that, for by so doing you will
save both yourself and your hearers.

---

the glorious gospel (cf. 4:16; 1:10, 11). There was a "form of doctrine," or a "standard of teaching" (Rom. 6:17; cf. Rom. 16:17) which was to be faithfully regarded.

[14-16] In addition to the "gift" which was imparted to Timothy by the laying on of the hands of the apostle Paul (see comments on 2 Tim. 1:6), there is in this verse strong indication that Timothy received another **gift** when the elders laid their hands upon him. There is no evidence elsewhere in the scriptures that an eldership was empowered to impart miraculous spiritual gifts. And there is little to support the idea that Paul's hands were the hands of the eldership. The context (13-16) indicates that the gift which Timothy was not to neglect is the same as **these duties** in verse 15, which is used in obvious reference to the things Timothy is to attend to in verse 13.

The use of the word **gift** (*charisma*) for a ministry, office, or function which is **given** (*edothē*) finds a parallel in Romans 12:4-8, where Paul speaks of ministries, offices, or functions as "gifts." Among the gifts listed in Romans 12 are **teaching** (*didaskalia*) and **exhortation** (*paraklēsis*) just as they appear in verse 13 in reference to the things Timothy is to attend to. Compare also "serving" (*diakonian*, Rom. 12:7) in light of 1 Timothy 3:8f., with reference to an office or ministry. In light of what Paul says in Romans 12, it seems altogether likely that Timothy's gift was his ministry of teaching and preaching to which he was appointed or ordained when the elders laid their hands on him. It was a ministry in which he could make **progress** by dedicating himself diligently to his **duties.** The concept of **gift** as a ministry that is **given** finds also a parallel in the words addressed to Archippus: "See that you fulfill the ministry which you have received in the Lord" (Col. 4:17).

The phrase **by prophetic utterance** (or alternatively "on account of prophecy") suggests that Timothy's appoint-

[1] Do not rebuke an older man but exhort him as you would a father; treat younger men like brothers, [2] older women like mothers, younger women like sisters, in all purity.

---

ment to his ministry as an evangelist, or missionary, was in circumstances much like those depicted in Acts 13:1-3. Timothy was appointed by the eldership, and he received his ministry **with the laying on** of their **hands.** The laying on of hands in New Testament times was an action involved in the following three important events: (1) *Healing* (Acts 28:8; 9:17; Mark 7:32). This action was not limited to the apostles. (2) *Imparting the Spirit* (Acts 8:17, 18; 19:6; cf. 2 Tim. 1:6, 7). This was an action performed by the apostles only. (3) *Appointing to a ministry* (Acts 13:3; 14:23; 1 Tim. 5:22 and 4:14). It is the latter action that involves Timothy and the eldership.

The action of laying on hands was a symbolic one, and it was appropriately accompanied by prayer. The action symbolized a blessing being bestowed upon someone. The prayer was the very heart of the ceremony, and the laying on of hands was an outward symbol of the prayer, which was a petition for divine blessing upon the candidate or appointee and was regarded as a personal benediction on the one being so commissioned. Jesus set an example for such action in his very familiar gesture of raising his hands to pronounce a benediction (Luke 24:50), and in placing his hands on individuals upon whom he pronounced a blessing (Mark 10:13-16).

Specific Instructions to Timothy, 5:1—6:2a

Timothy's Example, 5:1, 2. [1, 2] The family of God (3:15) is divided into the **older** and the **younger** (cf. Tit. 2:2-8; 1 Peter 5:5). Timothy's youth (4:12) placed him in the younger group to which he must relate as to brothers and sisters. The older group is to be treated as fathers and mothers. Paul's age placed him in a father-son relation to Timothy (cf. Phil. 2:22). Widows are also grouped as the younger and the older (5:9-11).

The word **rebuke** is not the same in meaning as the "rebuke" of 5:20, for here Paul is using a word (*epiplēssō*)

**[3] Honor widows who are real widows. [4] If a widow has
children or grandchildren, let them first learn their religious duty to their own family and make some return to
their parents; for this is acceptable in the sight of God.
[5] She who is a real widow, and is left all alone, has set her
hope on God and continues in supplications and prayers
night and day; [6] whereas she who is self-indulgent is dead
even while she lives. [7] Command this, so that they may be
without reproach. [8] If any one does not provide for his
relatives, and especially for his own family, he has disowned the faith and is worse than an unbeliever.**

---

which means to treat harshly. Metaphorically it means to strike against. Timothy is to urge or **exhort** in the sense of encouragement and comfort, as he would treat his own father (cf. Lev. 19:32). This is the word Paul himself used in speaking to Timothy: "I urged you" (1:3; cf. "urge" in 2:1 and 6:3). The only verbs of action in this verse are **rebuke** and **exhort.** The translators have supplied **treat.** So the admonition concerning not rebuking but exhorting pertains to Timothy's manner of exhorting the younger as well as the older. Timothy is to treat all with due respect and dignity in an encouraging manner. The phrase **in all purity** is descriptive of Timothy's relationship with all, not merely with the younger women. **Purity** (*hagneia*) is used in 4:12 with reference to Timothy's exemplary conduct before all believers; it is a word that signifies chastity and propriety.

Honor for Older Widows, 5:3-10. [3-8] These verses pertain to the duty of the church and the home to provide for the older **widows** who are deserving, i.e., who are left all alone. The word for honor (*timaō*) is used by Luke with the same meaning it has here when he records that the people of Malta "presented many gifts to us . . . whatever we needed" (Acts 28:10), literally "they honored (*timaō*) us with many honors" (*timē*). The idea of material or economic compensation for the widow is suggested by the words **some return** (*amoibē*) in verse 4 and the words **provide for** (*pronoeō*) in verse 8. Jesus used the word "honor" in reference to reward for service (John 12:26), and elsewhere in the New Testament the word is used in connection with taxes and revenues (Rom. 13:6, 7; 1 Peter 2:17). Compare also the reference to "double honor" for elders in 5:17. For the early church's care of widows see Acts 6:1. The word "visit" in James 1:27 means to care for or look after the widows and orphans.

An older woman deprived of her husband is not a **real widow** if she has **children or grandchildren** (5:4) or relatives (5:16) who are able to provide for her. The word **widow,** like the word orphan, suggests a state of being left desolate and unprovided for, **left all alone,** or deserted (5:5). The fact that she is older would place such a widow in a more serious predicament. Younger widows (11-15) were in a different predicament, but they were not in the same desperate plight from an economic viewpoint and from the viewpoint of a second marriage.

In verse 4, Paul uses one of the key words, *eusebeia,* discussed in 2:2, meaning godliness or piety, which is here translated **religious duty.** Christians are commanded and urged to practice true religion at home (cf. 5:7; James 1:27). A Christian worships God at home and shows piety toward God by providing for those of his own household. If he does not, **he has disowned the faith and is worse than an unbeliever.** The worship of God is expressed not only in the general assembly of the saints but also in one's faithfulness in fulfilling the everyday, practical responsibilities of the home (cf. 5:8, 14, 16; 2:10, 15; also Tit. 2:4, 5; Eph. 5:21-25; 1 Peter 3:1-6; Eph. 6:1-4).

The real widow, having no prospect or thought of marriage, and having no family, will henceforth give herself continually to **supplication** (*deēsis*) and **prayers** (*proseuchē;* cf. comments on 2:1 where these two terms are used). This suggests that she is a God-fearing, pious woman (cf. 2:10) who is willing to be of service to Christ and his church according to the measure of her talent and strength. The ministry of prayer is worthy of the increased attention of those who are free to devote more time to it (cf. 2:1). The word **continues** means to abide or remain (cf. Acts 11:23; 13:43). **Night and day** suggests "always" (cf. Mark 5:5). Compare the widow Anna (Luke 2:37, 38). It is used in reference to Paul's preaching (Acts 20:31) and

9 Let a widow be enrolled if she is not less than sixty years of age, having been the wife of one husband; 10 and she must be well attested for her good deeds, as one who has brought up children, shown hospitality, washed the feet of the saints, relieved the afflicted, and devoted herself to doing good in every way.

---

worship (Acts 26:7); also of working (1 Thess. 2:9), of praying (1 Thess. 3:10; 2 Tim. 1:3), and serving God in his temple (Rev. 7:15). Such a widow has proved through her younger years that she is not given to **self-indulgence** (*spatalosa*) which suggests a spoiled person who delights in luxury (cf. James 5:6).

[9, 10] Any Christian may be assisted, regardless of sex or age or marital status, so long as the person proves honest and in real need and unable to work. Here, however, Paul is referring to an **enrolled** widow, one placed on a list in view of being honored with permanent compensation during the last days or years of her life. She is thus promised perpetual care. It is understood, of course, that she will not marry again and that she has no other source of subsistence. The age when a person is regarded as having become "old" has varied through the centuries. In Old Testament times seventy was regarded as the span of life, with eighty as a possibility (Ps. 90:10). Sixty was considered "old" (cf. Lev. 27:3-7). Special consideration was given to those who were sixty and over, especially to women.

The honored widow must have been **the wife of one husband** in the same sense that an elder must be "the husband of one wife" (see comments on 3:2 for the meaning of this requirement). She must have established a good reputation as **one who has brought up children.** In this verse the emphasis is on the rearing of children more than on child-bearing (see comments on 2:15). The word for bringing up children (*teknotropheō*), found here only in the New Testament, means to nurture children or to rear a family (cf. Eph. 6:4).

The honored widow must also be one who has shown **hospitality** (see comments on "hospitable" in 3:2). The word used here implies the receiving of guests into one's

[11] But refuse to enrol younger widows; for when they grow wanton against Christ they desire to marry, [12] and so they incur condemnation for having violated their first pledge. [13] Besides that, they learn to be idlers, gadding about from house to house, and not only idlers but gossips and busybodies, saying what they should not. [14] So I would have younger widows marry, bear children, rule their households, and give the enemy no occasion to revile us. [15] For some have already strayed after Satan. [16] If any believing woman [i] has relatives who are widows, let her assist them; let the church not be burdened, so that it may assist those who are real widows.

[i] Other ancient authorities read *man or woman;* others simply *man*

---

home and giving them lodging (compare Lydia, Acts 16:15, and Phoebe, Rom. 16:1, 2; Phile. 22). Washing the saints' **feet** was one aspect of hospitality which indicated a humble spirit of service to others (cf. John 13:14; 1 Peter 5:5). She is deserving of relief and assistance if she herself assisted those **afflicted** or "troubled" (cf. Phil. 4:14, "we share our troubles").

Younger widows, 5:11-16. [11-16] These instructions concerning the **younger widows** must have been very helpful to Timothy not only in supplying a code of ethics but also in giving moral support in dealing with what must have been a most difficult matter.

Some interpret the enrolling of a widow as a sort of marriage ceremony in which the enrolled widow is regarded henceforth as a bride of Christ. Later, if she desired to marry some man this would be regarded as infidelity toward her Lord, Jesus Christ. Hence, the wisdom of enrolling only those who have determined never to marry again.

Paul's instructions concerning the younger widows are given in a spirit of encouragement and comfort (cf. 5:1), even as Timothy would speak and act toward a sister, or an older man to his daughter. What Paul is insisting on is for the spiritual well-being of the younger widow, not merely to relieve the strain on the church budget. The second marriage of a widow is not to be interpreted as infidelity on her part (cf. 1 Cor. 7:8, 9, 32-35). Paul's instructions on such matters are given in tenderness (1 Cor.

7:35). By reason of age, younger widows would find it much more difficult to keep the pledge involved in her enrollment. The church would be acting unwisely in placing her in a situation for which she is not ready. She would be more likely to be tempted by sexual desire and also desire for things that could not be obtained on the modest relief provided by the church. The difficulties and temptations posed by such a relationship to the church had evidently proved to be too much for some younger widows who had taken the pledge and had been enrolled, if this be the meaning of verse 15. Since a second marriage was not necessarily straying after Satan, it seems that an evil has resulted from enrolling younger widows and placing them in the position of violating a pledge if they were to marry again. This would create a strain in their relation to Christ and his church and bring them into criticism and reproach. If verse 15 does not refer to a bad experience with enrolling younger widows, then it suggests that in general such women showed a tendency to get into mischief, perhaps in pursuit of pleasure and luxury or entering into marriage with a man who was not a Christian in name or character (cf. 1 Cor. 7:39). Whatever the meaning of verse 15, Paul insists, in the spiritual interest of the young widow as well as the church, that she find security in marital love and find noble employment in the duties of the home. This would keep her from the temptations and snares of Satan, and becoming (1) an **idler,** meaning lazy (Tit. 1:12), useless (James 2:20), with nothing to do, or unemployed (Matt. 20:3); (2) one who is **gadding about** or wandering about with no house or home to keep her occupied (cf. Heb. 11:37); (3) a **gossip,** meaning one who talks foolishly about or falsely accuses someone, or as John said, "*prating against me with evil words*" (3 John 10 and see comments on "slander" in 3:11); (4) a **busybody,** a meddlesome person occupied with curiosity about other people's affairs (cf. 2 Thess. 3:11).

The younger widows need to **marry, bear children** (see comments on 2:15), **rule their households** (cf. Tit. 2:4, 5). They should do what the honored older widows have already done (cf. 5:9, 10). The word for **rule their households** (*oikodespoteō*) is found here only in the New Testa-

[17] **Let the elders who rule well be considered worthy of double honor, especially those who labor in preaching and teaching;** [18] **for the scripture says, "You shall not muzzle an ox when it is treading out the grain," and, "The laborer deserves his wages."**

---

ment. But it is a cognate form of *oikodespotēs*, meaning the master or ruler of a household, often translated "householder" (e.g., Matt. 24:43; 13:27) and usually in reference to a man. But its use here in reference to woman's place in the home compares perfectly with the virtuous woman of Proverbs (see Prov. 31:10, 13, 15, 19, 20, 26, 27).

Double Honor for Elders, 5:17-20. [17, 18] The meaning of the term **double honor** has been interpreted in various ways: (1) Properly honored and properly paid; (2) Honor (not pay) to elders who serve excellently, and honor for the excellency itself; (3) A double stipend, as compared with honor (compensation) for real widows; (4) More pay, not necessarily double, than that given to widows; (5) More honor (not pay) than that accorded widows and masters. Lenski allows only two meanings for **honor** (*timē*), i.e., "honor" and "price." He does not allow "wages," "pay," or "hire." If Paul had intended to imply "wages," says Lenski, he would have used *misthos*. We cannot be sure of this in view of Paul's metaphorical use of *misthos* concerning a wage or reward not measured in terms of money or material things. Paul's wage (*misthos*) or reward for serving the Corinthians was in not making full use of his rights in the gospel and in making the gospel free of charge (1 Cor. 9:18; cf. 1 Cor. 9:14, 15). The fact of the matter is that the word for **honor** (*timē*) is used in the New Testament in reference to supplying one's material needs. It has such a meaning concerning widows in 5:3-8. But it is also used to describe the supply of Paul's material needs by the inhabitants of Malta (see comments on **honor** for widows in 5:3, and compare Acts 28:10; Rom. 13:1-7).

It is also significant that the injustice symbolized by the figure of muzzling an ox when it is treading grain (Deut. 25:4) is used not only here but also in connection with Paul's own right in the gospel "to refrain from working for a living" (1 Cor. 9:6) and the Lord's command "that those who proclaim the gospel should get their living by the gospel" (1 Cor. 9:14). The second quotation in verse 18 is found verbatim in Luke 10:7. They have the right to receive "material benefits" for spiritual services rendered (1 Cor. 9:11; cf. 1 Cor. 9:4-18). It is not mere assumption, then, to allow **double honor** to mean that an elder who rules well and is occupied with preaching and teaching should not be dishonored and forced to serve at his own expense. An elder might choose not to insist on this right, but it is an important point of Christian ethics that the church must, as the imperative form of the verb in verse 17 indicates, see that his material needs are supplied.

It seems altogether possible that the **double honor** includes both the **honor** to be given widows (5:3) as well as the **honor** to be given masters by their servants (6:1), which was an honor that consisted of the respect and submissiveness which they owed to their masters. The **honor** of servants for masters was not measured in terms of wages they were to pay their masters. The honor to be given widows was not measured in terms of respectful submission but in terms of material benefits to supply their physical needs. Elders who rule well are worthy of respectful submission, but those who **labor in preaching and teaching** are worthy also of compensation in terms of their physical needs. The word **labor** (*kopiaō*) means to toil and work hard. It is used in reference to physical labor (e.g. Acts 20:35; 1 Cor. 4:12; Eph. 4:28; 2 Tim. 2:6). It is also used in reference to spiritual and mental labors which involve much physical energy and physical fatigue (e.g. 1 Cor. 15:10; 16:16; Gal. 4:11; 1 Tim. 4:10; Col. 1:29). It is significant that the word **labor** is used in a similar context in 1 Thessalonians 5:12, 13 concerning respect for "those who *labor* among you and are over you in the Lord and admonish you." Paul applies this same principle to certain elders in Ephesus who labored in **preaching** and **teaching.** The word translated **preaching** is *logos,* "word," which Paul used in reference to the preaching of the gospel (cf. 1 Cor. 1:17, 18; cf. Tit. 1:9). It is used of those who are "speakers" and suggests an ability to proclaim, or a gift of "utterance" (cf. Eph. 6:19; 1 Cor. 2:4).

[19] Never admit any charge against an elder except on the evidence of two or three witnesses. [20] As for those who persist in sin, rebuke them in the presence of all, so that the rest may stand in fear. [21] In the presence of God and of Christ Jesus and of the elect angels I charge you to keep these rules without favor, doing nothing from partiality.

Concerning the **teaching** role of elders see comments on 3:2.

[19, 20] The position of ruling and teaching sometimes exposes an elder to unfair gossip to a degree beyond that to which the average person is subjected. The fact that he is an elder, however, does not grant him immunity from accusation and guilt. The imperative **never admit** suggests that a charge is not to be accepted as true if it is not confirmed by a sufficient number of witnesses (cf. Deut. 19:15; Matt. 18:15-17). It seems that the integrity of the witnesses might also be checked out to insure against the possibility of false witness (see comments on 3:2 on the meaning of "above reproach" in regard to elders). The word **rebuke** (*elegchō*) in verse 20 is not the word translated "rebuke" in 5:1 (see comments on 5:1). Here it means to reprove, convict and correct, and does not imply the disrespect which is forbidden in 5:1.

A Special Encouragement to Timothy, 5:21-25. Any person placed in the position in which Paul has just placed Timothy (vss. 19, 20) will need to be sure his own house is in order. It is a very appropriate place for Paul to pause prayerfully and to give Timothy a special charge and word of exhortation on the great importance of keeping himself free of guilt and accusation in order that his leadership in matters of church discipline, both preventive and corrective, may not be hindered or made ineffective.

[21] The word translated **charge** means to bear witness, to testify solemnly and earnestly (cf. Acts 2:40; 8:25; 18:5; 20:21, 23, 24; 23:11; 28:23). The expression **in the presence of** (*enōpion*), meaning "before," is translated "in the sight of God" (5:4). Compare "before the Lord" (2 Tim. 2:14), and "in the presence of God and Christ Jesus" (2 Tim. 4:1). Here Paul adds the somewhat unusual words, **and of the elect angels.** Compare his reference to angels as spectators in 1 Corinthians 4:9 (cf. also Heb. 12:22, 23; 1:14; Col.

22 Do not be hasty in the laying on of hands, nor participate in another man's sins; keep yourself pure.

2:10; Eph. 1:21). The awareness by angels of events in the life of the church is also found in Luke 15:10 (cf. Luke 12:8; Acts 27:23; Heb. 13:2; 1:14). The term **elect angels** may suggest a contrast to the angels in Jude 6 who were condemned for disobedience. **Elect** means select, chosen. Compare "called and *chosen* and faithful" (Rev. 17:14).

Paul's reverent pause in the midst of his instructions is a most characteristic gesture, indicating his fervent conviction that the ministry of the word and the public functions of the preacher involving proclamation and discipline are much too serious to be undertaken without a solemn awareness of the presence and power of God through Christ and his Spirit. In the disciplinary action which he called for at Corinth he even promised them the presence of his own spirit, with the power of the Lord Jesus, when they assembled for the purpose of corrective discipline (1 Cor. 5:4, 5). Even the disciplinary action of one brother toward another should not be undertaken without first invoking the Lord's presence and power throughout the proceedings (see Matt. 18:15, 16, 19-22).

He was to enforce these things **without favor** (*prokrima*) which means without prejudice or prejudgment. Timothy was to be sure of his facts before forming his opinion. Paul's use of the word for pre-judgment (from *prokrinō*) is the same linguistic style used in 1 Corinthians 4:3-5 where he warns against judging or forming an opinion before the facts are fully known, using *krinō* (to judge) and *pro* (before). Timothy's role of pronouncing judgment on the basis of evidence is a position which Paul himself occupied in such matters; e.g., 1 Cor. 5:3-13. In such matters Timothy was to show **no partiality** (*prosklisis*, from *prosklinō*). A study of *klisis* and *klinō*, as used in the New Testament, suggests that the evangelist is not to bow down to certain persons in a preferential way.

[22] Not only is Timothy to guard against judging the guilt or innocence of an accused elder too quickly or in preferential manner, he is also to avoid public endorsement of a man as an elder in a manner that is too hasty. In light

[23] No longer drink only water, but use a little wine for the sake of your stomach and your frequent ailments.

---

of the context, it seems likely that **the laying on of hands** is a reference to the evangelist's role in ordaining, or appointing, elders in the church (cf. Tit. 1:5). For a discussion of ordination or appointment by the laying on of hands see comments on 4:14. Timothy, by the laying on of his hands, would be giving endorsement to the character and conduct of the man. He must be sure that the man being appointed is the kind of man described in 3:1-7. The ordaining of a man to an office of leadership in the church is an act of fellowship, and if the person is unqualified because of some sin that has not yet come to light (cf. vs. 24) Timothy would be placed in an embarrassing and compromising situation.

Another interpretation, based on post-New Testament practice, refers the laying on of hands to the reconciling of penitents to the church as a sign of the restoration of fellowship. Yet another interpretation suggested by the context is that the gesture belongs to a judicial ceremony (Lev. 24:14 and the apocryphal "Story of Susanna" added to the Greek version of Daniel) in which witnesses laid hands on the accused against whom they gave testimony.

Timothy is urged to **keep** himself **pure** (*hagnos*), i.e., to be on guard, watchful, to protect himself from incrimination. The word **pure** means innocent and clean, or holy, free from guilt. It is translated "guiltless" in 2 Corinthians 7:11, where the church had exercised disciplinary action toward a brother involved in a wicked deed, and in the process the church proved itself innocent and free of guilt in the matter.

[23] Why does Paul suddenly inject this admonition to Timothy concerning the drinking of **water** and **wine?** Is it related to what he has said in verse 22 and what he goes on to say in verse 24? This is very likely the case. The reference to the sins of another man and the injunction, "keep thyself pure," or free of guilt, suggests to Paul's mind a problem Timothy is having in his effort to keep a conscience that is free of a sense of guilt. Timothy was evidently a very conscientious person. He was avoiding any use whatsoever of wine, even for the sake of his own physical health, lest

he be guilty of an evil influence upon others. Perhaps in so doing he was manifesting a tendency toward asceticism which was somewhat extreme. There were false teachers in the church who classified certain food and drink as ceremonially unclean and ritualistically defiling (see 4:3 for the heretics' negative attitude toward creation). Timothy may have been yielding to them on this point out of charity. He did not want to be accused of drunkenness or being addicted to wine (cf. 3:3, 8; Tit. 2:34) and was protecting his reputation, just as Paul was urging him to do in verse 22. Paul sees a hint of false asceticism which might be an endorsement of the heresies concerning clean and unclean food and drink. Knowing Timothy's desire to keep a conscience void of offense, Paul gives him a word of encouragement, based on knowledge of the truth, which would keep Timothy from having any guilt feeling about using wine for his health (see comments on "good conscience" in 1:5; 3:9). Literally, Paul says "no longer drink water," here translated **no longer drink water only.** Compare Paul's use of "no longer" (*mēketi*) elsewhere (e.g., 2 Cor. 5:15; Eph. 4:14; Rom. 6:6; 1 Thess. 3:1, 5). Timothy's ministry may have been seriously hindered by his frequent ailments that were due to his drinking the water. Even today, the traveler is instructed not to drink the water in certain parts of the world. In Timothy's situation the use of a little wine was suggested both as a preventive and a cure. The mixing of wine with water has a purifying effect on the water, and a mixture of water and wine was the ordinary beverage of the Mediterranean world. It was a sign of asceticism to drink only water (Luke 7:33f.). Paul has much to say elsewhere concerning the use of wine. See Romans 14:14-23, where abstinence from wine is no more binding than abstinence from meats (see comments on 4:3 above).

Paul invokes the rule of love and good influence in deciding one's course of action. Since total abstinence was not required, according to knowledge and conscience, and the drinking of wine (not to be confused with drunkenness and addiction) is in the realm of expediency, Paul exercised his freedom in Christ to act according to the circumstances; hence, his instructions to Timothy do not violate his principle of acting out of love and in the interest of a good in-

[24] The sins of some men are conspicuous, pointing to judgment, but the sins of others appear later. [25] So also good deeds are conspicuous; and even when they are not, they cannot remain hidden.

[1] Let all who are under the yoke of slavery regard their masters as worthy of all honor, so that the name of God and the teaching may not be defamed. [2] Those who have believing masters must not be disrespectful on the ground that they are brethren; rather they must serve all the better since those who benefit by their service are believers and beloved.

Teach and urge these duties.

---

fluence. On the serious dangers and evils involved in the wrong use of wine see also Proverbs 20:1; 21:17; 23:21, 29-35 (cf. also Gal. 5:21; Eph. 5:18; 1 Cor. 5:11; 6:10; Isa. 5:11, 12; 1 Peter 4:3).

[24, 25] Having injected a note to Timothy on the difference between real and ceremonial defilement in the use of wine, a note which grew out of his injunction to "keep yourself pure," Paul continues to warn Timothy to be careful about quick judgments and appointments. Timothy would find that some men who are appointed as elders may turn out bad because of things that do not come to light until later. And, in time, if a man is really a good man, it will come to light. With some the evil is readily seen; with others it is hidden, perhaps by hypocrisy. So there will come times when the evangelist will have to rebuke and convict men who have been appointed but prove to be a disappointment. Compare Paul's warning in Acts 20:29, 30.

Honor for Masters, 6:1-2. [1, 2] The slaves were a part of a man's household, and Paul's inclusion of these instructions to servants and masters is in line with the theme of proper Christian behavior. The word **honor** (*timē*) is the same that Paul used in 5:3 and 5:17, as well as in the doxologies of 1:17 and 6:16. Here it implies that masters are worthy of respectful submission and service, especially those who are believers (see comments on 5:17, and 5:3). Slaves are not to be scornful or insubordinate (cf. Tit. 2:9, 10).

Elsewhere Paul instructed slaves to avail themselves of any legitimate opportunity to gain their freedom. If this

3 **If any one teaches otherwise and does not agree with the sound words of our Lord Jesus Christ and the teaching which accords with godliness,**

---

proved impossible, they were urged to be the Lord's free men, not slaves of men (1 Cor. 7:21-24). Paul urged them not to serve with eye-service as men pleasers but as servants of Christ (Col. 3:22-24; cf. Eph. 6:5-8). Believing **masters** were instructed to treat their slaves justly and fairly, just as their master in heaven has treated them (Col. 4:1; cf. Eph. 6:9). See also Philemon 10-20.

Once again Paul places emphasis on the importance of **the teaching** (see discussion of this in connection with 1:3 and 3:2). All the members of God's family are to conduct themselves in light of the fact that the church is the pillar and support of the truth (3:15). They should not act in such a way as to bring the name of their heavenly Father and his teaching into disrepute or cause it to be **defamed** or "blasphemed" (cf. Tit. 2:5; see comments on 2:2-4, 8).

Part Three, 6:3-21

The "man of God" is warned to avoid and oppose the spiritually sick who spread unhealthy teaching and use religion for morbid and mercenary reasons. He is urged to preach and teach the truth and to be content with the good and simple life.

A Description of the Enemy, 6:3-10

[3] Here Paul refers again to the false teachers mentioned in 1:3. For the meaning of **teaches otherwise** (*heterodidaskaloō*) see the comments on 1:3 where the same word is used of those who "teach any different doctrine." Such a teacher, says Paul, **does not agree** (*prosechō*, meaning to cling to, or to occupy oneself with) **with the sound words** of Jesus. The word translated **does not agree** is used in 4:13 where Timothy is told to "attend to" his three main duties as a preacher. In other words, the false teacher has not been attending to or occupying himself with the teaching of Christ. The same word is translated "addicted to," or given to, in reference to wine (3:8); so these teachers may be described as being addicted to teach-

[4] he is puffed up with conceit, he knows nothing; he has a morbid craving for controversy and disputes about words, which produce envy, dissension, slander, base suspicions,
[5] and wrangling among men who are depraved in mind and bereft of the truth, imagining that godliness is a means of gain.

---

ings that are contrary to the healthful words of the Lord. The metaphorical use of the medical term **sound**, meaning healthy and wholesome, is found only in Paul's letters to Timothy and Titus (cf. comments on 1:10).

[4, 5] The unhealthy teaching ("devilish doctrine," 4:1) issues from one who is himself spiritually ill. He is **puffed up with conceit** (see comments on "puffed up" in 3:6). He has **a morbid craving** for controversy and disputes about words. The word for **morbid craving** (*noseō*) is used figuratively for one who is ill or diseased (cf. *nosos*, illness, Acts 19:12; Luke 9:1; 4:40). And he **knows nothing**, signifying that he is without "understanding" (cf. James 3:13). Here it seems to be synonymous with the lack of knowledge on the part of those referred to in 1:7 who were professing to be teachers of the Law.

The word for **controversies** (*zētēsis*) is the same as the "speculations" in 1:4. **Disputes about words** (*logomachia*, cf. 2 Tim. 2:14) is a compound form using *machia* (fighting or striving), which is used concerning fighting against God (Acts 5:39). It is translated "fighting" (James 4:1; 2 Cor. 7:5), "quarreling" (Acts 7:26; 2 Tim. 2:23, 24; Tit. 3:9), and "disputing" (John 6:52). These controversies and disputes by sick men produce, in turn, five other serious diseases of the soul: (1) **Envy** is one of ten spiritual maladies mentioned by Paul (cf. Gal. 5:21, 26; Tit. 3:3, Phil. 1:5). (2) **Dissension** (*eris*) is a word peculiar to Paul in the New Testament, which he uses fourteen times (e.g., Phil. 1:15). A kindred word (*eritheia*), meaning strife or contentiousness, is descriptive of a "factious" person (Rom. 2:8). (3) **Slander** (*blasphēmia*), meaning evil speaking as in 1:20 and 6:1, is not the word used in 3:11 concerning the sin of slander (*diabolos*) to be avoided by the women. (4) **Base suspicions,** or evil conjectures, is used by John (3 John 10) to describe the malicious words of those who were

[6] There is great gain in godliness with contentment; [7] for we brought nothing into the world, and [m] we cannot take anything out of the world; [8] but if we have food and clothing, with these we shall be content.

[m] Other ancient authorities insert *it is certain that*

---

prating against, or gossiping about him. It is altogether possible that Paul is using a word which may, in this context, sustain a metaphorical relation to the word "sick" (cf. Luke 11:34). If so, the base suspicions are the sick imaginations of people who are spiritually ill. (5) **Wrangling** means constant quarreling, or vain argumentation.

The men, whose contrary teachings produce such an unhealthy condition, are **depraved in mind.** This may be synonymous with "defiled in conscience." The word **depraved** means defiled, corrupted, or ruined, in a moral sense. It is used elsewhere by Luke and Paul in reference to the corruption or decay of the mortal body. Only here is it used metaphorically. In the sense of physical corruption, Luke uses it five times (e.g. Acts 2:31; Luke 12:33) and Paul uses it once (2 Cor. 4:16). The figurative use of depraved, or corrupted, is found also in Revelation 19:2 in reference to fornication, or uncleanness. The false teachers with whom Timothy is dealing are also **bereft of the truth.** The word **bereft** (*apostereō*) is used passively here, suggesting that these men have been robbed, defrauded and deprived of the truth (cf. Tit. 1:13, 14; 2 Tim. 4:3, 4). The word **imagining** (*nomizō*) is found only in Luke and Paul. Luke is the only one who uses it in reference to false assumptions (cf. Acts 7:25; 14:19; 16:27; 17:29; Luke 2:44). Paul's one use of it elsewhere (1 Cor. 7:26) concerns a judgment of his own which he feels is true. The mercenary teachers Paul is denouncing here have a craving not only for controversy but also for material riches. They falsely assume that **godliness is a means of gain.** Paul warns evangelists and elders against such imaginings (cf. 6:6-11; 3:2; Tit. 1:7).

[6-8] In these verses Paul shows that **godliness with contentment** is in itself reward enough; it is truly **great gain.** Once again the significant word **godliness is used** (see comments on 2:5; cf. 3:15; 6:3). The word for **contentment**

[9] But those who desire to be rich fall into temptation, into a snare, into many senseless and hurtful desires that plunge men into ruin and destruction. [10] For the love of money is the root of all evils; it is through this craving that some have wandered away from the faith and pierced their hearts with many pangs.

---

is *autarkeia* which is used twice elsewhere in Paul in contexts of a sufficiency of life's necessities (2 Cor. 9:8; Phil. 4:11). This was a key word in Stoic philosophy, but for Paul the sufficiency was in God, not in self. Jesus himself urges us to be free of anxiety about **food** and **clothing** and promises that God will provide for those who seek first his kingdom (Matt. 6:25-34).

The word for **food** (*diatrophē*) implies not only subsistence but also the means of subsistence, that is, a job. Paul made tents (Acts 17:3) and commanded Christians to do honest work so they could help those in need (Eph. 4:28). If a man was able to work and would not, he should not eat, says Paul (2 Thess. 3:6-13). The word for **clothing** (*skepasma*) includes not only clothing but also a place of shelter. Verse 7 approximates Ecclesiastes 5:15. Compare Jesus' concern for Mary in providing a place of shelter for her (John 19:26, 27), Paul's own request for lodging (Phile. 22; cf. Acts 28:30), and his request for his cloak (2 Tim. 4:13).

[9, 10] Here Paul warns of the inevitable evils that plague the lives of those who **desire to be rich** and are obsessed with **the love of money.** The word for **desire** (*boulomai*) means to will and to determine (see comments on 2:8; cf. Tit. 3:8). The word **rich** (*plouteō*) means to be wealthy. It has the same meaning here as in James 2:6; 5:1-5, and with reference to the rich fool (Luke 12:16), and the rich ruler (Luke 18:23; cf. also Luke 18:25; 16:21). The same word is also used with reference to the true riches which one should set his mind on, e.g., the word of God (Col. 3:16), the Holy Spirit (Tit. 3:6), liberality (Luke 12:21; 2 Cor. 9:11), the unsearchable riches of Christ (Phil. 4:19; Eph. 3:8), spiritual riches (2 Cor. 6:10), the Lord's riches (Rom. 10:12).

Those who are obsessed with the desire to be rich in

11 **But as for you, man of God, shun all this; aim at righteousness, godliness, faith, love, steadfastness, gentleness.**

---

material things **fall into temptation, into a snare.** The word **temptation** (*peirasmos*) means enticement to sin. It is translated "trial" in James 1:12 (cf. also James 1:13-15). The word **snare** (*pagis*) is used in 3:7 (cf. 2 Tim. 2:26). It is translated "trap" in Matthew 22:15. The rich also fall into **many senseless and hurtful desires.** The word desire in this case (*epithumia*) is used elsewhere also of noble desires (cf. 3:1; Phil. 1:23; 1 Thess. 2:17). Here the desire is **senseless,** or foolish (cf. Rom. 1:14; Gal. 3:1; Tit. 3:3; 2 Tim. 3:9); it is **hurtful,** or injurious (cf. Luke 4:35). Paul describes the consequences of such fleshly desire in Galatians 5:16-21. With his use of the word **plunge** Paul changes the figure from snare or trap to perils of the sea. The word **plunge** occurs elsewhere only in Luke where it is translated "to sink" (Luke 5:7). A cognate form is used in reference to Paul's being adrift at sea following shipwreck (2 Cor. 10:25).

The term for **love of money** (*philarguria*) occurs only here in the New Testament, and a point is made of this by those who deny Paul's authorship. This word fits the known language of the Pauline circle. Compare "love of money" (*philarguros,* Luke 16:14) and free from the love of money (*aphilarguros* in Hebrews 13:5; cf. 1 Tim. 3:3). There are many parallels in contemporary moralistic literature. The figurative use of **root** (*rhiza*) and "to take root" (*rhizō*) is very Pauline (see Romans 11:16-18). If love of money is evil, it follows that the branches and fruit of such love will also be evil.

The word translated **heart** is literally "themselves" (*heautous*). They pierced or impaled themselves with many pangs (*odunē*), which means much suffering.

The Man of God, 6:11-19

[11] The reference to Timothy as a **man of God** calls to mind the frequent use of this appellation in reference to the prophets who spoke for God in the Old Testament (e.g. 1 Kings 17:24, 2 Kings 7:17; 8:2) and Peter's reference to the "holy men of God" who spoke from God (2 Peter

[12] Fight the good fight of the faith; take hold of the eternal life to which you were called when you made the good confession in the presence of many witnesses. [13] In the presence of God who gives life to all things, and of Christ Jesus who in his testimony before Pontius Pilate made the good confession,

---

1:21). The only other place in the New Testament where the exact phrase "man of God" is found is in 2 Timothy 3:17. Timothy is a **man of God** whose ministry is that of teaching, reproving, correcting, and training the people of God. The man who speaks for God must speak as the oracles of God (1 Peter 4:11; cf. Rom. 3:2; Heb. 5:12).

As God's man, Timothy is commanded to **shun** and **aim at.** These two words may be translated "run away from" and "run after," or "flee" and "pursue." **Shun** is translated "flee" (Acts 7:39; Luke 21:21), "escape" (Matt. 23:33), and "shun," meaning avoid (1 Cor. 6:18; 2 Tim. 2:22). The word for **aim at** is not the same word as the "aim" (*telos*) in 1:5. It is variously translated "pursue" righteousness (Rom. 9:30, 31; cf. 1 Peter 3:11), "practice" hospitality (Rom. 13:13), "strive for" peace (Heb. 12:14), "seek" to do good (1 Thess. 5:15), and make love your "aim" (1 Cor. 14:1). The good soldier who is involved in the good fight of the faith (vs. 12) will find that there is much to be said for the spiritual strategy of retreat and pursuit. He is to avoid the vices and evil attributes mentioned in 6:4, 5, 9, 10, and in light of the great lesson of 6:6-8, he is to aim at certain virtues listed here (cf. 2 Tim. 2:22-25).

Righteousness, or goodness and uprightness (cf. Rom. 9:30-31; 1 John 2:29; 3:7) is the breastplate of Ephesians 6:14 (cf. 2 Peter 2:5). **Godliness** is discussed in connection with 2:2; 3:16; 6:3. The next two virtues, **faith** and **love** are discussed in connection with 1:5. In addition to these, Timothy is to aim at **steadfastness** (*hupomonē*), which implies patient endurance (cf. 1 Thess. 1:3; 2 Cor. 6:4; Heb. 10:36; 2 Tim. 3:10; Tit. 2:2; James 1:3). **Gentleness** is related to the word translated "courtesy" in Titus 3:2, where the word for "gentle" is a different word.

[12, 13] Here Paul makes a significant use of verb and noun combinations. He urges Timothy to fight (*agōnizō*) the good **fight** (*agōna*) and to lay hold of life eternal to which he was called when he **made** (or confessed, *homologeō*) the good **confession** (*homologia*). The verb for **fight** is a figurative use of the word Jesus used with Pilate (John 18:36). Both literally and figuratively it means to engage in a conflict. Paul's figure may be military or athletic. This word is translated "striving" in describing Paul's labors as a teacher and preacher (Col. 1:28, 29; 3:1). It is used in reference to the fervent prayers of Epaphras, "remembering you earnestly," or who "labors" fervently for you in his prayers (Col. 4:12). The same word is translated "contend" (Jude 3). The noun **fight** (*agōna*) is translated "conflict" (Phil. 1:30; Col. 2:1), "opposition"or "contention" (1 Thess. 2:2). It is transliterated in describing the "agony" of Jesus' struggle in the garden of Gethsemane (Luke 22:44).

It is significant that Paul used two different words in reference to the **confession** that Timothy **made,** or confessed (*homologeō*) and the **confession** that Jesus **made,** or witnessed (*martureō*). Timothy confessed (*homologeō*) before many witnesses (*martus*). Jesus witnessed (*martureō*) the confession (*homologia*) before Pilate. The play on words may be related to the reference to **the eternal life** Timothy laid hold of when he made the good confession. Paul may be reminding Timothy that Jesus met death when he made that same confession. Jesus was martyred when he remained faithful to his profession, or confession, of the good and great truth represented by the word of his mouth during his trial. If such is the meaning suggested by the use of *martureō* in describing the act of Jesus before Pilate, it seems to be the only instance of such a use of the verb in the New Testament (but see Rev. 2:13 for the noun). This may be the beginning of the tradition among later Christians, when the term "to witness" (*martureō*) became synonymous with martyrdom.

The **good confession** that Jesus made was made with the mouth (cf. John 18:36, 37; Luke 23:2-3). Jesus suffered humiliation and death because he gave such an utterance (cf. Mark 15:17-20). The good confession with which Timothy laid hold of eternal life is also made with the mouth as a public profession of submission and loyalty to Jesus Christ as Lord (cf. Rom. 10:9, 10; Matt. 10:32; Phil. 2:11; John

[14] I charge you to keep the commandment unstained and free from reproach until the appearing of our Lord Jesus Christ; [15] and this will be made manifest at the proper time by the blessed and only Sovereign, the King of kings and Lord of lords,

---

9:22; 12:42). It is not only called **good**, but it is also called "great" in 3:16, where Paul used the adverb "confessedly" (*homologoumenōs*) in reference to the revealed mystery of the Christian religion. The good confession included the great aspects of the faith which are set forth in the hymnic terminology of 3:16, that Jesus was God manifest in the flesh (cf. 1 John 4:2; 2 John 7). It includes the fact that he is the Son of God (1 John 4:15), that he died for our sins (cf. 2:6; 1 Cor. 15:3), that he was raised from the dead (Rom. 10:9; Eph. 1:20; 1 Cor. 15:4), and that he ascended into glory to be glorified as Lord of the church (3:16; Eph. 1:20-23). Compare the good and great confession of Jesus as Faithful and True, the Word of God, King of kings and Lord of lords (Rev. 19:11, 13, 16).

The usage of the language of "confession" in the New Testament suggests a baptismal setting for Timothy's confession. The immediate context lends support to the possibility that Paul refers to some confession made, as Jesus did, before Roman governmental authorities. Less likely is a reference to a pledge made by Timothy at his ordination.

Timothy, in making the good confession, accepted the call to **the eternal life**, which was with the Father, who is the living God (cf. 3:15; 1 John 1:2). This life was "manifested unto us" (cf. 3:16; 1 John 1:3). God has given this life in Christ: "And this is the testimony (*marturia*), that God gave us eternal life, and this life is in his Son" (1 John 5:11, 12; cf. 1 John 5:20).

Paul uses two words to Timothy, pursue or **aim at**, and **take hold**, which he also uses in Philippians 3:12: "I press on" (pursue) . . . "to make it my own" (take hold), "because Christ Jesus has made me his own" (or, laid hold on me). In that context the aim is expressed in terms of knowing Christ and attaining the resurrection.

[14, 15] In God's presence (cf. 5:21) Paul **charges** (cf. 1:3; 4:11) Timothy to keep **the commandment**. The word

[16] who alone has immortality and dwells in unapproachable light, whom no man has ever seen or can see. To him be honor and eternal dominion. Amen.

---

for **commandment** (*entolē*) is used here with the same force and meaning as in 2 Peter 2:21 where reference is made to "the holy commandment." It may signify the entire covenant or the commandment of the Lord and Savior through the apostles (2 Peter 3:2; Heb. 9:20). **Free from reproach** (*anepilēmptos*) is translated "above reproach" in reference to elders (3:2) and widows (5:7).

The word **appearing** is a reference to the second coming or "manifestation" of the Lord. Paul refers to the first appearing in 3:16 (cf. Tit. 1:2, 3; 2 Tim. 1:10). Both manifestations, or appearances, are mentioned in Tit. 2:11-13. Timothy is admonished to persevere until Jesus comes again. Compare "until he comes" (1 Cor. 11:26). In 2 Timothy the idea of faithfulness unto death is the dominant thought (see 2 Tim. 1:8; 2:12, 13; 3:12; 4:16; cf. Rev. 2:10). The second appearing of Jesus, as the judge of mankind, will be manifested **at the proper time,** just as the first appearing to save mankind was at its proper time (see comments on 2:6 and 2 Tim. 4:1). The time is known to the Father only (Matt. 24:36).

The description of God as the **only Sovereign** (*dunastēs*) is found only here, although the word is found in Mary's song in which she magnifies the Lord who has put down (dethroned) the mighty (rulers, *dunastēs*) from their thrones (Luke 1:52; cf. Dan. 4:17). The word derives from *dunamai* which implies ability and strength. It is generally thought that the word **Sovereign** refers to God (the Father) and not to Jesus (cf. 1:17), although the next two titles have a counterpart as titles of Jesus (Rev. 19:16). The term **only Sovereign** may also suggest one dynasty (cf. Dan. 7:13, 14; 2:44).

[16] Not only is he the only (*monos*) sovereign, but it is he **alone** (*monos*) who **has immortality.** He is the living God (4:10), "who gave life to all things" (6:13; see comments on 4:10). The word **immortality** (*athanasia*) is found only here and in 1 Corinthians 15:53, 54. The word translated "immortal" in 1:17 is *aphthartos,* meaning "incorrup-

17 As for the rich in this world, charge them not to be
haughty, nor to set their hopes on uncertain riches but on
God who richly furnishes us with everything to enjoy.
18 They are to do good, to be rich in good deeds, liberal
and generous, 19 thus laying up for themselves a good
foundation for the future, so that they may take hold of
the life which is life indeed.

---

tible," which Paul also uses (Rom. 1:23; 1 Cor. 15:52; 9:25; cf. 2 Tim. 1:10). The word for immortality (*athanasia, athanatos*) is a cognate form of "death" (*thanatos*) and "to die" (*thanatoō*) used by Paul (Rom. 7:4, 10; 8:6; cf. 1 John 3:14; James 1:15; 5:20). As far as man's ability and power is concerned, God dwells in **unapproachable light,** which is explained by the words **whom no man has ever seen or can see** (cf. 1:17; Col. 1:15; John 1:18; Ex. 33:20).

Paul's insertion of the doxology here is typical (see comments on 1:17; cf. Eph. 3:19-21). He always uses the word **glory** (*doxa*) in such doxologies, but here, as in 1:17, he adds the word **honor** (*timē*) which is not found in his doxologies elsewhere. It is found in the doxology of Revelation 5:13. See comments on 1:17 for the possible significance of the word **honor** in relation to the emphasis on honor in this particular epistle (cf. 5:3; 5:17; 6:1).

[17-19] Having given Timothy his special charge in verses 11-14, and having inserted the doxology in verses 15, 16, Paul returns to his original subject and adds his final word to the rich on the proper stewardship of the blessings they enjoyed in greater abundance. He urges them to be **liberal** and **generous.** His words **laying up for themselves** calls to mind the Lord's parable of the rich fool in Luke 12:13-21 (cf. Matt. 19:23, 24), and his precepts in the Sermon on the Mount concerning laying up treasures in heaven (Matt. 6:19-21). Paul urges the rich to **take hold of the life which is life indeed,** just as he had urged Timothy to "take hold of the eternal life" (6:12). The rich are not to be **haughty,** proud or high-minded; (cf. Rom. 11:20; 12:16), nor to **set their hope on riches** but on the living God (cf. 4:10; 5:5; 6:6-10).

20 **O Timothy, guard what has been entrusted to you. Avoid the godless chatter and contradictions of what is falsely called knowledge,** 21 **for by professing it some have missed the mark as regards the faith.**

Grace be with you.

A Final Charge to Timothy, 6:20, 21a

[20, 21] In conclusion Paul says, **O Timothy,** using an interjection that expresses deep feeling. This interjection is especially characteristic of Jesus and Paul in the New Testament. He pleads with Timothy to **guard** what had been **entrusted** to him. For a discussion of the meaning of these terms as they are used here in the final charge, see comments on **guard,** and the deposit which was **entrusted** to Timothy in 2 Timothy 1:12-14; 2:2. The word **avoid** (*ektrepō*) means to turn away from. It is also used in 1:6 and 5:15 (cf. 2 Tim. 4:4), concerning those who turn away (wander or stray) from the truth. Timothy is to turn away from **the godless chatter.** The word **godless** (*bebēlos*) means "profane" (see comments on 4:7). The word **chatter** means empty talk (see comments on 2 Tim. 2:16). He is also to turn away from **the contradictions of what is falsely called knowledge.** Ignorance had disguised itself as knowledge, and falsehood had assumed a pseudonym called truth (see comments on 1:3, 4, 6, 7; 4:7, 8; 6:3-5). Some were already **professing,** or proclaiming (*epangellō*) these unholy contradictions. Contrast the reference in 2:10 to women who "profess" reverence for God. These professors of godless falsehood had **missed the mark** (*astocheō*) **concerning the faith** (see comments on 1:6; cf. 2 Tim. 2:18). There is no reason to see in **knowledge** (*gnōsis*) and **contradictions** (*antithesis*) the technical language of Marcion and second century Gnostics.

Benediction, 6:21b

Paul's last sentence is somewhat brief, as in Colossians 4:18, but it is typical (cf. Tit. 1:3; Gal. 6:18; 2 Tim. 4:22). The word **grace,** used commonly in such benedictions, was also very common in Paul's letters. For the plural **you,** see comments on the end of 2 Timothy and Titus.

III

The Second Letter of Paul to Timothy

Introduction

Date of Writing

About A.D. 67 Paul was in chains in Rome awaiting execution. He had been freed from his first imprisonment in Rome and had engaged in the activities recorded in 1 Timothy and Titus, which were written during the time of freedom (*circa* A.D. 63-67). For a fuller discussion of the facts and problems related to the date of the letters to Timothy and Titus see the discussion of the historical setting and the date of writing in the General Introduction to this volume and the comments on 2 Timothy 4:16, 17.

Probably serving as Paul's scribe was Luke. The deep emotional involvement in the situation does not interfere with a definite plan and purpose in the letter.

Theme and Content

Timothy's loyalty to Christ and the gospel was to be given a fiery test in the crucible of Paul's tragic circumstances in Rome. He was summoned to Rome in courageous fulfillment of a twofold commitment which is briefly stated in 1:8. In this verse Paul charges Timothy to take his share of suffering for the cause of Christ by committing himself (1) to unashamed testimony on behalf of Christ and the gospel, and (2) to unashamed testimony on behalf of Paul, the Lord's prisoner. He is to suffer humiliation for the cause of Christ by identifying himself openly with Paul's humiliation in Rome. These two aspects of Timothy's charge and commitment shine brilliantly and echo loudly throughout the letter (see comments on 1:8). Paul's charge summons him to witness and to suffer.

The style employed by Paul in giving this charge to Timothy is both definite and unique. He hangs the body of his message on a basic framework suggested by the two words: *remembering,* and *reminding.* Within this framework Paul gives his solemn charges to Timothy, together with gems of truth that sparkle brightly against a background of loving remembrance and bold reminders that call Timothy to full fellowship in the company of the committed.

Paul writes in this manner to help Timothy to understand what is happening. This word "understanding" is a key word in interpreting the words which Paul addresses to him (cf. 2:7; 3:1). Paul is looking back over a vigorous, dedicated ministry which is nearing an ending that is both glorious and tragic. He is interpreting his present situation for the benefit of his "beloved child" (1:2) who is about to become personally, and perhaps dangerously, involved in Paul's predicament in Rome. It seems rather obvious that Paul is not only writing to summon Timothy to Rome (cf. 4:9) but also to help him understand the shocking, frightening, and disheartening events which were conspiring to make Paul, and perhaps Timothy also, a martyr for the cause of Christ.

Again and again Paul speaks of preaching the gospel and the suffering that results. It is the theme of this letter (e.g., 1:8, 12; 2:9, 11; 3:12; 4:5, 6). Timothy, by following Paul's teaching and example, will continue to testify and to suffer hardship, perhaps imprisonment and death, as a result of such faithful witness to the gospel of Christ. And his decision to go to Rome will give proof of his willingness to suffer (see comments on 2:7).

Outline of 2 Timothy

I. Salutation, 1:1, 2

II. Part One, 1:3—2:7

- A. An Introductory Remembrance, 1:3-5
- B. A Reminder, 1:6, 7
- C. The Twofold Charge, 1:8—2:7

II. PART TWO, 2:8—3:9
- A. Remember the Suffering of Christ and His Disciples, 2:8-13
- B. Remind the Brethren of the Proper Way to Handle the Word of Truth, 2:14—3:9

III. PART THREE, 3:10—4:5
- A. Remember Paul and his Suffering, 3:10-13
- B. Reminder of What Learned, 3:14-17
- C. A Solemn Charge, 4:1-5

IV. PART FOUR, 4:6-21

V. BENEDICTION, 4:22

Commentary

Salutation, 1:1, 2

[1, 2] Paul's introductory reference to his apostolic commission from the Lord is characteristic (cf. Rom. 1:1; 1 Cor. 1:1; 2 Cor. 1:1; Gal. 1:1; Eph. 1:1; Tit. 1:1). The meaning of Paul's apostleship is discussed in connection with 1 Timothy 1:1.

The **promise of life** seems to be in the forefront of Paul's thinking as he writes his last letter to Timothy. This keen awareness of the life to come is seen in such passages as 1:10; 2:8, 9; 4:6-8, 18. The language of verse two is the same as in 1 Timothy 1:2, with the exception of his use here of the term **beloved** (see comments on 1 Tim. 1:2). Paul's reference to Timothy as his **beloved child** calls to mind his appraisal of Timothy in 1 Corinthians 4:15-17 (see comments on 1 Timothy 1:2). For other instances of Paul's use of "beloved" (*agapētos*) in reference to those who were close to him in the fellowship of the gospel, see Colossians 4:7, 9, 14 (cf. Eph. 5:1; 6:21; Phile. 1:1, 16; Phil. 2:12; Rom. 16:5, 12). The significance of the words **grace, mercy,** and **peace** as used by Paul here is discussed at 1 Timothy 1:2.

Part One, 1:3—2:7

The first of the remembering-reminding sections of this letter is to be found in 1:3-7, after which Paul gives the basic twofold charge of the epistle (1:8). This is followed by a brief and comprehensive discussion of the implications of this commitment (1:9-2:7).

An Introductory Remembrance, 1:3-5

[3] This verse may be divided into two parts for discussion: (1) **I thank God . . . , when I remember you constantly in my prayers,** and (2) **whom I serve with a clear conscience, as did my fathers.**

**1 Paul, an apostle of Christ Jesus by the will of God ac-
cording to the promise of life which is in Christ Jesus,
2 To Timothy, my beloved child:
Grace, mercy, and peace from God the Father and
Christ Jesus our Lord.
3 I thank God whom I serve with a clear conscience,
as did my fathers, when I remember you constantly in my
prayers.**

The linguistic style employed here serves to connect two things: Paul "has thanks" (**I thank**) toward God and "has remembrance" (**I remember**) of Timothy. This style of utterance is characteristically Pauline as in "have not love" and "have faith" (1 Cor. 13:1, 3), and "the love I have for you" (2 Cor. 2:4; Phil. 2:2). Compare also "holding faith" (1 Tim. 1:19) and "having thanks" (1 Tim. 1:12).

Paul begins his message to Timothy with the significant words **I thank God.** The use of *charin* (literally "grace") in the sense of thanks and gratitude is Pauline. Elsewhere it is found only in Luke 17:9 and Hebrews 12:28. Paul uses it in this way frequently (e.g., 1 Cor. 10:30; 2 Cor. 9:15). It conveys Paul's sense of divine grace and favor. In keeping with his exhortation to the church at Philippi, which Timothy would remember (Phil. 1:1), Paul seems to be gloriously free of fearful anxiety, continuing in his "prayers and supplications with thanksgiving" (see Phil. 4:4-6).

Paul's way of saying **I remember,** or "I have you in remembrance," is found elsewhere only in 1 Thessalonians 3:6. The closest parallels are also Pauline, "I make mention of you always in my prayers (Rom. 1:9; cf. 1 Thess. 1:2; Phile. 4; Eph. 1:6). The word translated **constantly** (*adialeiptos*) is found elsewhere only in Romans 9:1, where it is translated "unceasing." The adverbial form "constantly" (*adialeiptōs*), or "without ceasing," is also uniquely Pauline in the New Testament (cf. Rom. 1:9; 1 Thess. 1:2; 2:13; 5:17). With the exception of "unceasing anguish" in Romans 9:1, Paul always uses it in reference to prayer. For the meaning of **prayer** (*deēsis,* "begging") see the comments on 1 Timothy 2:1 (cf. Phil. 1:3, 4).

The word for **serve** (*latreuō*) may also be translated "worship" (cf. Phil. 3:3; Heb. 12:28; Rom. 12:1). It is the

**4 As I remember your tears, I long night and day to see
you, that I may be filled with joy. 5 I am reminded of your
sincere faith, a faith that dwelt first in your grandmother
Lois and your mother Eunice and now, I am sure, dwells
in you.**

---

word used in Romans 1:9 where Paul's language is much like it is here in regard to his thanks to God, "whom I serve with my spirit," and his unceasing remembrance of them in his prayers. Paul served, or worshiped God with **a clear conscience.** This is the terminology used in reference to deacons in 1 Timothy 3:9. The word for **clear** means "pure." It is used in 1 Timothy 1:5 in reference to "a pure heart." A striking linguistic parallel is found in Hebrews 10:2, where the vocabulary of **serve, conscience, clear** (or pure) is used in reference to the worship of God under the Mosaic system, which is the system Paul is referring to in the words as **did my fathers** (cf. Acts 24:14-16).

An exact translation of as **did my fathers** would be "from my fathers." Paul's language here may be indicative of a state of mind induced by the testimony he had given in connection with his trial in Rome. He was not guilty of propagating some illegal religion in the name of a strange deity, as he was so often accused.

[4] Paul remembered Timothy's **tears** which symbolized Timothy's love for Paul. Paul also referred to his own tears as proof of his love for others (cf. 2 Cor. 2:4), just as the tears of the sinful woman spoke eloquently of her love for Christ (Luke 7:38, 44, 47). Paul's love for Timothy is expressed in the tender words, **I long night and day to see you.** The word **long** (*epipotheō*) and its cognates occur fifteen times in the New Testament, thirteen of these being found in Paul (e.g. Phil. 4:1; 2 Cor. 5:2; Rom. 1:11; 1 Thess. 3:6; 2 Cor. 7:7). Paul's love is the source and reason for the great joy he will experience when he sees Timothy again. The relationship between love and joy is expressed in Paul's words to Philemon, "I have derived much joy and comfort from your love" (Phile. 7; cf. Phil. 2:2; 4:1).

[5] Paul remembered also Timothy's **sincere faith.** This brings to mind the charge to Timothy in the first letter (1 Tim. 1:5). In fact, the charge given there echoes here in

6 Hence I remind you to rekindle the gift of God that is within you through the laying on of my hands; 7 for God did not give us a spirit of timidity but a spirit of power and love and self-control.

---

verses 3, 5, and 7 (see comments on 1 Tim. 1:5). Here Paul also witnesses to the fact that Timothy's faith was a faith which he received from his forebears, just as Paul had worshiped God "from his fathers."

The only other reference to Timothy's family is in Acts 16:1. It seems that Timothy's father, who was a Greek, was not a Christian. Timothy had received his sincere faith from his mother and grandmother. The verb **dwells in** (*enoikeō*) is a word peculiar to Paul in the New Testament. Compare the indwelling Spirit (1:14; Rom. 8:11), indwelling sin (Rom. 7:17), the indwelling word of Christ (Col. 3:16), and God's dwelling in his people who are his temple (2 Cor. 6:16).

Paul's confidence, or conviction, expressed in the words **I am sure**, deserves attention. It is used again in 1:12 concerning Paul's certainty about God's ability to guard that which he had committed to Paul. The word for **I am sure,** or I am persuaded (*peithō*), is translated with several shades of meaning, such as to be convinced, to trust in, to believe, or to be certain.

An Introductory Reminder, 1:6, 7

[6, 7] In the word for **I remind you,** Paul makes a switch to another term in the category of remembering and reminding (*anamimnēskō;* cf. 1 Cor. 4:17). Paul's use of the term may be a play on words in relation to the word **rekindle** (*anazōpureō*). Paul's reminding Timothy would be an exercise in thoughtful recollection which would serve to fan the glowing embers of God's spirit into a new flame, thus stirring up the spirit of **power, love,** and **self-control,** which he would need in good measure if he accepted Paul's summons to Rome where he would face the prospect of sharing the persecution and suffering that had befallen Paul.

Concerning **the gift of God** that was in Timothy through the laying on of Paul's hands, see comments on 1 Timothy

4:14. The conclusion reached there was that Timothy's gift was his ministry and not the same as the gift in 1:6. If, however, one concludes that the gift is the same in both places, then it may be that the nature of Timothy's gift is explained by the words "teaching" and "exhortation" which were among the gifts that God gave to men (cf. Eph. 4:7-12; Rom. 12:7; 1 Tim. 4:13, 14).

If, on the other hand, Timothy's gift was one of the spiritual gifts of 1 Corinthians 12:1-11, the text does not indicate which one it was. Some suggest that in Timothy's case it was probably prophecy, or discerning of spirits. Or it could have been "faith," in light of 1:5 and 1 Corinthians 12:9. Those who possessed the miraculous gifts also possessed the indwelling Spirit (1 Cor. 6:19; 12:11) which apportioned to each one individually as he willed. Paul's teaching on miraculous spiritual gifts was accompanied by an exhortation to each person who possessed such gifts that they should "earnestly desire the higher gifts" (1 Cor. 12:27-31). He added very plainly that the gift of prophecy was a higher gift than speaking in tongues (1 Cor. 14:1-5) because it accomplished the edification of the church. But, significantly, he went on to emphasize that prophetic power, knowledge, and faith were nothing without love (1 Cor. 13:2, 3) and he proceeded to show them a "more excellent way" (1 Cor. 12:31; 13:1-13). In exhorting Timothy to **rekindle the gift of God** which was in him, Paul does not dwell on a particular spiritual gift which Timothy may have received from the indwelling Spirit, but he does emphasize the more excellent manifestations of the Spirit which are described in verse 7.

Whatever these possibilities, it seems that the point Paul is concerned about here is found in verse 7 which clarifies what particular manifestations of the Spirit he wants Timothy to demonstrate. The **for** of verse 7 connects the **gift of God** with the **spirit** which God gives. In Romans 5:5 Paul affirms that the Holy Spirit has been given to us and that God's love has been poured into our hearts through the Holy Spirit (cf. Eph. 3:16). Verse seven, if it does not identify the particular spiritual gift Timothy may have possessed, does define the particular manifestations of the indwelling Spirit which Paul wants Timothy to demonstrate.

The "gift," like the "faith" of 1:5, Paul says, is **in you** (*en soi*). Paul's language here concerning the **spirit of power and love and self-control,** in contrast to the spirit of timidity, closely parallels his teaching in Romans 8:9-18. There Paul spoke of an indwelling Spirit which has resurrection "power" (Rom. 8:11). It is a spirit of self-control and discipline (Rom. 8:12-13), and it is not a spirit of timidity, fearfulness or cowardice but one of sonship (Rom. 8:14, 15). And, in the same context, Paul adds a word about suffering (Rom. 18:17, 18). Paul's emphasis on the indwelling Spirit in Romans seems to parallel 2 Timothy 1:6-8, 14. This does not rule out the possibility of Timothy's possessing a miraculous gift, but it does place the emphasis on a more important aspect of the Spirit's indwelling.

The **gift** God has **given,** says Paul, is not a spirit of **timidity.** The word **timidity** (*deilias*) is translated "afraid," or "fearful" in John 14:27 and signifies a fear that results from lack of faith (Matt. 8:26; Mark 4:40). Compare "the cowardly" (*deilos*) and "the faithless" in Revelation 21:8.

Paul affirms three things about God's gift to himself and to Timothy. (1) God's **gift** is a spirit of **power** or might. Paul spoke of the power of Christ which makes one strong and gives him the ability to face insults and persecutions and calamities (2 Cor. 12:9, 10). It is an immeasurably great **power** or strength whereby God is able to do more than we ask or think (Eph. 1:19; 3:16; Col. 1:11). It is an "energy," says Paul, which God "mightily inspires within me" (Col. 1:29; cf. Phil. 4:13; 2 Thess. 1:11-12; see comments on "he is able" in connection with 1:12 below).

(2) God's **gift** is a spirit of **love** (cf. Rom. 5:5). This is a most important aspect of Paul's appraisal of the spirit of God (see comments on 1 Timothy 1:5).

(3) God's **gift** is a spirit of **self-control.** The word for **self-control** (*sōphronismos*) is translated "sensible," meaning sober-minded, in reference to the elders (1 Tim. 3:2). A striking parallel on love and self-control is found in 2 Corinthians 5:13, where Paul says, "If we are in our right mind" [sensible, or self-controlled] it is for you. For the love of Christ controls us." Timothy would need such love and such self-possession if he accepted the mission to Rome.

[8] Do not be ashamed then of testifying to our Lord, nor of me his prisoner, but take your share of suffering for the gospel in the power of God,

---

The Twofold Charge, 1:8—2:7

[8] On the basis of what he remembers and knows about Timothy (vss. 4, 5) Paul has confidently reminded him to rekindle the gift of God's spirit (vss. 6, 7). In so doing, Paul has laid the foundation for a most demanding two-fold charge which calls for a twofold commitment on Timothy's part, a commitment which many had been too fearful and ashamed to make. Paul connects verse 8 to verse 7 by his use of **then,** meaning therefore, or accordingly. It is the same linguistic style Paul uses in Romans 6:12 (cf. Gal. 5:1; Col. 2:16; 1 Cor. 10:31) in giving commands or charges based on preceding considerations.

Here Paul solemnly charges Timothy to take his **share of suffering** by committing himself to: (1) unashamed testimony on behalf of Christ and the gospel, and (2) unashamed testimony on behalf of Paul himself, his integrity, and the truthfulness of his gospel. Timothy was to do this by coming to Rome to stand by Paul in his death and to carry on from there the cause for which he is to die. To Timothy it is a moment of truth: if he lets Paul down and is ashamed to identify with Paul in the Roman crisis, it will amount to being ashamed to own Jesus Christ as his Lord (cf. 1:15; 2:1, 3, 8-9).

The first aspect of his commitment, loyalty to Christ, echoes loudly through this letter in such passages as 1:8-11; 2:1, 2, 8, 9, 11-13, 22-26; 3:1-9, 14-17; 4:1-5. The second aspect of his commitment, loyalty to Paul, also appears in the following passages, 2:8, 13-15; 2:1-3, 7, 8; 3:10-15; 4:6-11, 16-18, 21.

Paul's word for **ashamed** (*epaischunomai*) is the same word Jesus used when he spoke of his being ashamed of any one who was ashamed of him and of his words (Luke 9:26). It is the word Paul used when he said, "I am not ashamed of the gospel" (Rom. 1:16). It seems that many were ashamed of Paul's chains (cf. 1:15). Noble examples

9 who saved us and called us with a holy calling, not in virtue of our works but in virtue of his own purpose and the grace which he gave us in Christ Jesus ages ago, 10 and now has manifested through the appearing of our Savior Christ Jesus, who abolished death and brought life and immortality to light through the gospel.

---

of those who were not ashamed were Onesiphorus (1:15-18), Luke (4:11), as well as Crescens, Titus, and Tychicus (4:10-12). Paul's description of himself as a **prisoner** of the Lord is characteristic of his letters written during times of imprisonment (cf. Eph. 4:1; Phile. 1, 9; Phil. 1:13).

[9] Having called for unashamed testimony by Timothy, Paul himself testifies unashamedly to the great truths of the gospel which he had preached and for which he was suffering (cf. 1:11, 12; 4:6-8). In another letter, which was probably available to Timothy, Paul had written at greater length on the grand theme of salvation by the **grace** and **purpose** of God. Compare his evaluation of the **virtue of our works** (Eph. 2:7-10), his emphasis on the **grace** of God (Eph. 2:4-10; 3:7), and the **purpose** of God (Eph. 3:11-12). Paul's reference to salvation as a gift which God **gave us in Christ ages ago** compares with Ephesians 2:8-10; 3:9-11. His reference to the **holy calling** also has an interesting parallel in Ephesians 3:20—4:1.

[10] Here, as in 1 Timothy 3:16, Paul speaks of the manifestation of God's purpose and grace in the first advent or **appearing** of Christ, which was at its proper time (cf. 1 Tim. 2:5-7; Tit. 2:11). The first appearing was to **abolish death** and to bring **immortality to light through the gospel** (cf. John 3:16-19; Tit. 1:2, 3; 1 Tim. 2:3-6). Elsewhere Paul speaks of the second appearing of Christ, at its proper time (cf. 1 Tim. 6:14, 15) to judge the living and the dead and to reward the faithful with a crown of righteousness (see comments on 4:1, 8; cf. 2 Thess. 1:7-10).

Living in the shadow of death, Paul must have found much comfort in the good news that Jesus **abolished death.** It is significant that Paul does not say that Christ will come some day to abolish death (as in 1 Cor. 15:26), but that he has **now** abolished death and brought **life and immortality to light through the gospel.** The word **abolished** means to annul. Jesus annulled death by "abolishing in his flesh the law of commandments and ordinances, that he might create in himself one new man" (Eph. 2:15). He abolished death by raising from the dead those who were "dead in trespasses" and making them alive together with him, having forgiven their trespasses (Col. 2:12, 13; 3:1-4). The wages of sin is death (Rom. 6:23), so he **abolished death** by dying for our sins (1 Cor. 15:1-4; cf. 2 Cor. 5:21).

Jesus brought **life.** The word for life is *zōē,* and its use here seems to be a reference to the life of grace and holiness rather than to life in the eschatological sense. Paul does use it in such a sense elsewhere, as in his reference to those who are alienated from the **life** of God (Eph. 2:18). In this sense he also speaks of the law of the Spirit of **life** in Christ Jesus which had made him free from the law of sin and death (Rom. 8:2). For one "to set the mind on the Spirit is **life** and peace" (Rom. 8:6). According to Paul, to be saved is to live, and to this end God "through us spreads the fragrance of the knowledge of him everywhere . . . a fragrance from **life** (*zōē*) to **life** (*zōē*)" (see 2 Cor. 2:14-16). **Life** in Christ is a promise that can be realized both here and hereafter (cf. 1:1; 1 John 5:11, 12).

This life and **immortality** were **brought to light** (*phōtizō*) by Jesus through the gospel. This word, in the sense that it is used here, is not used often in the New Testament (cf. John 1:9; 1 Cor. 4:5; Eph. 3:9; Heb. 6:4; 10:32). The use here may be compared with Ephesians 1:18, where Paul also uses it in connection with **life** in Christ. Significantly, Paul connects this enlightenment with the power of God in raising Jesus from the dead and making us alive in Christ (see Eph. 1:18-20; 2:1, 5-10; cf. John 1:9). The spiritual experience of passing from death to resurrection life is described in terms that are both present and future. It is something that can take place **now** (cf. Eph. 2:1, 5:10; John 5:25, 26), just as eternal life can be a present reality (1 John 5:11-16). It is also something that is to happen in the future (1 Cor. 15:22; John 5:28, 29), just as eternal life is also the Christian's hope of the future (1 Cor. 15:22; John 5:28, 29).

The word for **immortality** (*aphtharsian*) means undying and incorruptible (cf. 1 Cor. 15:42f., 50, 52, 57; see discus-

[11] **For this gospel I was appointed a preacher and apostle and teacher,** [12] **and therefore I suffer as I do. But I am not ashamed, for I know whom I have believed, and I am sure that he is able to guard until that Day what has been entrusted to me.**[a]

[a] Or *what I have entrusted to him*

---

sion of another word for immortality in 1 Tim. 6:16). The word here is used by Paul in reference to "undying love" (Eph. 6:24), and he uses it in speaking of God (Rom. 1:23; 1 Tim. 1:17). So Paul speaks of **life** in Christ as undying. Note Paul's confident affirmation in Philippians 1:20, 21.

[11] Having defined the gospel in terms of God's saving grace through Christ in abolishing death and creating an undying life, Paul reaffirms his calling as a **preacher** and **apostle** and **teacher** of this glorious gospel. These are the three words used to describe his ministry in 1 Timothy 2:7. These three facets of Paul's ministry are integral parts of his office as a minister of the word. "Of this gospel," said Paul, "I was made a minister according to the gift of God's grace which was given to me by the working of his power" (Eph. 3:7). His apostolic ministry was primarily to the Gentiles, or the uncircumcision, a ministry which he magnified and in so doing suffered much at the hands of the Jews who instigated most of his persecutions (cf. Rom. 11:13; Gal. 2:7-9; Acts 17:4, 5; 18:12, 13; 13:45-50; 14:1, 2).

[12] The verb for **suffer** in this verse is *paschō* and is the only use of it in this letter. Elsewhere Paul's word is *kakopatheō* (see comments on 2:3; cf. 1:8; 2:9; 4:5). If *paschō* here has the connotation it seems to have in Paul's other writings, it signifies suffering which may or may not result in death (e.g. 1 Cor. 12:26; Phil. 1:29; 2 Thess. 1:5). If it has the connotation here it has in Luke-Acts, it signifies the suffering of death (e.g. Luke 22:15; 24:46; Acts 1:3; 3:18; 17:3).

Paul uses **therefore** to connect the fact of his suffering with the fact that he has been a preacher and an apostle and teacher of the gospel of Christ. Paul does this to encourage Timothy to suffer the hardship for the gospel and not to be timid, fearful, or **ashamed** (cf. 1:6-8), just as he himself was unashamed of the gospel (Rom. 1:13-17).

Next, Paul gives the twofold reason and source of his courage and fidelity in fulfilling his ministry:

(1) **For I know whom I have believed.** Paul is stressing the fact that he knows God personally on the basis of a close fellowship with God. Paul also spoke of knowledge of certain facts of truth (cf. 2 Cor. 5:1, 11), but here he rejoices that he knows God on the basis of his past and present experience of his divine power and grace in his own personal life. This experiential knowledge is a confirmation of the knowledge gained through an academic study of revealed truth. This kind of knowledge is not only a strong degree of faith, but it is a knowledge based on the actual experience of the grace of God which one has access to by faith (Rom. 5:1-5). The knowledge Paul rejoices in here is an assurance and conviction that springs from his vital fellowship with God and his love for those made in God's image (see 1 John 3:7, 8).

(2) **I am sure that he is able to guard until that Day what has been entrusted to me.** Paul's knowledge of God and his conviction that God **is able** is not fully comprehended apart from what he said to Timothy in verse 7, that God gives a spirit of power and love and self-control.

Paul did not say, "I am sure that he is able to guard that which I have committed unto him until that Day," but **I am sure that he is able to guard until that Day what has been entrusted to me.** This fits the context of what Paul has just said and is seen more clearly if verses 11 through 14 are treated as one unit of thought. They are organically tied by certain key words such as **guard** and **entrusted.** These four verses fall into two couplets without disturbing the organic unity. Verses 11 and 12 belong together in a special way, and verses 13 and 14 also go together. And the second couplet (13, 14) is organically tied to the first couplet (11, 12). In the first couplet, Paul states that he was appointed to the ministry of the gospel as a preacher, apostle, and teacher. God thus entrusted to him the truth to be proclaimed and the ministry of proclamation. And the God who committed to or entrusted such a deposit and such an office was able also to guard, protect, and safely keep that which

[13] Follow the pattern of the sound words which you have heard from me, in the faith and love which are in Christ Jesus; [14] guard the truth that has been entrusted to you by the Holy Spirit who dwells within us.

---

he had committed to Paul by giving to him the spirit of power and love and self-control. This power of God to protect what he had committed to Paul, by protecting Paul and empowering Paul, is a thing Paul is very certain about (cf. Phil. 4:5-7). The ministry came from God and the power belongs to him, not his ministers (2 Cor. 4:1, 7).

[13, 14] Having reminded Timothy of his experience of the power of God in fulfilling his own ministry, Paul charges Timothy to be true to the deposit of truth which had been committed to him from God through Paul (vss. 13, 14). There is a seeming discrepancy in the fact that Timothy is told to **guard** what has been **entrusted** to him, but Paul had said plainly that God would guard what had been entrusted to Paul himself. This seeming discrepancy vanishes in the words **through the Holy Spirit who dwells in us.** The indwelling Spirit would empower Timothy to protect the deposit of truth entrusted to him. The phrase **by the Holy Spirit** goes with **guard, not entrusted.** Timothy, therefore, like Paul is to let God's Spirit (cf. 1:7) enable him to guard the truth and the trust deposited with him.

Paul's use of the noun meaning "deposit" (*parathēkē*) which is translated **what has been entrusted to me** in verses 12 and 14 (cf. also 1 Tim. 6:20), is regarded by some as a linguistic innovation that suggests a new theological concept of a deposit of truth or a creed that is to be passed on. It should be noted, however, that this noun belongs to a working vocabulary that is especially familiar to Paul and Luke. It is the noun equivalent of the verb *paratithēmi* meaning (1) to entrust something to someone's keeping (cf. 2:2; 1 Tim. 1:18; Luke 12:48; Matt. 13:24, 31), and (2) to entrust someone to someone's keeping (Acts 14:23; 20:32; Luke 23:46; 1 Peter 4:9). The idea of entrusting truth to some one is suggested by the cognate language of Paul (*paratithēmi*) in 2:2 in reference to the truth to be entrusted by Timothy to other faithful men.

**15 You are aware that all who are in Asia turned away
from me, and among them Phygelus and Hermogenes.
16 May the Lord grant mercy to the household of Onesiphorus, for he often refreshed me; he was not ashamed of
my chains, 17 but when he arrived in Rome he searched for
me eagerly and found me— 18 may the Lord grant him to
find mercy from the Lord on that Day—and you well know
all the service he rendered at Ephesus.**

[15-18] The words **all who are in Asia** are not to be interpreted to mean all Christians in Asia, for Tychicus was not one of those who repudiated Paul (see Acts 20:4; 2 Tim. 4:12; Tit. 3:12). No information is given concerning Phygelus and Hermogenes other than in this verse. (The latter is mentioned in the apocryphal *Acts of Paul and Thecla* 14 along with Onesiphorus.) The word for **turned away** (*apostrephō*) is translated "deserted" in 4:16. It signifies rejection (cf. 4:4; Tit. 1:14). These men were ashamed to testify for Paul and thus to be identified with him in the humiliation to which he was being subjected. Onesiphorus had **searched eagerly** until he found the place where Paul was being held and **refreshed** him often. The word **refreshed** is found elsewhere only in Acts 3:20 and Romans 15:32. It seems to imply both spiritual and physical refreshment and relief, but in the three instances where it is used the predominant thought seems to be spiritual. Paul's spirit was greatly encouraged by the visits of Onesiphorus.

There has been much speculation on the import of Paul's language concerning **Onesiphorus.** Some think that he had already suffered martyrdom as a faithful witness. Others feel that he is probably in prison as a consequence of his devotion to Paul. One thing is certain: all of Paul's words about him are in terms of what is past. Some suggest that Paul's prayer for him indicates that he is alive, otherwise it would be a prayer for the dead. Paul's words, **may the Lord grant him to find mercy from the Lord on that Day,** need not suggest anything more than prayers on behalf of those who are out of human hands and in the hands of God. It may be that Onesiphorus was also in prison awaiting execution. If so, Paul would have been cautious in making

[1] You then, my son, be strong in the grace that is in Christ Jesus, [2] and what you have heard from me before many witnesses entrust to faithful men who will be able to teach others also.

---

any reference to the fact. Or perhaps Onesiphorus was in jail awaiting trial and Paul avoids language that might be used against him.

[1] The first three verses of this chapter should be regarded as a unit of thought. The words **You then** in verse 1 serves to connect what follows with what he has been reminding Timothy of in 1:15-18. Briefly stated, Timothy is to leave Ephesus for Rome as soon as possible. His mission in Ephesus (see 1 Timothy) must now be delegated to others, in order for him to accept the summons to suffer with Paul and Christ in Rome (cf. 4:6, 9; 1:8) and to resume his primary function as a missionary, or evangelist by traveling to testify and suffer for the gospel (cf. 1:8; 4:5-9). The urgent admonition to **be strong** (*endunamoō*) serves to connect this admonition with his words in 1:7, 8, 12-14, where he speaks of the grace of God in Christ as a source of strength or power (see comments on 1 Tim. 1:14; cf. 2 Thess. 2:16, 17; 1 Cor. 15:10). Timothy will need a full measure of the power which God's spirit gives (cf. 1:7).

[2] Paul does not depart from the main burden of his message to give Timothy this instruction. Timothy had been commissioned by Paul to an important task in Ephesus which was related to the serious threat caused by false teachers who were leading Christians into moral and religious apostasy. This meant that Timothy's primary job in Ephesus was one of teaching, charging, and exhorting the church (see the discussion of 1 Tim. 2:7 and 4:14). He was to lead the church in securing the right kind of men to carry on the work of teaching and admonishing and serving the church (cf. 1 Tim. 3:1ff.). Now Timothy is to turn the work over to these men in fact and to leave Ephesus as soon as he can (cf. 4:9, 21). Timothy must now entrust to these men what the Lord and Paul had entrusted to him (cf. 1 Tim. 6:20; 4:11-16; 2 Tim. 1:13f.; 3:14).

Timothy is to entrust to faithful men what he had **heard from** Paul (cf. 3:10-17). Paul's thought here is closely

[3] Take your share of suffering as a good soldier of Christ Jesus. [4] No soldier on service gets entangled in civilian pursuits, since his aim is to satisfy the one who enlisted him.

---

paralleled by his language in 1 Corinthians 11:2: "you remember me in every thing and maintain the traditions even as I have delivered them to you" (cf. also 2 Thess. 2:15; 3:6). The phrase **before many witnesses** has a different preposition from that in 1 Timothy 6:12, "in the presence of many witnesses." Here the preposition is "with" or "through." It may be that Paul is speaking out of his experience of having witnesses called to testify concerning his teaching. In other words, Paul may be using witness (*marturos*) in a legal sense (cf. Matt. 26:65; Acts 6:13; 7:58; 2 Cor. 13:1; 1 Tim. 5:19). It may carry something of the same import as his words to the Thessalonians, "while we preached to you the gospel of God. You are witnesses, and God also, how holy and righteous and blameless was our behavior" (1 Thess. 2:9b, 10).

On the great importance of appointing men who are **able** teachers who can be entrusted with the truth, see the comments on 1 Timothy 3:2 (cf. also Tit. 1:5, 9). The word **able** (*hikanos*) means "qualified" and "competent." It is translated "fit" (1 Cor. 15:9) and "sufficient" (2 Cor. 3:5). Paul used the verbal equivalent when he said that God had "qualified" him to be a minister of the new covenant (2 Cor. 3:6). Timothy must now hasten to complete his mission of committing the truth to men whom God had qualified to be entrusted with the teaching that accords with godliness.

[3] Paul's summons to Timothy to **take his share of suffering** by coming to Rome is clearly the main burden of this letter (see 1:8, 12; 2:9, 11; 3:8-13; 4:5, 6; cf. 1:10, 11, 16-18). The reference to **soldier** introduces the first of three illustrations.

[4] Paul's use of "be strong" (verse one) in admonishing Timothy to be a **good soldier** compares with his earlier language to the church in Ephesus, where his command to be strong is followed by the command to put on the whole armor of God. On both occasions of writing, Paul is in chains guarded by Roman soldiers (see Eph. 6:10-20). The

[5] An athlete is not crowned unless he competes according to the rules. [6] It is the hard-working farmer who ought to have the first share of the crops.

---

word for **soldier** (*stratiōtēs*) in verse 3 is not found elsewhere in Paul's writings. For some reason it was not included in the list of words classified by Harrison and others as unPauline. But the word translated **enlisted** (*stratologeō,* "to enlist a soldier") is listed. Both Paul and Luke had many encounters with the military, and both show familiarity with the language of the army (cf. *strateuō,* "to serve as a soldier," 1 Cor. 9:7; 2 Cor. 10:3; cf. also Luke 3:14; 21:20; 23:36; Acts 10:7; 28:16; 2 Cor. 10:3, 4).

The word translated **entangled** (*empleketai*) presents the picture of a sheep whose wool is caught in thorns. It is used figuratively here and in 2 Peter 2:10, where Peter speaks of being entangled in the defilements of the world. The word for **civilian pursuits** (*pragmateia*), found only here in the New Testament, is derived from a word meaning to carry on a business or a trade, which Luke uses twice (Acts 19:13, 15). Paul uses a kindred word meaning "a business matter" (1 Cor. 6:1, translated "grievance").

[5, 6] Paul moves quickly through three illustrations about the soldier, the athlete, and the farmer. This change of metaphors or analogies is typically Pauline (cf. 1 Cor. 9:7). He does this in discussing the church (Eph. 2:19-22; 4:12-16; 5:21-32), and refers to Christians as "babes," and a "field," and a "building" (1 Cor. 3:1-4, 5-9, 9-19; cf. also 1 Tim. 1:18, 19). The word translated **athlete** is really a verb referring to one who contends in the games. It is used here only in the New Testament, but Paul does use it in a compound form (*sunathleō,* Phil. 1:27; 4:3) meaning to contend or to strive together (cf. also *athlēsis,* "contest" in Heb. 10:32). Athletics supplied a favorite metaphor for Paul (1 Cor. 9:25f.). In 4:7, 8 Paul will return to the analogy of the athlete and the crown which one receives when he finishes the race. The reference to the reward due the **hard-working farmer** is paralleled in 1 Corinthians 9:10, 11 where Paul speaks of rewards due for his service performed. In these three analogies Paul is urging Timothy to suffer

[7] Think over what I say, for the Lord will grant you understanding in everything.

[8] Remember Jesus Christ, risen from the dead, descended from David, as preached in my gospel,

---

hardship for the crown of righteousness (cf. 4:7, 8), just as a soldier and athlete and farmer persevere through danger, rigid discipline, and hardship to the point of pain and fatigue in the hope of achieving victory and receiving a well-earned reward.

[7] Paul's words **think over what I say** are really an urgent demand that Timothy must perceive or comprehend (*noeō*), or gain insight into what Paul is talking about. And the word **understanding** (*sunesis*) also signifies "insight." Since the main burden of this letter seems to be Timothy's call to suffering (cf. notes on verse 3), Paul is writing and praying that Timothy will comprehend the will of God for his life and be able to understand the meaning of the events that are pushing him toward Rome.

Part Two, 2:8—3:9

The second of the remembering-reminding sections of this letter follows a pattern suggested by the language of 2:8 and 2:14. Timothy is charged to remember the sufferings of the Lord and of Paul, and then he is to remind the brethren of the place and necessity of such suffering on behalf of the gospel and the church.

Remember Jesus Christ, 2:8-13

[8] Paul now goes deeper into the mystery of God's will for Timothy, especially in reference to the call to suffering and hardship. To further Timothy's insight and understanding of the mystery of the cross he not only admonishes Timothy to **remember Jesus Christ,** but he also helps him to see that Paul's suffering is the ultimate and inevitable consequence of preaching the gospel. Timothy is to remember Jesus Christ, not simply as the crucified, but especially now as one who is **risen from the dead.** He must, with God-given insight, see beyond the cross to the crown (cf. 4:6-8).

**9 the gospel for which I am suffering and wearing fetters
like a criminal. But the word of God is not fettered.
10 Therefore I endure everything for the sake of the elect,
that they also may obtain the salvation which in Christ
Jesus goes with eternal glory.**

His brief description of the **gospel** for which he is suffering compares with his earlier utterances: (1) **Jesus Christ, risen from the dead** (cf. 1 Cor. 15:1-4); (2) **descended from David** (Rom. 1:3-4; 1 Tim. 2:5; 3:16); (3) **as preached in my gospel** (cf. Gal. 1:11; Rom. 2:16; 16:25; 2 Cor. 4:3; 1 Thess. 1:5).

[9] Paul's words here echo the same thought expressed earlier and later in this letter (cf. 1:8; 11, 12; 3:11, 12; 4:6, 7). The words translated **wearing fetters like a criminal** mean literally, "suffer hardship unto, or even to the point of, bonds like an evildoer."

The word for bonds or **fetters** (*desmōn*) is a cognate form of the word for prisoner (*desmios;* cf. Phile. 1:9; Eph. 3:1; 4:1). Paul's word for bound or **fettered** (*deō*) is the word translated "in prison" in Colossians 4:3, where Paul glories in the fact that even though he is behind barred doors, he has "an open door for the word" for which he is "in prison" (*deō,* bound). Just as Paul made a play on the idea of an open door for the word of a man behind locked doors, even so he draws an analogy from his own fetters by declaring that the words of a fettered man are not fettered or imprisoned (cf. Phil. 1:12-14; John 8:32).

[10] Timothy must also understand that Paul's suffering and death is a vicarious offering of himself on behalf of the church (Eph. 3:13; Col. 1:24), just as Christ loved the church and gave himself for her (Eph. 5:25-27; Acts 20:28). Paul was committed to dying that others might live, "always carrying about in the body the death of Jesus, that the life of Jesus may also be manifested in our bodies" (2 Cor. 4:10).

Paul reminds Timothy that he is willing to **endure** (*hupomenō*) everything. In 4:5 he uses the same word in challenging Timothy to **endure** suffering in fulfilling his ministry (cf. 3:10; 1 Tim. 6:11).

11 The saying is sure:
If we died with him, we shall also live with him;
12 if we endure, we shall also reign with him;
if we deny him, he also will deny us;
13 if we are faithless, he remains faithful—
for he cannot deny himself.

[11-13] These verses are arranged strophically on the assumption that Paul is quoting the words of a hymn that was being sung by the early church. While this is possible, it is also possible that Paul is simply uttering great truths without any effort to be poetic. The language is very, at times uniquely, Pauline in comparison with the rest of the New Testament. The language of verse eleven is the same as in 2 Corinthians 7:3 (cf. Rom. 6:8), and the great idea expressed is very Pauline (e.g., Rom. 6:3-11; Phil. 3:10, 11; cf. 2 Cor. 4:10, 11; Col. 3:1-4). The same can be said of the first line in verse twelve; in fact, the verb translated **to reign with** (*sumbasileuomen*) is found elsewhere only in Paul's language (1 Cor. 4:8). To **endure** in the context of suffering is very Pauline (e.g., 2 Thess. 1:4; Rom. 12:12; cf. Rom. 8:17). The word for **deny** (*arneomai*) is used in 1 Timothy 5:8 (cf. 2 Tim. 3:5; Tit. 1:6), but is not found elsewhere. However, Luke, Paul's scribe, uses it in expressing the very truth found in verse twelve (see Luke 12:9; cf. Luke 9:23; Matt. 10:33). The truth of verse thirteen, that God cannot deny himself, finds a unique parallel in Hebrews 6:13-18. The faithfulness of God is frequently stated (2 Cor. 1:18; 1 John 1:9). Verse thirteen is Pauline both in thought and language (e.g., Rom. 3:3, 4; cf. Rom. 8:31-39). So it is altogether possible that the apostle expresses himself here in prose that has a poetic quality, especially in the rhythm of thought which is the essential nature of biblical poetry. See comments on 1 Timothy 1:15 for **the saying is sure.**

The Proper Way to Handle the Word of Truth, 2:14—3:9

Paul's words in this section (2:14—3:9) may be divided into the negative aspects of what Timothy is to avoid and deny and the positive aspects of what he is to affirm in his

[14] Remind them of this, and charge them before the Lord[b] to avoid disputing about words, which does no good, but only ruins the hearers.

[b] Other ancient authorities read *God*

---

speech and behavior. The force and meaning of these words is comparable to what he said about the "man of God" in 1 Timothy 6:11-14, 20, 21 (cf. 2 Cor. 2:17; 4:1-4).

On the negative side, the correct handling of the truth means: (1) to avoid disputing about words (2:14), godless chatter (2:16-19), and senseless controversy (2:23, 24a); (2) to avoid youthful passions (2:22); and (3) to avoid such persons as described in 2:16-19 and 3:1-9 (cf. 3:5).

On the positive side handling aright the word of truth means: (1) to purify and consecrate oneself as a vessel of honor, fit and ready (2:20, 21); (2) to aim at righteousness, faith, love, and peace in company with the people who call upon the Lord out of a pure heart (2:22); and (3) to be kindly to everyone, an apt teacher, forbearing, and gentle in correcting opponents (2:24, 25a), keeping the right motivation in the hope of their conversion (2:25b, 26).

By such handling of the truth Timothy will demonstrate to the faithful men (2:2) how they also must conduct themselves as the Lord's servants in teaching the truth to others.

[14] Timothy is to remember what Paul has said in verses 8-13, and he is to **remind them of this, and charge them before the Lord.** His language here is the same as that used in charging Timothy in the presence of the Lord Jesus Christ (see comments on 1 Tim. 5:21). Now he commands Timothy to do the same thing in committing the truth to faithful men (cf. 2:3), charging them to avoid **disputing about words.** This, too, is the language he used earlier (see comments on 1 Tim. 6:4). Such disputation **does no good,** or literally, is not "profitable" or "useful." Earlier Paul spoke to Timothy on the useful or lawful use of the Law in teaching sound doctrine that accords with the glorious gospel (see 1 Tim. 1:8). The terrible evil of such **disputing** is judged and measured in light of the tragic fact that men like Paul are suffering and dying for the sake of the gospel of saving truth while others are addicted to indulging in vain argumentations that **ruin** rather

15 Do your best to present yourself to God as one approved, a workman who has no need to be ashamed, rightly handling the word of truth.

---

than save the hearers (cf. comments on 1 Tim. 1:3-6; 6:3-5).

[15] The word for **do your best** (*spoudazō*) signifies diligence, zeal, and earnest activity. No doubt Timothy felt the force of Paul's four uses of this word. He used it first adverbially in reference to the diligence and earnestness with which Onesiphorus had searched for him in Rome (1:17). Now he uses it to describe Timothy's diligence in the handling of the truth which he is committing to the men of 2:2, 2:14. His next two uses of the word will pertain to Timothy's activity in trying to reach Rome before winter (4:9, 21).

The word for **present yourself** (*paristēmi*) signifies to put oneself at God's disposal. It also serves to introduce the thoughts expressed later (e.g., vss. 19, 21, 24). Timothy is to make total commitment of himself as the Lord's servant. The idea of presenting oneself is typical of Paul (cf. Rom. 6:13b, 16, 19; 12:1; Col. 1:22). An **approved** (*dokimon*) workman is one who is purified, consecrated, useful, and ready (cf. vss. 19, 21). The word for **workman** (*ergatēn*) is translated "laborer" in 1 Timothy 5:18 (cf. James 5:4). Here the workman **who has no need to be ashamed** is pictured in contrast to the "deceitful workmen" of 2 Corinthians 11:13-15 (cf. Phil. 3:2). The word **unashamed,** along with such words as "suffering" and "understanding," is a key word in his message (see comments on 1:8; cf. 1:12, 16).

The compound word for **rightly handling** (*orthotomeō,* meaning "to cut straight") occurs only here. The only other instance in the New Testament of a compound verb from *ortho* (*orthopodeō,* meaning to walk straight, uprightly, or straightforward) is in Paul (Gal. 2:14). The meaning would be to cut a straight path through the word, giving it a proper interpretation. Paul's use of the term **the word of truth** compares with Ephesians 1:13 (cf. also Gal. 2:5; 5:7; 2 Thess. 2:12-13; Rom. 1:18; 1 Tim. 6:5). See the comments on 1 Timothy 3:15 for the important significance of the **truth** in Paul's letters to Timothy.

[16] Avoid such godless chatter, for it will lead people into more and more ungodliness, [17] and their talk will eat its way like gangrene. Among them are Hymenaeus and Philetus, [18] who have swerved from the truth by holding that the resurrection is past already. They are upsetting the faith of some.

[16, 17] Timothy is urged to **avoid** (*periistēmi*) or "go around," using a word that is found only here and in Titus 3:9. Similarly, Paul had earlier urged Timothy to "charge certain persons" at Ephesus not to teach or occupy themselves with such things (see 1 Tim. 1:3, 4, 6, 7). **Hymenaeus** was one of the certain persons (1 Tim. 1:20), as was Alexander, who is perhaps the same Alexander mentioned in the warning given in 4:14. This is the only reference we have to **Philetus.**

The words **godless chatter** (cf. 1 Tim. 6:20) are Paul's description of the disputing about words in verse 14, and his words **it will lead people into more and more ungodliness** explains how such disputing **ruins** the hearers. For the meaning of godless (*bebēlous,* profane) see comments on 1 Timothy 4:7 (cf. also 1 Tim. 1:9; 4:7; 6:20; Heb. 12:16). The word **chatter** (*kenophōnias*) means "empty talk." The use of "empty" (*kenos*) in compound words is peculiar to Paul in the New Testament. Compare "empty conceit," or "vain glory" (*kenodoxia*) in Philippians 2:3 (cf. Gal. 5:26). Paul frequently uses "empty" in a figurative sense meaning to be without any basis of truth: e.g., empty words (Eph. 5:6), empty deceit (Col. 2:8). The talk of Hymenaeus and Philetus is both profane and untrue.

The word translated **it will lead** (*prokoptō*) means to progress, advance, or go far. It is used again in 3:9 and 3:13, and is found only in Paul and Luke (e.g., Gal. 1:14; Luke 2:52; Phil. 1:1, 22, 25). The word for **eat,** a term used metaphorically by the medical men of Luke's day, is derived from the pastoral scene of sheep spreading out for pasture and signified such diseases as the cancer of spreading ulcers, or gangrene, which spreads or advances by eating its way along.

[18] Having described the chatter of Hymenaeus and Philetus as gangrene, Paul specifically identifies one of the

[19] But God's firm foundation stands, bearing this seal: "The Lord knows those who are his," and, "Let every one who names the name of the Lord depart from iniquity."

---

main points in their profane and false teaching. The reason for selecting this particular point of doctrine is obvious. It is not only a basic and cardinal truth of the gospel (2:8; cf. 1 Cor. 15:4), but it is also one that is especially relevant to the present suffering and impending death of Paul (2:11-12; 4:6-8). If **the resurrection is past already,** Paul himself would not be able to rejoice in such hope for himself and Timothy, and the message of 2:11-13 would be robbed of its comforting meaning. Such a false doctrine was **upsetting the faith of some** (cf. Tit. 1:11) just as it had disturbed the church in Thessalonica. For Paul's teaching see 1 Thessalonians 4:14-18 and 2 Thessalonians 2:1-11. The truth is, the resurrection is to take place in connection with the second coming of Christ, and the "dead in Christ will rise first, then we who are alive, who are left, shall be caught up together with them in the clouds to meet the Lord" (see 1 Thess. 4:14-18). The second advent is still future (2 Thess. 2:1-11); therefore the resurrection is still a future event to be hoped for.

Hymenaeus and Philetus, being professed Christians, did not deny that Christ was raised nor that Christians experience a resurrection. They simply taught that it had already happened. The form of their teaching may have been a compromise with Greek prejudices by teaching that the Christian's death and resurrection is a mystical experience that has nothing to do with the resurrection of the physical body. In this respect it may have been somewhat like the Gnostic heresy of Menander who, according to Irenaeus, was a disciple of Simon the sorcerer (Acts 8.9ff.) and taught his disciples that they could, by the exercise of magic powers, overcome the angels who made the world. He promised them that "they obtain the resurrection by being baptized into him, and can die no more, but remain in possession of immortal youth" (Irenaeus, *Against Heresies,* I. xxiii. 5).

[19] The words here relate especially to what has been said in verse 18, and they serve as a basis for the continued

admonitions on handling the truth which he resumes in verse 20. Verses 19 through 21 have been somewhat confusing and have been interpreted in several different ways. Some try to make the three verses fit into one continuing metaphor. Others see a shift or change in metaphor in verses 20 and 21. Some even see a slight metaphorical shift in the terminology of verse 21 as compared with verse 20. Much of the controversy over the interpretation of Paul's metaphor, or metaphors, centers around the term **God's firm foundation.** Does it refer to Christ and the apostles, or to the truth of the gospel, of the church as a whole, or to the faithful in the church?

The word **firm** in its figurative use is found in 1 Peter 5:9 and Acts 16:5, meaning firm or strong. The word for **foundation** (*themelios*) is used metaphorically in reference to several different things: (1) the truth of Jesus' words (Luke 6:48f.); (2) the work of another man (Rom. 15:20); (3) Christ himself (1 Cor. 3:10-12); (4) elementary doctrines (Heb. 6:1); (5) the apostles and prophets, with Christ as the chief cornerstone (Eph. 2:20). (6) Compare also his figurative use of the verb to lay a foundation or to establish (*themelioō*) in Ephesians 3:17 and Colossians 1:23. In which of these senses is Paul speaking or is he using it in a still different sense?

The word for **seal** (*sphragis*) may be the key that unlocks the meaning. But it is probably through the verb (*sphragizō*), meaning "to seal," that the best insight is gained. The word for **seal** is found only twice in Paul: (1) his words, "you are the seal of my apostleship in the Lord" (1 Cor. 9:2) and (2) his reference to circumcision as a mark or sign (Rom. 4:11). Both of these passages involve other metaphors. Paul's use of the verb "to seal" seems more closely akin metaphorically to the context of the words to Timothy. The figurative uses are found in three places: "he has put his **seal** upon us and given us the Spirit in our hearts as a guarantee" (2 Cor. 1:22); "In him you also, who have heard the word of truth, the gospel of your salvation, and have believed in him, were **sealed** with the promised Holy Spirit, which is the guarantee of our inheritance until we acquire possession of it" (Eph. 1:13, 14; cf. 4:30). It seems that in all instances above, the seal is more than a mere mark of identification; it is also a guarantee of divine power. Of all the above references, the language of Ephesians 1:13, 14 most closely parallels the language of 2 Timothy: e.g., "the word of truth" (2:15), "the gospel of salvation" (cf. 2:8, 10), "sealed" (2:19), and the "Holy Spirit" (1:14; cf. 1:7, 12).

If **God's firm foundation** refers to the faithful in the church, it signifies the solid, reliable, dependable element in the membership in contrast to the unreliable, false element represented by Hymenaeus and Philetus. As a foundation bears an inscription, faithful Christians are inscribed with the Holy Spirit. Such a metaphorical sense would not be at all foreign to Paul. Compare his metaphor in 1 Timothy 3:15 concerning the church as the "pillar and support of the truth." Paul's use of **foundation** metaphorically is characterized by a shifting of meaning (e.g., Eph. 2:19-21; 1 Cor. 3:10-12; 1 Tim. 3:15).

Not only does the word **seal** or **sealed** serve as a key, but the words of that seal also help to interpret the message in verses 19 through 21 as well as the entire context (2:14—3:9). The value of the two quotations seems to be twofold. In the first place, Paul reassures God's children that the resurrection has not already happened, an eventuality that would have left them hopeless in the face of suffering and death, by the words, **"The Lord knows those who are his."** Then he urges them to live in hope and readiness by saying, **"Let everyone who names the name of the Lord depart from iniquity."** This is the same line of reasoning and admonition as that which he used in 1 Corinthians 15:30-33 and 1 Thessalonians 4:17, 18 and 5:2-11. Confusion over the doctrine of the resurrection had a discouraging and demoralizing effect on believers, with disastrous consequences in matters of faith and morals.

In the second place, these two quotations help to mark Hymenaeus and Philetus as false teachers in opposition to Timothy and the "faithful men" to whom Timothy is committing the charge of responsibility as able teachers of the church (see comments on 2:2 and 2:14). And it may be that these faithful teachers, along with Timothy, are the particular "vessels of honor" implied in verses 20, 21. The two quotations are apparently taken from the story of the

[20] In a great house there are not only vessels of gold and silver but also of wood and earthenware, and some for noble use, some for ignoble. [21] If any one purifies himself from what is ignoble, then he will be a vessel for noble use, consecrated and useful to the master of the house, ready for any good work.

---

gainsaying of Korah and those who joined in revolt against Moses and Aaron. For the first quotation see Numbers 16:5, and for the second quotation see Numbers 16:26 (cf. Isa. 52:11). With these quotations God sets his seal upon Timothy and the faithful brethren in the church with whom he is working so diligently, and at the same time he sets his seal to the fact that only such vessels of honor will be cherished as precious by the Lord (cf. 20-22). With these quotations he also withholds his seal from the people who are to be avoided (cf. 3:5), not only people like Korah, but also false leaders like Hymenaeus and Philetus. By withholding his seal he also promises that such men "will not get very far" (see comments on 3:7-9). In light of the context of his instructions on rightly handling the word of truth (2:14—3:9) such an interpretation of the metaphors of verses 19-21, which occur in the midst of these instructions, does not seem strained.

[20, 21] If the metaphor of God's firm foundation, bearing God's seal, is a reference to the faithful in the church at Ephesus, the metaphor in these verses probably has the same meaning. Paul simply changes the figure to speak of the vessels of honor in God's house. Thus there is a different metaphor from 1 Corinthians 3:12 where the various materials are built on the foundation. Just as he used three different illustrations to make one point in 2:4-6, so he may be using different metaphors here in reference to those who are the Lord's true servants.

A very unique parallel in Paul's use of vessel is found in Romans 9:21-23. In Romans 9:21 he says the potter makes one vessel for beauty and another for menial use. In the next verses he makes a figurative application to the vessels of mercy to whom God makes known the riches of his glory (Rom. 9:23), and the vessels of wrath made for destruction (Rom. 9:22). Paul himself is called a "chosen

[22] So shun youthful passions and aim at righteousness, faith, love, and peace, along with those who call upon the Lord from a pure heart.

---

vessel" (Acts 9:15). The figurative use of vessel in his words to Timothy follows much the same pattern, with a shift in the point of truth being illustrated. If one stretches the metaphor too far in trying to make too many points, confusion results. The only point Paul seems to be making is that there are in the church both noble and ignoble men. The problem in Ephesus has to do with enemies of the truth who are in the church, not with foes outside.

There were men in the church who were vessels of dishonor unfit for any good works. On the other hand there were also vessels of honor who were useful for **noble** deeds. In verse 21 he applies the metaphor of verse 20 by urging Timothy and the men to whom he is committing stewardship of the truth (cf. 2:2, 14) to separate themselves from dishonorable men, such as Hymenaeus and Philetus, and to prepare themselves to be both precious and useful to the Lord for any good works. The word for **purifies** is *ekkathairō,* a word which puts emphasis on a purging which means to separate oneself from the ignoble vessels.

[22] Paul's reference to Hymenaeus and Philetus suggested the metaphors of verses 19-21. Now he returns to what he started in verses 14, 15 by interpreting the metaphors in terms of how the Lord's servant must handle the word of truth as a vessel of honor. He must separate himself from ignoble vessels and make himself serviceable or useful for any good work.

The vessel of honor will **shun youthful passions.** The word for **shun** (*pheugō*) means to flee from or avoid. The word for **youthful** (*neōterikas*) is from a word (*neōteros*) meaning "younger" (cf. 1 Tim. 5:1-2; cf. also "youth, *neotēs,* in Acts 26:4; Luke 18:21). The word for **passions** (*epithumias*) is used in a bad sense in Romans 7:7, 8 (cf. 1 Cor. 10:6). It is used in a good sense in 1 Timothy 3:1 where it is translated "desire" (cf. also 1 Thess. 2:17; Luke 22:15). The distinction is made between unlawful and lawful desires.

[23] **Have nothing to do with stupid, senseless controversies; you know that they breed quarrels.** [24] **And the Lord's servant must not be quarrelsome but kindly to every one, an apt teacher, forbearing,**

The vessel of honor will **aim at** (see comments on 1 Tim. 6:11) certain honorable things: (1) **Righteousness** (*dikaiosunē*), meaning what is right or just (Heb. 11:33) or what pertains to mercy and grace (2 Cor. 9:9). It signifies doing what is right (1 John 3:7; Rom. 5:7; cf. Tit. 2:12; see the comments on "training in righteousness" in 3:16). The **righteousness** Paul refers to here is synonymous with the "good works" of 2:21. In this respect he seems to be emphasizing what he did in Ephesians 2:8-9; 6:14 (cf. Phil. 1:10-11). (2) **Faith** is discussed in connection with 1 Timothy 1:5. (3) **Love out of a pure heart** is discussed in connection with 1 Timothy 1:5. (4) **Peace** is discussed in connection with 1 Timothy 1:2.

The Lord's servant as a vessel of honor is urged to keep company with those **who call on the Lord out of a pure heart** (cf. 1 Tim. 1:5). Just as he is to purge himself, or separate himself from the vessels of dishonor, he is to associate with vessels of honor.

[23] The word for **have nothing to do with** (*paraiteomai*) is also found in Titus 3:10 concerning the factious person. The vessel of honor will thus avoid such things as **stupid, senseless controversies.** The word for **stupid** (*mōras*) means "foolish" (Tit. 3:9), or "silly" (Eph. 5:4). Compare also "fools" (Rom. 1:22) and "folly" (1 Cor. 3:19). The word for **senseless** (*apaideutos*) means untaught, ignorant, or undisciplined. It is used only here in the New Testament. It belongs to a family of words used by Paul. The word for **controversies** (*zētēsis*) signifies disputes over controversial questions (see comments on 1 Tim. 1:4; 6:4; cf. Rom. 14:1; Acts 15:1, 2).

[24] The word for **servant** (*doulos*) is used in connection with **master** (*despotēs*) in Titus 2:9 (cf. also 1 Tim. 6:1; 1 Peter 2:18), and the word **Lord** (*kurios*) is the word Paul used in speaking of the **master** (*kurios*) of the **slaves** (*doulos*) in Colossians 3:22—4:1. **The Lord's servant** is here a special minister of God, for this was the designation

[25] correcting his opponents with gentleness. God may perhaps grant that they will repent and come to know the truth, [26] and they may escape from the snare of the devil, after being captured by him to do his will.[c]

[c] Or *by him, to do his* (that is, God's) *will*

---

of Moses and Joshua in the Greek Old Testament (Josh. 14:7; 24:29). He **must not be quarrelsome.** The word for **must** (*dei*) was used in stating the qualifications of elders in 1 Timothy 3. It is a key word in Christian ethics.

The Lord's servant **must be:** (1) **Kindly to every one.** The word for **kindly** signifies gentleness or mildness. It is not the same word as "gentle" in 1 Timothy 3:3. The word here is found only in 1 Thessalonians 2:7, where it is used in describing the gentleness of a nurse taking care of her children. (2) **An apt teacher** (*didaktikon;* see the comments on elders as **apt teachers** in 1 Timothy 3:2; cf. Tit. 1:9). (3) **Forbearing** (*anexikakos*), a word used only here, is derived from "to bear with" (*anechō*) which Paul uses in 1 Corinthians 4:12 in reference to bearing evil without resentment (cf. also Eph. 4:2; Col. 3:13). In Hebrews 13:22 and 2 Corinthians 11:1 it suggests the act of listening to someone, indicating a willingness to listen.

[25, 26] The forbearing of verse 24 seems to go well with **correcting his opponents with gentleness.** The word for **correcting** (*paideuonta*) means to teach (cf. Tit. 2:12). The word translated "correction" in 3:16 (*epanorthōsin*) signifies restoration. The Lord's servant is to teach his opponents with forbearance and gentleness in the hope that they will **repent and come to know the truth,** or come to acknowledge the truth (see comments on 1 Tim. 2:3-7).

The word for **repent** (*metanoian*) signifies a change of mind (see the comments on 1 Tim. 3:15 for Paul's emphasis on **the truth;** cf. 2 Tim. 3:15). His words that **God may perhaps grant** that they will repent and acknowledge the truth blends perfectly with his teaching that God opens doors for the word (Col. 4: 3), God brings the growth from the teaching of the truth (1 Cor. 3:6), and the power in the word is God's power (2 Cor. 4:7).

By leading his opponents to repentance and the acknowledging of the truth, the Lord's servant will be work-

[1] **But understand this, that in the last days there will come times of stress.** [2] **For men will be lovers of self, lovers of money, proud, arrogant, abusive, disobedient to their parents, ungrateful, unholy,**

---

ing with God in helping them to **escape the snare of the devil.** For the meaning of **snare** (*pagis*) see the comments on 1 Timothy 6:9. The word for escape (*ananēphō*) means to wake up (cf. "temperate" in 1 Tim. 3:2) or come to one's senses. These people have been **captured** (*zōgreō*). The only other place where this word is found is in Luke 5:10 where Jesus said to Peter, James and John, "henceforth you will be catching," or "capturing, men."

[1] Verses one through nine are closely related to the metaphor in 2:20, 21 and the admonition to the vessels of honor to separate or purify themselves from the vessels of dishonor. The faithful vessels of honor are described in 2:22-26. Now Paul describes the vessels of dishonor—men of corrupt mind and counterfeit faith.

The word for **understand** (*ginōskō*) means to comprehend, or perceive. Here it means more than to be sure about what is happening but also to comprehend why it is taking place and to gain a true perspective (cf. "insight" in 2:7).

The expression **in the last days** is not the same as "in later times" (see comments on 1 Tim. 4:1). The expression here is the same as in Acts 2:17 where Peter refers to the Christian age or the age of the church on earth. Paul seems to be saying that during the Christian age there will be **times of stress,** indicating that such a condition may be at intervals rather than as one continuing crisis. The word for **stress** (*chalepos*) suggests violence and fierce danger. The only other instance of its use is in Matthew 8:28 where it is translated "fierce." Timothy can expect to experience dangerous times, even violence, because of the activities of dangerous men (e.g., Alexander, 4:14, 15). There **will be** evil men, and as a consequence of their presence **there will come** the violence and danger which their presence promotes.

[2] This list of the sins of the evil men begins with one which is synonymous with the cardinal sin of pride: **lovers**

of self (*philautos*). This is the only place in the New Testament where this word is found. It is a compound made up of the word for loving, devoted, or beloved and dear (*philos*) and the word for self (*autos*). There are also three other words compounded from *philos* used here in verses 2-5 which are not to be found elsewhere in the New Testament. At first glance this might seem to indicate a linguistic problem concerning Paul's authorship. The fact is that the presence of these words suggests just the opposite when a comparison is made with the vocabulary of the rest of the New Testament. Of the fifteen words (twenty-two, counting close cognates) using *philos* in word formation as it is used here, all are found in the vocabulary of Paul or Luke, or both.

Paul's word for **proud**, meaning boastful and egotistical, is included in his list of vices in Romans 1:20, the only other place where it is found. The word for **arrogant**, meaning "haughty," suggests one who makes himself too conspicuous, who parades himself before others proudly (cf. also Matt. 6:5; Rom. 1:30; James 4:6; 1 Peter 5:5).

Evil men will also be **abusive** (*blasphēmos*), using slanderous speech (see the comments on 1 Tim. 1:13, 20; and cf. Acts 6:11; 2 Peter 2:11). This evil is included in the list of vices found in 1 Timothy 6:20 and Mark 7:22 (cf. also Eph. 4:31; Col. 3:8; Matt. 15:19).

Under their influence children will become **disobedient to parents.** Elders and deacons are commanded to lead out in an exemplary manner in keeping their children in respectful submission (see comments on 1 Tim. 3:4, 5, 12; cf. Tit. 1:6; Eph. 6:1-4; Col. 3:20, 21).

The word for **ungrateful** is found only here and in Luke 6:35. This sin is the opposite of Paul's virtue of thankfulness (see the comments on 1:3).

The word for **unholy** is synonymous with irreligious conduct. Compare Paul's use of holy (*hosios*) in Ephesians 4:24 and 1 Thessalonians 2:10 (cf. also Tit. 1:8; 1 Tim. 1:9). **Unholy** is found only here and in 1 Timothy 1:9, but it seems somewhat strained to attempt to classify it as foreign to Paul. One who used the word holy would likely be familiar with **unholy**, just as he would know **ungrateful** if he knew the word grateful.

**3 inhuman, implacable, slanderers, profligates, fierce, haters
of good, 4 treacherous, reckless, swollen with conceit, lovers
of pleasure rather than lovers of God,**

---

[3] The word for **inhuman** means to be without natural, or family affection. In exhorting the brethren to be genuine in their love (*agapē*) Paul urges them to be devoted in brotherly, or human love (Rom. 12:10; cf. Rom. 1:31). The word for **implacable** is found here only, but an alternate reading based on a manuscript variation includes it in the list of vices in Romans 1:31. It describes one who is irreconcilable, which is indeed an evil thing in light of the fact that the gospel ministry is one of reconciling man to God as well as man to man (2 Cor. 5:18-20; Matt. 5:23, 24). People who are **implacable** cannot be persuaded to enter into an agreement or covenant.

For the meaning of the word **slanderers** (*diabolos*) see the comments on 1 Timothy 3:11 (cf. Tit. 2:3) and the reference to the devil in 2:26. The word for **profligate** means incontinent. Paul discusses incontinence in 1 Corinthians 7:5. It is translated "rapacity" in Jesus' condemnation of the hypocrites in Matthew 23:25. These three instances are the only times this word, with its cognates, is found in the New Testament.

The evil men who cause times of stress or violence for God's people are men who are **fierce** (*anēmeros*), meaning not gentle or merciful (cf. 3:1 above). They are **haters of good** (*aphilagathos*) or, literally, they do not love the good. Compare Titus 1:8, 16 where such people are described as reprobate to every good work because they love evil rather than good.

[4] The description of wicked men in the church continues: They are **treacherous,** meaning they betray God's servants. This word is found elsewhere in the New Testament only in Luke's language where Stephen denounces those who betrayed Jesus (Acts 7:52) and in reference to Judas as a traitor (Luke 6:16).

The word for **reckless** means rash and thoughtless. It is used only one other time, in Acts 19:36, where it is translated "rash." It suggests headlong, irrational behavior prompted by strong emotions of prejudice and hatred. The

[5] **holding the form of religion but denying the power of it. Avoid such people.**

---

word translated **swollen with conceit** means "puffed up" and conceited. See the warning concerning appointing a neophyte to be an elder (1 Tim. 3:6); also Paul's description of the sick, morbid teachers of error (1 Tim. 6:4). The use of the metaphor for swollen or inflated in reference to spiritual evil is especially characteristic of Paul. Compare his use of the word for "puffed up" or "conceited" or "proud" in 1 Corinthians 4:6, 18; 5:2; 8:1; 13:4.

The evil workers in the church are **lovers of pleasure.** Peter says "they count it pleasure to revel in the daytime" (2 Peter 2:13b). The only other places where this word for **pleasure** occurs are in James 4:1, 3, where it is translated "passions," Luke 8:14, where it is translated "pleasures," and Titus 3:3.

[5] These evil men profess **religion.** The context indicates they are members of the church (cf. 2:17-21). The word translated **form** (*morphōsin*) is found elsewhere only in Romans 2:20 where it is translated "embodiment." The sin of these people in the church who hold to a **form** (body) suggests that their religion is merely outward, not inward (cf. James 2:26). Such pious hypocrisy is denounced by Jesus in Matthew 23:23-32.

The word translated **denying** (*arneomai*) is the same as in 2:13 (see comments there, and cf. Heb. 11:24; Tit. 1:16; 2:12; 1 Tim. 5:8). The word for **power** (*dunamis*) as used by Paul elsewhere sheds some light on his meaning here. In 1 Thessalonians 1:5 he said, "our gospel came to you not only in word, but also in power and in the Holy Spirit and with full conviction." He issued a challenge to false teachers in the church in similar words: "I will find out not the talk of these arrogant people but their power. For the kingdom of God does not consist in talk but in power" (1 Cor. 4:19, 20). Earlier in 2 Timothy he has stressed the importance of power in the Spirit (see comments on 1:7 and 1:14). Compare also Paul's reference to God's power in his own ministry in 1:12. For the meaning of the word translated **religion** (*eusebeia*) see the comments on 1 Timothy 2:3 and 2:10. It is one of the key words in 1 Timothy.

[6] For among them are those who make their way into households and capture weak women, burdened with sins and swayed by various impulses, [7] who will listen to anybody and can never arrive at a knowledge of the truth.

Timothy and the other faithful vessels of honor are urged to **avoid such people.** The word for **avoid** (*apotrepō*) means to turn away from. It is essentially the same in meaning as the word in 1:15 (*apostrephō*) in reference to those who rejected Paul.

[6] Among the evil people described above there are men (the word being masculine) who **make their way into houses.** This verb (*endunō*), meaning to enter in, is found here only in the New Testament and is used figuratively. Its metaphorical meaning, to creep or to sneak in, suggests that these false teachers slip into a man's house while he is away from home and seduce a woman into false religious practices. The word for **capture** (*aichmalōtos*) and its cognates, with one exception, are used figuratively in reference to captivity of a spiritual nature.

The word for **weak women** is an uncomplimentary description of one who is morally weak or little. These "little" women are persons who are not truly adult or mature spiritually. They are "silly," which is another translation of this word. Paul does not imply that all women are like this. He does, however, warn women in the church of their unique and basic nature which might make them an easy prey of evil men who would lead them captive and use them in a false way either religiously or morally. The exploitation of weak women for immoral and irreligious purposes, however, is seen in Acts 13:50; 16:16-18; and Revelation 2:20 (cf. 1 Tim. 5:13). On the other hand, spiritually mature women were useful and active in many good works, as seen in Acts 9:36; 16:13-15; 17:4, 12, 34; 18:18; Romans 16:1-4 (cf. also 1 Tim. 3:11; Tit. 2:3-5). But the weak, silly women in Ephesus were **burdened with sins and swayed by various impulses.** The word for **swayed** is from a word which means literally "to lead." The word for **various** means manifold or many. The word for **impulses** (*epithumiais*) means lust or desire (see comments on 2:22; cf. also Tit. 3:2-3).

[8] As Jannes and Jambres opposed Moses, so these men also oppose the truth, men of corrupt mind and counterfeit faith;

---

[7] The words translated **they will listen to anybody** mean "they are always learning." The word for **listen,** *manthanō,* is used in 3:14 (cf. also 1 Tim. 2:11; Col. 1:7). But, Paul says of these women, they **can never arrive at a knowledge of the truth.** The noun for **knowledge** (*epignōsis*) occurs fifteen times in Paul's writings. Peter is the only other New Testament writer who uses this noun (cf. 2 Peter 1:2, 3, 8; 2:20). The verb form (*epiginōskō*) is used often by both Paul (ten times) and Luke (fifteen times). For comments on Paul's use of the noun, see 1 Timothy 2:4; and for his use of the verb see 1 Timothy 4:3. Both the noun and the verb may signify a thorough knowledge of, or awareness of, or an acknowledgment of the truth.

[8] Paul's purpose in using **Jannes and Jambres,** two magicians who opposed Moses, may be simply to show the inevitable doom of those who oppose the truth, men like Hymenaeus, Philetus, and Alexander. But it seems that they may also serve to identify Hymenaeus and Philetus with the sin of seducing people by their magical practices. There is the possibility of a close relationship between the doctrinal error concerning the resurrection, and the existence of an heretical group of professed Christians who resorted to magic. The names Jannes and Jambres are not given in the Old Testament (Ex. 7:11), but they are mentioned in other literature dealing with Mosaic traditions. Paul compares Hymenaeus and Philetus with Jannes and Jambres (cf. 2:10; 3:8), who **oppose the truth** (cf. Acts 13:8, 10 for **oppose** and 19:19 for Ephesus as a center of magic.

These religious sorcerers were men **of corrupt minds.** The word for **corrupt,** or "utterly corrupted," means seduced, ruined, and depraved (see 2 Cor. 11:3; Eph. 4:22). The word translated **counterfeit** (*adokimos*) signifies something which does not stand the test. It is a word that is found in only six places in the New Testament (1 Cor. 9:27; 2 Cor. 13:5-7; Tit. 1:6; Rom. 1:28; Heb. 6:8). Paul puts great emphasis on standing the test and proving qualified

9 but they will not get very far, for their folly will be plain to all, as was that of those two men.

10 Now you have observed my teaching, my conduct, my aim in life, my faith, my patience, my love, my steadfastness.

---

in God's sight (Phil. 2:22; 2 Cor. 8:8, 22; 13:5; 1 Thess. 2:4). Paul's emphasis on "approved," or genuine (*dokimos*), in his charge to ministers of the word in 2:15, finds its counterpart in his description of false teachers in the church as men who were "counterfeit" or not approved (*adokimos*).

[9] All that Paul has been saying, especially in the section which began in 2:14 and ends with 3:9, has been dealing with the approved vessels of honor, and the unapproved vessels of dishonor. His conclusion about the vessels of dishonor is simply, **they will not get very far, for their folly will be plain to all,** just as in the case of Jannes and Jambres. For the meaning of **they will not get far** see the discussion in 2:16 above. Their folly will be **plain,** meaning fully exposed or manifest.

Part Three, 3:10—4:5

This is the third of the remembering and reminding sections which consists of memories and charges that are written in terms of the unique personal relationship between Paul and Timothy: (1) You Timothy, have observed me, my ministry and my suffering, 3:10-13. (2) As for you, continue in what you have learned, 3:14-17, and suffer for the gospel as I have, 4:5. A special charge is given concerning Timothy's duties as a minister of the word, especially in reference to completing his mission in Ephesus (cf. 2:7; 4:14) and resuming his missionary ministry by coming to Rome to preach and to suffer hardship for the gospel (cf. 4:6-9).

You Have Observed Me and My Sufferings, 3:10-13

[10] The word for **you have observed** (*parakoloutheō*) is found only three times elsewhere. In the sense that it is used here it occurs in 1 Timothy 4:6 where it is translated "followed," and in Luke 1:3 where it is translated "having

11 **my persecutions, my sufferings, what befell me at Antioch, at Iconium, and at Lystra, what persecutions I endured; yet from them all the Lord rescued me.**

---

followed all things closely." In a somewhat different sense it is used in Mark 16:17 where it is translated "attended," or "accompanied."

Much can be said about each of the items Paul includes in his list of things Timothy can remember from personal observation. They serve as a sort of check list for Timothy to use as he reflects on his close companionship with Paul through the years: (1) **My teaching**—see the comments on Paul's ministry as a teacher (1 Tim. 2:7), the importance of sound teaching (1 Tim. 1:10) and the meaning of "apt teacher" (1 Tim. 3:2). (2) **My conduct,** meaning manner of life. (3) **My aim in life** (*prothesis*), meaning my purpose of heart (cf. "steadfast purpose," Acts 11:23). (4) **My faith** (*pistis*) may also be translated "my faithfulness," or "loyalty" (cf. "true fidelity" in Tit. 2:10). Paul elsewhere emphasizes the importance of being sound in the faith (cf. Tit. 1:13). Here he may also imply his own personal faith or confidence in God which he steadfastly demonstrated (cf. 1:12 and 4:7). (5) **My patience,** which is the word translated "longsuffering" or "forbearing" in 2 Corinthians 6:6. Paul exhorted the brethren to "admonish the idle, encourage the fainthearted, help the weak, be *patient* with them all" (1 Thess. 5:14). For an example of the patience of Paul which Timothy had observed read 2 Corinthians 1:1; 2:1-11; 4:5, 8-12, 15; 6:3-13. (6) **My love**—see the comments on 1 Timothy 1:5. Paul urged brethren to exercise genuine love, love without hypocrisy (cf. Rom. 12:9-13) and he maintained in his own heart and life a genuine love (2 Cor. 6:6). (7) **My steadfastness** signifies endurance, one of the virtues Timothy was to aim at (see 1 Tim. 6:11).

[11] Paul continues with things Timothy could remember from his own personal observations: (8) **My persecutions**—see the comments on verse 12 below. Paul's attitude toward his own persecution is reflected in Romans 8:31-37 and 2 Corinthians 12:10. (9) **My suffering** is the word used in 2:9 with the prefix *kako,* meaning evil. See also his charge to Timothy to take his share of suffering (*kako-*

[12] **Indeed all who desire to live a godly life in Christ Jesus will be persecuted,** [13] **while evil men and impostors will go on from bad to worse, deceivers and deceived.**

---

patheō) in 2:3 above and 4:5 below. Here the word signifies misfortune and is used by Paul in reference to "the sufferings of this present time" (Rom. 8:18). (10) **What befell me at Antioch, at Iconium, and at Lystra.** For **Antioch** see Acts 13:14, 44-50. For **Iconium** see Acts 13:51—14:5. For **Lystra,** see Acts 14:5-7, 19-20. For the list in general, see 2 Corinthians 6:4-10.

Out of all these difficulties, says Paul, **the Lord rescued me.** The phrase is substantially the same as Psalm 34:19. The word for **rescued** (*rhuomai*), meaning delivered, is used with reference to being rescued from evil men (cf. 3:13 and 2 Thess. 3:2), also in reference to being delivered from this body of death (Rom. 7:24), to his deliverance from the lion at his first defense (4:17), and to his final deliverance and salvation in the heavenly kingdom (4:18). This is the word used in Matthew 27:43 concerning Jesus' cry for deliverance on the cross (cf. Ps. 22:1, 7-8, 19, 24).

[12] The word for **desire** (*thelō*) means to wish, but here it signifies more than mere desire. With the desire there is a will, resolution, or purpose of heart. It is used in 1 Timothy 2:4 concerning God's wish or will that all men be saved (see comments on 1 Tim. 2:4, 8; cf. Phil. 2:13). So Paul says that all who have desired and determined to be saved will suffer, reminding Timothy of the inevitability of his own suffering, if he accepts the challenge to follow in Paul's steps and to accept the summons to share Paul's suffering for the sake of the gospel in Rome. The word for **a godly life** (*eusebōs*) is an adverb meaning piously.

[13] The word for **evil men** is a figurative use of a word that means "sick," also virulent, or extremely venomous and noxious, or malignant. Figuratively, as Paul is using it here, it may signify evil, vicious and degenerate. See the comments on the spiritually sick men described in 1 Timothy 6:4-5 whose lives and teaching are like an infectious disease. The word for **impostors** may signify a sorcerer (see comments on 3:8) or a swindler and a cheat. Such evil men **will go on,** or advance, just as their teaching will spread

**14 But as for you, continue in what you have learned and
have firmly believed, knowing from whom you learned it
15 and how from childhood you have been acquainted with
the sacred writings which are able to instruct you for
salvation through faith in Christ Jesus.**

---

or advance like a malignancy (see 2:16). But, as Paul has said, these impostors will not get very far (see 3:9). For the meaning of **deceiving and deceived** see the discussion of the deceitful spirits in 1 Timothy 4:1. The word for "deceive" means to lead astray or to be misled (see Tit. 3:3; 1 John 1:8; 2:26; 1 Thess. 2:3). Paul's language in 2 Thessalonians 2:9-12 seems especially near in meaning.

Continue in the Scriptures, 3:14-17

[14, 15] Paul's word for **continue** (*menō*) means to live or abide. Note the use by Jesus, "If you continue in my word, you are truly my disciples" (John 8:31; cf. John 15:4-7), and "if you keep my commandments, you will abide in my love" (John 15:10; cf. 1 John 4:16).

The word for **learned** is the same as in 3:7 above, where it is translated to "listen," and in 1 Timothy 2:11 concerning women who must learn in silence. As Paul is using it here in his charge to Timothy, it finds close parallels in Paul's language to the Corinthians, "that you may learn by us to live according to the scriptures" (1 Cor. 4:6).

The word for **firmly believed** suggests that Timothy was fully convinced or persuaded on the basis of his own personal observations (cf. 3:10). And his sources of information about the truth of God were reliable sources. Paul suggests three sources from which or from whom Timothy had learned the truth: (1) From Paul himself (3:10, 14). (2) From his parents (cf. 1:5). The word for *childhood* means "infant," or "babe." (3) But the basic source of Timothy's knowledge, whether through Paul or his parents, was the **sacred writings** (see comments on "scripture" in verse 16). These sacred writings are **able** or powerful **to instruct** one for **salvation through faith in Christ Jesus.** The word for **instruct** means to make one wise. Paul frequently connected true wisdom with what one learns, or is taught,

16 All scripture is inspired by God and [d] profitable for teaching, for reproof, for correction, and for training in righteousness, 17 that the man of God may be complete, equipped for every good work.

[d] Or *Every Scripture inspired by God is also*

---

from the word of God. He prayed that God's children "may be filled with the knowledge of his will in all spiritual wisdom and understanding" (Col. 1:9), and added, "Let the word of Christ dwell in you richly, as you teach and admonish one another in all wisdom" (Col. 3:16; cf. Col. 1:28; Rom. 16:17-19; Ps. 19:7; Eph. 5:15-16).

[16, 17] All scripture, or sacred writing, **is inspired of God.** This does not mean that all writings are inspired, but that all that Paul regarded as sacred writings (vs. 15) are inspired of God. To Paul there was a definite canon or collection of writings which he regarded as "sacred" or holy. The writings which Timothy had been taught from his infancy were the Old Testament manuscripts kept in sacred trust in the Synagogues where people gathered to hear men read publicly or aloud from God's word. This was one of Timothy's duties as a minister of the word (see comments on 1 Tim. 4:13). Christians also regard the twenty-seven books of the New Testament as sacred or holy writings, each one inspired of God. But the scriptures to which Paul is referring here are those of the Old Testament. From these sacred writings Jesus and his apostles, and other evangelists, preached **salvation through faith in Christ Jesus.** For example: (1) Jesus in Luke 24:25-27, 32, 45 (cf. Luke 4:16-21; Matt. 21:42; 22:29); (2) Philip in Acts 8:32-35; (3) Paul in Acts 17:2, 11; (4) Apollos in Acts 18:24-28.

Paul describes the holy scriptures as **profitable** (*ōphelimos*), which is derived from *ōpheleō* meaning to be useful or beneficial. It is translated "of value" (Rom. 2:25; 3:1), "benefit" (1 Cor. 14:6), "advantage" (Gal. 5:2), and "profit" (Luke 9:25). A significant parallel is found in Hebrews 4:2, where the glad tidings did not "benefit" or "profit" those who heard it because the message did not meet with faith in the hearers.

The word for **inspired by God** (*theopneustos*) is found only here in the New Testament. It is of a class with other words compounded with "God": "haters of God" (*theo-*

[1] **I charge you in the presence of God and of Christ Jesus who is to judge the living and the dead, and by his appearing and his kingdom:**

---

stugēs), found only in Romans 1:30; "fighting against God" (*theomacheō*), found only in Acts 23:9; 5:39); "taught of God" (*theodidaktos*), only in 1 Thessalonians 4:9; "reverence for God" (*theosebeia*), found only in 1 Timothy 2:10.

If read in faith, the holy Scriptures will instruct and equip the **man of God** for every good work. See 1 Timothy 6:11 for comments on the meaning of the term **man of God,** and compare this with the "Lord's servant" in 2:21-25 above. These sacred writings are profitable in four respects: (1) **For teaching,** see the discussion of the importance of both "teaching" and "the teaching" in 1 Timothy 1:3 and 4:13. (2) **For reproof,** which means to convict or to show someone. Jesus used this word when he said, "If your brother sins against you, go and *tell* (show or convict) him his fault, between you and him alone" (Matt. 18:15). This is the word Paul used in instructing Timothy to "rebuke" those who sinned (see comments on 1 Tim. 5:20). It is translated "conviction" or proof, in Hebrews 11:1. (3) **For correction.** This word is kin to the one meaning to cut straight (2:15 above) and means to set straight, as in "make straight paths for your feet" (Heb. 12:12). (4) **For training in righteousness.** The word for **training** is translated "discipline" in Ephesians 6:4 (cf. Heb. 12:7-9). It signifies also "instruction." The Law (Old Testament) is called an instructor to bring us to Christ (Gal. 3:24). A knowledge of the Old Testament scriptures will instruct or make one wise unto salvation through faith in Christ (cf. 3:15). For a discussion of righteousness see the comments on 2:22, 25, and compare 1 Timothy 6:11. The phrase **every good work** is the same as that used in 2:21 in reference to the vessel of honor, who is here called **the man of God.** It is also used concerning women (see the comments on 1 Tim. 2:10; cf. 1 Tim. 5:10).

A Solemn Charge 4:1-5

[1] The word for **I charge you** means to testify solemnly, and is used earlier in 2:14 (see also the comments on 1 Tim.

5:21). In these earlier instances the charge is given in the presence of the Lord, or of God, Christ, and the elect angels, with no suggestion of adjuration. Here, however, it is possible that the charge takes on this meaning, by virtue of the use of *kata* (by, or according to) followed by the accusative case for **his appearing,** and **his kingdom.** It is also possible that Paul's use of *kata* with the accusative suggests that he is pointing toward the coming of Christ and the future glory of his heavenly kingdom. In this sense he may be giving solemn testimony in view of the fact that Jesus will appear again to judge the living and the dead and to save those who have longed for his coming, rewarding them with a place in his heavenly kingdom (cf. 4:8 and 4:18). In 1:18 and 4:8 Paul looks forward to "that Day," in accord with his teaching in Romans 2:1-11, as a day of wrath and a day of glory and honor. Paul's charge here also accords with his teaching that God has appointed Christ to be the judge in that Day (cf. Acts 17:30-31; 10:42). See the discussion of Christ "the righteous judge" in 4:8 below. Christ **is to judge** the living and the dead, which may suggest the idea of intent and certainty as well as the fact that it may be in the not too distant future. For other instances of Paul's use of the word for **judge** in reference to the divine administration of justice, the vindication of the innocent and the punishment of the wicked, see 1 Corinthians 4:3-5, Romans 2:16, and 1 Thessalonians 4:15-17 (cf. 4:8; 1 Tim. 5:24; Heb. 10:30, 31; James 5:9; 1 Peter 4:5; Rev. 20:11-13).

Paul's references to the **appearing** (*epiphaneia*) and **kingdom** (*basileia*) of Christ are sometimes in terms of the past, and in some cases they point to the future. Consider the following arrangement of passages pertaining to the Lord's epiphanies or manifestations: (1) was manifested, i.e. his first appearing—1 Timothy 2:6; 3:16; 2 Timothy 1:10; Titus 1:2-3; 2:11; (2) will be manifested, i.e., his second coming, 1 Timothy 6:14-15; 2 Timothy 4:1; 4:8; Titus 2:12 (cf. 2 Thess. 1:7-10; 2:1-12). The following arrangement of passages pertains to Christ's **kingdom,** his kingship or royal rule: (1) his past and present reign as King—1 Corinthians 15:20-28; Colossians 1:13 (cf. Rev. 1:5, 6); (2) his future sovereignty and power—1 Timothy 2:24; 2 Timothy 4:18. As far as his present kingship is concerned, Paul teaches

[2] preach the word, be urgent in season and out of season, convince, rebuke, and exhort, be unfailing in patience and in teaching .

---

elsewhere that the second coming of Christ and the general resurrection and judgment were to be the final acts of Jesus as King (1 Cor. 15:28). See the comments on the sovereignty of God and Christ in 1 Timothy 6:15.

[2] Paul charges Timothy to **preach the word,** using the word for preaching (*kerussō*) which he did not use in giving his charges in 1 Timothy. For the significance of this and for a discussion of the important meaning of Timothy's ministry as a preacher (*kērux*) of the word, see the discussion of 1 Timothy 2:7.

Paul also charges Timothy to **be urgent,** meaning to stand by or to be at hand. The same word is translated "has come," or is at hand, in 4:6. For the sense of being on hand or showing diligence in standing by, see Acts 22:13, 20; 12:7; Luke 24:4. The meaning "be on guard duty" occurs in the papyri. Timothy, too, is to be on the job, ready for any good work (cf. 2:21; 3:17). The words for **in season** (*eukairōs*) and **out of season** (*akairōs*) mean whether it is convenient or inconvenient, opportune or inopportune, favorable or unfavorable. The only other use of **out of season** is in Philippians 4:10. The word for **in season** is used in verb form, meaning to find an opportunity or a time (1 Cor. 16:12; cf. Lk. 22:6 and Heb. 4:16). For Paul's own practice see Acts 20:20, 31.

Timothy is also charged **to convince.** For a discussion of the meaning of this word see 1 Timothy 5:20. He is to **rebuke,** meaning to reprove, censure, warn, or punish. Timothy is also charged to **exhort.** This is one of the words used to describe his ministry in Ephesus (see the comments on 1 Timothy 1:3).

He is to **be unfailing in patience and in teaching.** The words for **be unfailing,** in the sense employed here, are very characteristic of Paul and signify the fullest measure of devotion. The language of verse 2 has a close parallel in Ephesians 6:18b, "To that end keep alert with all perseverance." For the meaning of **patience** see the comments on 3:10 above. For the important meaning and place of **teach-**

[3] For the time is coming when people will not endure sound teaching, but having itching ears they will accumulate for themselves teachers to suit their own likings, [4] and will turn away from listening to the truth and wander into myths. [5] As for you, always be steady, endure suffering, do the work of an evangelist, fulfil your ministry.

---

ing in the ministry of the word, see the comments on 2:24, 25 above, as well as the comments on 1 Timothy 2:7 and 3:2.

[3, 4] On the meaning of the words **the time is coming,** see the discussion of 3:1 and 4:2 above. The word for **will not endure** (*anechō*) means they will not listen willingly. The same word is used in Hebrews 13:22, "bear with my word of exhortation." The word for **sound** (*hugiainō*), meaning healthy, is a key word, in both 1 Timothy and Titus, in describing the doctrine which accords with the gospel and with holiness (see 1 Tim. 1:10).

The word for **itching** is derived from a word that means to scratch. Metaphorically Paul is saying that there is something wrong with their ears and they want someone to scratch them, or say something that is soothing to their ears. Those who will not listen to the truth **accumulate** or heap up **teachers to suit their own liking.** Compare "who will listen to anybody" in 3:7 above. Jesus warned, "take heed what you hear" (Mark 4:24), and "take heed how you hear" (Luke 8:18; cf. Heb. 5:11 on "ears dull of hearing"). The word for **turn away** means to reject (see the comments on 1:15 above.) For comments on **the truth** see 1 Timothy 3:15. And for the meaning of **wander into myths** see the comments on 1 Timothy 1:4-6 and Titus 1:14.

[5] The word for **steady** means "sober" (see the comments on 1 Tim. 3:2, 11). It is also translated "temperate," meaning self-possessed and well-balanced. For the serious import of the words **endure suffering** see the discussion of 2:3 above (cf. 1:8; 2:9-10).

Timothy is now charged to **do the work of an evangelist.** This is the only place the word **evangelist** is found in the three letters to Timothy and Titus. And the only other instances of its use are in Ephesians 4:11 and Acts 21:8. The term is always used in specific reference to a particular

6 For I am already on the point of being sacrificed; the time of my departure has come.

---

ministry in the church. For Paul's definition of the work of an evangelist, see the discussion of preaching in 1 Timothy 1:1 and 2:7 and the comments on Timothy's work as a preacher in 1 Timothy 4:13. The word for **fulfil** is synonymous with the word used in 4:17, where Paul speaks of proclaiming the word fully. To fulfill one's ministry means to live it fully and bring it to full fruition. For the meaning of the word **ministry** (*diakonia*) see the discussion of 1 Timothy 1:1 (compare also the word "minister" in 1 Cor. 3:5 and 4:5).

Part Four, 4:6-22

Paul informs Timothy of the status of things in Rome. He takes a quick forward and backward look (4:6-8), then proceeds with a series of instructions involving Timothy's immediate departure for Rome and things to do and to avoid en route to Rome. These instructions are mixed with several quick recollections and instructions concerning other people. This is followed by his benediction in 4:22.

A Backward and Forward Look, 4:6-8

[6] The word Paul uses in speaking of his being **sacrificed** (*spendō*) is most significant. The only other place where this word is used in the New Testament is in Philippians 2:17, written by Paul during his first Roman imprisonment. Now, as he writes to Timothy, he is again in Roman imprisonment, definitely facing the prospect of execution, and speaks again of his death as a drink offering which is poured out upon the sacrifice (see Num. 15:1-10; 28:4-8). It is difficult to determine just what thought was in Paul's mind in the use of these words. Elsewhere Paul speaks of his body as a living sacrifice (*thusia*) presented to God (Rom. 12:1). If he thinks of his life and ministry as something offered in the sacrifice and service of the faith of Christians, his death would be a most appropriate drink offering that is poured upon the sacrifice and giving it a fragrant aroma. Typically, Paul chooses to put his mind on

**7 I have fought the good fight, I have finished the race, I
have kept the faith. 8 Henceforth there is laid up for me the
crown of righteousness, which the Lord, the righteous
judge, will award to me on that Day, and not only to me
but also to all who have loved his appearing.**

---

the fragrant and pleasant aspects of his unpleasant suffering. So he thinks of the gift of himself in terms of a fragrant aroma or sweet smell.

His word for **departure** (*analusis*) is found nowhere else in the New Testament, but it is derived from a verb (*analuō*) meaning "to depart," which is found in the same sense as here in reference to death in Philippians 1:21-23: "My desire is to depart (*analuō*) and be with Christ."

[7] In this verse Paul gives a summary evaluation and appraisal of his life as a servant of Christ and a minister of the gospel: (1) **I have fought the good fight.** Here he uses the same words he had used in 1 Timothy 4:10 and 6:12 (see the comments on the latter). The figure is from the wrestling match at the games. (2) **I have finished the race.** The word for **race** calls up another athletic metaphor. There are only two other places where it is so used, and both are in Paul's language as recorded by Luke: in Acts 13:25 where Paul refers to John the Baptist "finishing his course," and in Acts 20:24, where he said, "If only I may accomplish my course." The word for **finished** means "accomplished" and is the word Jesus used on the cross after he had "accomplished" his mission (John 19:28, 30). (3) **I have kept the faith.** The word for **kept** (*tēreō*) may signify that Paul had guarded it well, keeping it unharmed, or that he had observed it fully and faithfully. This is the word he used to Timothy about keeping himself pure (1 Tim. 5:22) and in charging him to keep the commandment unstained and free from reproach (1 Tim. 6:14; cf. 1 Thess. 5:23). If **the faith** does not refer to the pledge by contestants in the games to keep the rules, then Paul refers to the doctrinal content of Christianity (as in 1 Tim. 4:1).

[8] Paul looks forward confidently and joyfully to the prospect of standing before **the righteous judge** in the supreme court of the universe. He had appeared for trial

many times before human tribunals to face false charges (cf. Acts 18:25; 24:10; 26:6). He declared that he would not refuse to die if he was found guilty of wrongdoing (Acts 25:11), but he also insisted that he be given a fair trial and the opportunity to testify in his own behalf and in behalf of the cause he represented (Acts 25:10, 11; 26:4-8). Having tried and failed to receive justice in the courts of Rome, he now looks forward to his appeal to Christ, who is to judge the living and the dead (cf. 4:1; 1 Cor. 4:3-5). This final judgment was to be according to the word of God which Paul had proclaimed, when all men would be judged according to the gospel which Paul had preached (cf. Rom. 2:16). He was prepared in all good conscience for this appearance before Christ, and he confidently hoped to receive **the crown of righteousness** from the one whose righteousness he had faithfully proclaimed and written about, the righteousness from God that depends on faith (Phil. 3:9; Rom. 1:16-17).

Paul's **crown** was not to be a symbol of his own righteousness, nor was it to be an award that he had merited (see the discussion of Paul the "sinner" saved by grace in 1 Timothy 1:14-17). The figurative use of **laid up** is found only in Colossians 1:5 and Hebrews 9:27. Paul's crown being "laid up" seems to be synonymous with "the hope laid up in heaven" (Col. 1:5). Victors in the games were crowned with a wreath of garlands (1 Cor. 9:25).

Paul's crown was not merely some garland which he would wear on his head. Just as the brethren in Philippi, whom Paul loved and longed for, were his joy and crown, so his hope of heaven and his **crown of righteousness** were thought of in terms of gaining Christ. Paul was not merely trying to win a race that he might gain a crown. He was trying to gain Christ and this was to be his true reward (cf. Phil. 3:8, 13-14). But, Paul says, his crown or award is not only laid up for himself, but also for **all who have loved his appearing.** The word for **have loved** (*agapaō*) as used here, signifies a longing or desire which causes one to strive for something. So Paul speaks of those who love, or long for, the **appearing** of Christ (see the discussion of 4:1 above for the significance of this term).

[9] **Do your best to come to me soon.** [10] **For Demas, in love with this present world, has deserted me and gone to Thessalonica; Crescens has gone to Galatia,** [e] **Titus to Dalmatia.** [11] **Luke alone is with me. Get Mark and bring him with you; for he is very useful in serving me.**

[e] Other ancient authorities read *Gaul.*

A Series of Instructions, 4:9-21

[9] This is the second time Paul has said to Timothy **do your best** (cf. 2:15). The same word describes the diligence of Onesiphorus in seeking Paul when he came to Rome (cf. 1:17). For the meaning of **soon,** signifying quickly and without delay along the way, see the comments on 4:21 below and on 1 Timothy 3:14.

[10] **Demas** had ceased loving and longing for the coming of Christ (cf. verse 8), and was **in love with this present world,** or the "present age." (See the comments on 1 Timothy 6:17.) In his case "the cares of this world and the delight in riches" had choked the word (cf. Matt. 13:22). Paul had warned against this in 1 Timothy 6:6-10, 17-19. Demas had **deserted** Paul (cf. 4:16) like the others who had turned away from him (cf. 1:15). Demas who, with Luke, was a "fellow worker" (Phile. 24; cf. also Col. 4:14), has either quit the ministry, or he has decided to shun the kind of ministry that involved sacrifice and hardship. Neither **Crescens** nor **Titus** had so deserted, but they had left Rome for other fields of service. Some Greek writers use **Galatia** for Gaul, so the latter reading may be an interpretative variant. Titus had gone to **Dalmatia,** which was a part of Illyria across the Adriatic Sea from southern Italy. Earlier, Titus had left Crete and joined Paul in Nicopolis and continued with him to Rome (cf. Tit. 3:12).

[11] Of all Paul's team of special co-laborers, **Luke alone** is with him as he writes to Timothy. This definitely suggests Luke's role as Paul's scribe. See the General Introduction on Luke's important role as Paul's companion through many years and his vital role as Paul's scribe in writing this letter as well the two earlier letters to Timothy and Titus.

John **Mark** (Acts 13:5), who had been an earlier disappointment to Paul (Acts 13:13; 15:37ff.), is now regarded

[12] Tychicus I have sent to Ephesus. [13] When you come, bring the cloak that I left with Carpus at Troas, also the books, and above all the parchments.

---

by the apostle as **very useful** to him in the ministry. Mark had been to Rome before and had been associated with Paul there as indicated by earlier letters Paul had written from there during his first imprisonment (cf. Col. 4:10; Phile. 22). His later experience in Rome is reflected in the Gospel according to Mark, which we think of as the gospel to the Romans. Mark is **useful** (*euchrēstos*), the word he used for the "vessel of honor" in 2:21.

[12, 13] Paul had sent **Tychicus** to Ephesus, probably in view of Timothy's leaving there as soon as possible. At one time Paul had debated sending Tychicus to Crete to enable Titus to join him in Nicopolis. It seems that he probably sent Artemas instead, since both Titus and Tychicus were in Rome with Paul after Titus left Crete (cf. 4:9 above with Tit. 3:12).

The reference to **the cloak** which Paul had left in Troas indicates that his visit there was during the time following his first Roman imprisonment, else it would have to have been left prior to his two years in jail in Caesarea and the two years in Rome recorded in Acts 24-28. Why would Paul want the cloak? There is the prospect of winter coming on and the date of execution was not certain (cf. verse 21), so it would be of comfort to him. If the cloak was something Paul cherished, he might just want Timothy to have it.

What were the **books** (*biblia*) or papyrus rolls which he had left at Troas? Paul's experience as a student in the school of Gamaliel and his missionary journeys, would have given him many opportunities to gather such materials. They might have included portions of the sacred Scriptures. But we do not know what these books were. But the **parchments** (*membrana*) seem to have been more precious for some reason. Were they pieces of skin or vellum which Paul needed for his own writing purposes? Such materials were somewhat precious. Or they may have been writings which Paul wanted for his own personal study. Being confined in prison gave him much time for study. Another possibility is that they were materials which he needed as

[14] Alexander the coppersmith did me great harm; the Lord will requite him for his deeds. [15] Beware of him yourself, for he strongly opposed our message. [16] At my first defense no one took my part; all deserted me. May it not be charged against them!

---

evidence in the next stage of his trial. This depends on whether Paul really expected to have such a hearing (see the comments on verse 16).

[14, 15] The mention of **Alexander** in connection with Troas may indicate that he was there and Timothy would have to be cautious in stopping there to pick up the things Paul had left with Carpus. The word **coppersmith** may also signify one who works with metal. We cannot assume that this is the same Alexander as the one mentioned in Acts 19:33, but it may be safe to identify him as the person referred to in 1 Timothy (see the comments on 1 Tim. 1:20). The word for **requite** is translated "repay" in Paul's reference to the judgment in Romans 12:17; (cf. 1 Thess. 5:15). The statement is a commonplace in the Old Testament (e.g. Ps. 62:13; Prov. 24:12). Paul warns Timothy to **beware,** meaning to be on guard against and to avoid. The words translated **our message** probably signify that Alexander had strongly contradicted the "statements" made by Paul and others who had testified in his behalf. If one interprets the word for message (*logos*) in line with 1 Timothy 5:17, it would signify "preaching." But in this context it may be, and perhaps should be, translated to signify that Alexander had strongly contradicted the "statements" or testimony made by Paul and others who had witnessed in his behalf.

[16] Different interpretations have been put on Paul's words **at my first defense.** Some suggest that it refers to his first appearance before the Sanhedrin (Acts 23:1-10) and take the language of verse 17 below to refer to the vision in Acts 23:11. Others think it refers to the appearance before Felix (Acts 24: 1-23). The view rather commonly subscribed to is that he is referring to his first appeal to Caesar (Acts 25:11, 12) which eventually took him to Rome for his first appearance and trial before Caesar (Acts 28:19, 30-31). Paul was not executed then, but was set free. This compares favorably with verse 17 below. But some find it difficult

[17] **But the Lord stood by me and gave me strength to proclaim the word fully, that all the Gentiles might hear it. So I was rescued from the lion's mouth.**

---

to believe that all forsook Paul at this first appeal to Caesar in Acts 28, in light of the many friends he had in Acts 28:30, 31. Another view, which seems to be increasingly accepted, is that Paul is referring to the preliminary hearing or investigation, the *prima actio* of Roman jurisprudence, which took place when he was arrested and taken to Rome this second and last time. This first action of the court was not equal to trial. If the judge was still in doubt, there could also be a second hearing, the *secunda actio*. Whether Paul went through two actions, there is no way of knowing. But Paul seems certain now that he is to be executed, which means the trial has already gone against him, or that he is pessimistic about the outcome on the basis of the preliminary hearings. If **first defense** does not mean the trial itself, has the final trial already taken place, or is it still pending? If it is already over, why doesn't Paul say that everybody forsook him at the final trial? If the trial is pending, and Timothy is on his way to be a witness for the defense, why Paul's pessimism in verses 6-8 if things went favorably at the first defense? All interpretations face some difficulties, but it seems obvious here that he is already aware of the verdict from his second appeal or appearance before Caesar. Nevertheless, Paul always allowed for the possibility that God might intervene and change the future as Paul envisioned it.

Paul's language in verses 16 and 17 is like that which was used in connection with the crucifixion of Jesus. His expressed desire that the sin of those who had deserted him **may not be charged against them** recalls the words on the cross (Luke 23:34; cf. Acts 7:59, 60). No one, says Paul, **took my part** signifying that they would not appear publicly in his defense, refusing to come to his aid. The word **deserted** is the same word used about Demas in 4:10. It is also the word Jesus used in Matthew 27:46, from Psalm 22:1, "why hast thou *forsaken* me?"

[17] **But the Lord stood by me**, says Paul. The word for **stood by** means to give aid to (cf. Rom. 16:2). Here again

[18] **The Lord will rescue me from every evil and save me for his heavenly kingdom. To him be the glory for ever and ever. Amen.**

[19] **Greet Prisca and Aquila, and the household of Onesiphorus.** [20] **Erastus remained at Corinth; Trophimus I left ill at Miletus.**

---

is a remarkable comparison between Paul's language and the language connected with Jesus' crucifixion. Feeling "forsaken" by God, Jesus cried out in the language of Psalm 22:1. It was a cry for help: "O thou my help, hasten to my aid . . . Save me from the mouth of the lion" (Ps. 22:19, 21), and the Lord heard his cry (Ps. 22:24). So Paul, likewise, being forsaken by others, received help when the Lord stood by or came to his side to help. And he was **rescued from the lion's mouth.** Paul's language here is figurative, referring to his being saved from execution, rather than literal, since Roman citizens were not thrown to the lions.

[18] Paul is not anticipating deliverance from the lion's mouth. But his execution will simply be his final rescue by the power of God to be saved into the heavenly kingdom. The doxology following the reference to God's power is typical of Paul. His language in Galatians 1:4, 5 closely parallels this, where he speaks of the Lord's ability "to deliver us from the present evil age, according to the will of our God and Father; to whom be the glory for ever and ever" (cf. also Rom. 9:5; Phil. 4:19-20; Eph. 3:21).

[19, 20] Paul's special word of salutation to **the household of Onesiphorus** is intended to comfort them in their bereavement over Onesiphorus (see comments on 1:16 above.) **Prisca and Aquila** were long-time friends and coworkers in Christ. For some reason her name appears before his. It may be mere coincidence, or it may signify that her station in life, or her personality, distinguished her in a unique way which tended to overshadow Aquila. But this is mere speculation. (See the references to these friends of Paul in Acts 18:1-3, 18, 26-29, Rom. 16:3-5, and 1 Cor. 16:19.)

Erastus was probably the same person who went with Timothy to Macedonia (Acts 19:22), rather than the city treasurer at Corinth (Rom. 16:23). The word **left** signifies

[21] **Do your best to come before winter. Eubulus sends greetings to you, as do Pudens and Linus and Claudia and all the brethren.**

[22] **The Lord be with your spirit. Grace be with you.**

---

that Erastus stayed behind. Paul's arrest may have taken place in Corinth. **Trophimus** had been with Paul on the trip to Miletus, and then in Jerusalem (Acts 20:4; 21:19). This suggests that they were together a second time in Miletus, following the release from the first Roman imprisonment.

[21] This is the third time Paul says **do your best,** meaning to be diligent (cf. 1:15; 4:9). Timothy is to do his best to reach Rome **before winter,** probably because of the difficult, if not impossible, conditions for travelling by sea to Rome after winter set in. This would cause delay and he would not be able to come without delay (cf. 1 Tim. 3:14, 15).

The four names given here are all of Latin character, and probably indicates that they were friends who lived in Rome.

The Benediction, 4:22

[22] The singular form of **your** means Timothy himself. And the plural form for **you** suggests that the last word includes all the brethren. Even though the language is used in other benedictions (as Phile. 25), it seems that his words to Timothy, **The Lord be with your spirit,** take on deeper meaning, especially in light of 1:7, 8, 14; 2:1-3, 7; 3:5.

IV

The Letter of Paul to Titus

Introduction

Titus

Titus has been described as "the most enigmatic figure in early Christian history" (W. M. Ramsay, *St. Paul the Traveller and Roman Citizen,* p. 58). The details of the pattern of his life and ministry as Paul's co-laborer are somewhat obscure, even puzzling and inscrutable at times. This is due mainly to the fact that the book of Acts does not make any mention of Titus. Timothy is rather conspicuous in the book of Acts, as well as in all of Paul's letters, except Galatians, Ephesians, and Titus. Titus is mentioned only in Galatians and 2 Corinthians and 2 Timothy. He was one of Paul's truly great helpers, especially in Corinth and on the island of Crete. He also came to Paul's help in Nicopolis, Rome, and Dalmatia (Tit. 3:12; 2 Tim. 4:10).

The events described by Paul in Galatians 2:1-9 involve the great controversy over circumcision. Titus played a significant role in this controversy; in fact, he seems to have been exhibit "A" in Paul's prosecution of those who made circumcision a test of fellowship. Luke's supplementary and explanatory account of these same events does not mention Titus by name (cf. Acts 15:1-35). The mention of Titus by

Paul was essential to the point he was making, but the account given by Luke did not require such reference to Titus. It is obvious that Titus was with Paul on the trip to Jerusalem, but he was not one of the official delegates Luke mentions in Acts 15:2. Titus may have been privately selected by Paul to be his associate and assistant on this important mission. Luke's concentration on the chosen messengers of the churches probably explains, at least in part, why Titus is not named in the Acts account.

Titus faded from recorded activities for a few years. Paul's next mention of him is in connection with plans to meet Titus in Troas (2 Cor. 2:12f.). Titus was then on his way from Corinth to Macedonia, where he did join Paul in Philippi. The background of these activities is found in 2 Corinthians where Titus is mentioned prominently as one of Paul's most trusted associates. He is mentioned nine times in this letter. Paul's failure to mention him in 1 Corinthians may be due to the fact that at that stage Titus was the one selected to deliver the letter. Titus became especially interested in the work in Corinth (2 Cor. 7:15; 8:16) and returned later to serve very effectively in that field (2 Cor. 8:22).

One can safely conclude that Titus was with Paul in Ephesus in A.D. 55 and had been with the apostle on the third missionary journey. If Paul did not take him along on the first and second journeys, the reason might have been very simple: Titus was an uncircumcised Greek. Paul steadfastly refused to have Titus circumcised (Gal. 2:3-5). This would have posed some very serious problems for both Titus and Paul, if Paul had chosen him to be a close associate during the trials with the Jews that occurred on those first two journeys.

Titus, like Timothy, became Paul's "true child" (Tit. 1:4; 1 Tim. 1:2). This gave Paul, the Jewish apostle to the Gentiles, two "sons," one circumcised and one uncircumcised, who worked with him as with a father in reconciling Jew and Greek in Christ.

Date of Writing

During his years of freedom following his first Roman imprisonment, Paul preached on the island of Crete and left Titus behind to correct certain serious defects. In the summer or fall of A.D. 66 or 67, Paul wrote this encouraging letter urging Titus to do his best to complete his assignment and to join him, probably before winter, in Nicopolis on the Adriatic Sea, about one hundred and fifty miles northwest of Corinth in Achaia. It seems that Paul had not yet reached Nicopolis, judging by his use of "there" rather than "here" (see comments on 3:12).

The Island of Crete

In 141 B.C. the Jews on the island had become strong enough to win the political support of Rome, which made them even more prosperous and influential. Because of the religious ties of the Cretan Jews with Jerusalem, the people were exposed to influences from the east. Rome annexed Crete in 67 B.C. and combined it with Cyrene, a part of Lybia in north Africa, as one province. Politically and geographically Crete was in a position of exposure to influences from Europe on the north and from Egypt, Lybia and Cyrene to the south. It was favorably situated as the largest in a chain of islands which served as a convenient series of stepping stones for the traffic that moved between Greece and Asia Minor. Its harbors were very important to the ships that sailed the Mediterranean, especially in bad weather (cf. Acts 27:7-14). Ships going west from Egypt to Rome usually sailed north toward Asia Minor, then westward to reach the shelter of the coasts of Crete (cf. Acts 27:5-7).

According to Acts 2:10, 11, on the day of Pentecost there were devout Jews from Crete who heard the gospel and witnessed the establishment of the church. The conversion of some of these men and their subsequent return to their island home was likely the beginning of the churches with which Paul and Titus later worked. Even though Paul's ambition was to preach the gospel where Christ had not been named, lest he build on another man's foundation (Rom. 15:20), yet, when he found the time and the opportunity, he rejoiced in strengthening and confirming churches established by others (Rom. 15:22-24). Paul's first recorded visit to Crete (Acts 27:7ff.) was due to a sudden shift from gentle south winds to a tempestuous northeaster, probably the famous Euraquilo rushing down the slopes of the island's historic Mt. Ida. We do not know how much contact Paul may have had with Christians during his brief time of refuge at Fair Havens, but there may have been some, judging by the kindly treatment of Julias in allowing Paul freedom to visit with friends while the ship was docked at Sidon (Acts 27:3). In any event, Paul's influence among the churches on the island was evidently strong.

Outline

I. Introduction, 1:1-5
   - A. Formal greeting, 1:1-4
   - B. Basic twofold charge, 1:5

II. The Appointment of Elders, 1:6-16
   - A. The qualifications of elders, 1:6-8
   - B. The twofold duty of elders, 1:9-16

III. Amending What Is Defective in Christian Behavior, 2:1—3:11
   - A. Various Groups in the Church, 2:1-10
     1. The older men and women, 2:2-4a
     2. The younger men and women, 2:4b-8
     3. The slaves in the church, 2:9-10
   - B. Christian morality based on salvation by grace, 2:11-14
   - C. A charge to Titus, 2:15
   - D. Remind them: seven rules for all, 3:1, 2
   - E. Remind them: seven aspects of their behavior before they were saved by God's goodness, 3:3, 4
   - F. Good deeds: an obedient response of one who has believed the goodness and love of God, 3:5-8
   - G. Evil things and people to be avoided, 3:9-11

IV. Conclusion, 3:12-15
   - A. Two final instructions, 3:12-14
   - B. Final greeting and benediction, 3:15

Commentary

Introduction, 1:1-5

The Salutation, 1:1-4

[1] This salutation, which is longer than those in most of Paul's letters, compares in length with the ones in Romans and Galatians. The term **servant of God** is not used elsewhere. The closest parallel is in James 1:1. Paul does refer to himself as the servant of Christ (Rom. 1:1; Phil. 1:1). The word for **servant** is the same as "slave" in 2:9 below. It was a term commonly used in association with the word for "master" (*despotēs*). In this connection, see the comments on 1 Timothy 6:1-2 and 2 Timothy 2:24.

The phrase **to further** is supplied to interpret the preposition *kata,* meaning according to, in agreement with, or with reference to. The preposition is used again in this verse in the phrase **according to godliness.** In 3:3 the same word is translated by, or in accord with, God's command (cf. also 1 Tim. 1:11). Here it signifies that Paul's apostolic ministry is for the purpose of promoting or furthering the faith and the knowledge of God's people. His reference to the **elect** compares with Romans 1:5, 6, where he says that his ministry as an apostle is "to bring about the obedience of faith" and among those "who are called to belong to Jesus Christ" (cf. also 2 Tim. 2:10). God's elect are those who have accepted the call of Christ through the gospel.

For a discussion of **the faith,** see the comments on 1 Timothy 3:9. A discussion of **the knowledge of the truth** is given in connection with 1 Timothy 2:4; 3:15 (cf. also 2 Tim. 2:25; 3:7). Since the word **godliness** (*eusebeia*) is one of the key words in 1 Timothy, the readers is referred to 1 Timothy 2:2.

[2] The **hope of eternal life** is the promise of life in

**1 Paul, a servant[a] of God and an apostle of Jesus Christ,
to further the faith of God's elect and their knowledge of
the truth which accords with godliness, 2 in hope of eternal
life which God, who never lies, promised ages ago 3 and
at the proper time manifested in his word through the
preaching with which I have been entrusted by command
of God our Savior;**

4 To Titus, my true child in a common faith:

Grace and peace from God the Father and Christ Jesus our Savior.

[a] Or *slave*

Christ Jesus (cf. 2 Tim. 1:1). It is the hope of all who are longing for his second coming (2 Tim. 4:1, 8), and it will come to those who are waiting for him (Tit. 2:13). See the comments on "Jesus Christ our hope" in 1 Timothy 1:1. Paul's hope in the promise of God is based upon the truth that God **never lies** (cf. Heb. 6:18). Paul also knew that he himself was not lying when he spoke the truth in God (Rom. 9:1; cf. Rom. 3:4; 1 John 1:10). Contrast verse 12.

[3] This hope of eternal life was promised **ages ago** (cf. 2 Tim. 1:9; Rom. 1:2) and was manifested **at the proper time** (cf. 1 Tim. 2:6; Gal. 4:4) through **the preaching** with which Paul had been **entrusted.** For Paul's ministry as a "preacher" see the comments on 1 Timothy 2:7 (cf. also 2 Tim. 1:10, 11). The faithful proclamation of the gospel is to continue until the second coming of Christ (cf. 1 Tim. 6:14, 15 and 2 Tim. 4:1, 2). For a discussion of **by the command of God our Savior** see the comments on 1 Timothy 1:1, and for **entrusted,** 1 Timothy 1:11.

[4] Titus, like Timothy, is regarded by Paul as his **true child,** the meaning of which is discussed at 1 Timothy 1:2. A very close tie bound Titus to Paul as a son to a father. The word **in** is a translation of *kata;* it signifies that Titus was Paul's true child in harmony with or in accord with **a common faith.** The use of the adjective **common** (*koinos,* cf. Jude 3) is a cognate form of the word for Christian fellowship, meaning to share (*koinōneō;* cf. 1 Tim. 5:22; Rom. 15:27), and the word meaning a partnership, or a sharing (*koinōnikos;* cf. 1 Tim. 6:18; Phil. 1:5; 1 Cor. 1:9).

[5] This is why I left you in Crete, that you might amend what was defective, and appoint elders in every town as I directed you,

---

Paul's use of **grace and peace** is the same here as in the salutations of his other epistles, with the exception of the two letters to Timothy where he inserts the word "mercy."

The Basic Twofold Charge, 1:5

[5] The word translated **I left you** is the word used in reference to leaving his cloak at Troas and leaving Trophimus ill at Miletus (cf. 2 Tim. 4:13, 20), and indicates that Paul had been with Titus on the island and had left him behind there. This would have been during the years of freedom following his first imprisonment in Rome (see the General Introduction to this volume).

Before leaving Titus in Crete, Paul had given him a twofold charge which this letter repeats and expands:

(1) **To amend what is defective.** The word **amend** means to set things straight, to line them up in the right order. For Paul's use of "straight" in various combinations with other words, such as "cutting straight," see the comments on 2 Timothy 2:15 on "rightly handling the word of truth." The word for **defective** means what is lacking. The text of the letter indicates that there were several serious defects in the individual and corporate life of the churches of Crete, such as (a) lack of spiritual leadership (1:5), (b) false teachers (1:10-11), and (c) immoral conduct among the members of God's family, both young and old (2:1-10).

(2) **To appoint elders in every town as I directed you.** The word for **appoint** means to ordain, to constitute, to set over, or to put in charge (Acts 6:3; 7:10); it also signifies to place one in position of ruling or judging (cf. Luke 12:14; Heb. 5:1; 8:3). Compare also "to set over" (Matt. 25:21, 23). For the method Titus was to use in making these appointments see the discussion of laying on of hands in 1 Timothy 4:14 (cf. also 1 Tim. 5:22 and 2 Tim. 1:6).

Paul **directed** Titus to appoint a plurality of **elders** in **every town** (cf. his own practice in Acts 14:23). The words to Titus make it obvious that the terms bishop (vs. 7) and elder refer to the same person and ministry. The plural

[6] if any man is blameless, the husband of one wife, and his children are believers and not open to the charge of being profligate or insubordinate.

---

elders in 1 Timothy 5:17 compares with Titus 1:5. And the singular for elder in 1 Timothy 5:19 compares with the singular for bishop in Titus 1:7 (cf. 1 Peter 5:1).

The word for **I directed you** means to command or to lay down a rule. Compare "this is my rule" (1 Cor. 7:17; cf. 1 Cor. 11:34). It is translated "commanded" in 1 Corinthians 9:14. It signifies the command given by one in a position of authority. The manner in which Paul exercised authority and gave commands in the name of Christ is discussed in connection with 1 Timothy 1:3, 18.

The Elders, 1:6-16

Their qualifications, 1:6-8

[6] Paul's orders to Titus included not only the command to appoint men to the task, but also directions concerning the character, conduct, and ability of the men to be appointed. Titus is to appoint a man **if** he **is blameless.** The word for blameless is the word used in reference to the deacons in 1 Timothy 3:10. Another word, meaning above reproach, is used in reference to the bishops, or elders, in 1 Timothy 3:2. The fact that Paul uses **blameless** two times in his directions to Titus (1:6 and 7) suggests that it is not merely one of the qualifications in the list, but that the elders are to be blameless in respect to the certain essentials that are given here. These qualifications consist of things that **must be** (1:7), as in 1 Timothy 3:2.

One of the characteristics of an unimpeachable elder involves his marital status: he must be **the husband of one wife.** This is the same language as in 1 Timothy 3:2.

He must have children who **are believers and not open to the charge of being profligate or insubordinate.** He must manage his own household, keeping his children submissive and respectful in every way (cf. 1 Tim. 3:3, 4). **Children** is generic and includes one or more (cf. the plural in Eph. 6:4). The word for **believers** means "believing." It may at

[7] For a bishop, as God's steward, must be blameless; he must not be arrogant or quick-tempered or a drunkard or violent or greedy for gain,

---

times mean "faithful" as in 1 Timothy 1:12 and Matthew 25:21, 23; or "trustworthy" as in 1 Corinthians 4:2. The word believer, literally "believing children" or "faithful children," would indicate a relationship of the child to the elder as his father, suggesting trustworthiness and loyalty. On the other hand the word is also synonymous with being a Christian, as in the case of the masters in 1 Timothy 6:2 (cf. 1 Tim. 4:3; 4:10; and Acts 10:45). Whether the word means one who is trustworthy and reliable, or one who is a Christian, is determined by the context. The meaning here in Titus has been much debated. The context does imply the children's relationship to their fathers, as in 1 Timothy 3:4, 5, signifying obedience to them as parents. But, the context here suggests more than this. The words that follow immediately are also definitive: **not open to the charge of being profligate,** which suggests that they are old enough to be Christians. The word for **profligate** is the word used in Ephesians 5:18 in describing the conduct of one who is drunk with wine. It is used in Luke 15:13 to describe the son who was guilty of "loose living," or dissipation and debauchery. It seems safe to conclude that children who are old enough to conduct themselves in such a manner are also old enough to obey the gospel and to embrace the Christian faith, with its moral demands. Also the word for **insubordinate,** meaning undisciplined and rebellious, is used in 1 Timothy 1:9 to describe those who are lawless (cf. also Tit. 1:10). This suggests that they are old enough to fulfill the ethical requirements of the Christian life. In such a context, the use of **believers in the** sense of being a Christian is defensible.

[7] Here Paul uses the term **bishop** (*episkopos*) to describe the ministry of an elder. The **for** shows that the **bishop** here is the same as elder in verse 5. There is a similar change from the plural to the singular in the instructions about women at 1 Timothy 2:11. For a study of the episcopal ministry in the early church, see 1 Timothy 3:1, 2.

The word for **steward** (*oikonomos*) designates an office of administration, the office of a manager who has been en-

[8] **but hospitable, a lover of goodness, master of himself, upright, holy, and self-controlled;**

---

trusted with responsibility of oversight (cf. Luke 16:2-4). It recalls the image of the church as God's household (1 Tim. 3:15).

On the significance of **must** and **blameless** see comments on the discussion of 1 Timothy 3:2, and verse six above.

The word for **arrogant,** meaning self-willed and stubborn, is found in the New Testament only here and in 2 Peter 2:10 where it is translated "wilful" (cf. also "arrogant pride" in Prov. 21:24). A **quick-tempered** man is one who is inclined toward the human emotion of indignation and wrath and is easily provoked to anger. This word is found only here in the New Testament, but cognate forms are used by Paul elsewhere: e.g., "anger" (1 Tim. 2:8; Eph. 4:31), and "to be angry" (Eph. 4:26; cf. Luke 14:21).

For a discussion of **drunkard,** and **violent** (a striker) see 1 Timothy 3:3; **greedy for gain** is discussed in connection with 1 Timothy 3:8.

[8] For a discussion of **hospitable,** see 1 Timothy 3:2. The word for **lover of goodness** compares with the word for "no lover of good" which is translated "haters of good" in 2 Timothy 3:3. The word for **master of himself,** meaning self-control and mental soundness, is one of the important words in Paul's message to Titus, as well as to Timothy. It is used again in 2:2 and 2:5 where it is translated "sensible." In verb form it is used in 2:4 concerning older women training, or putting younger women in a right mind; and again in 2:6 where Titus is to urge the younger men to control themselves, be discreet, or to be in their right mind (cf. Luke 8:35; Rom. 12:3). As an adverb it is used in 2:12 where it is translated "sober," meaning with self-control and good judgment. See the comments on 2 Timothy 1:7 where it is translated "self-control." In 1 Timothy 2:9 it is translated "sensibly," meaning rationally and with sound mind (cf. Acts 26:25). Since the Christians on the island are seemingly very much in need of developing this quality of mind and conduct, it is especially important that the elders, as overseers, also be of sound mind, mature thinking, using good judgment and self-control. It

[9] **he must hold firm to the sure word as taught, so that he may be able to give instruction in sound doctrine and also to confute those who contradict it.**

---

is a practical kind of wisdom which reflects itself in the practical application of Christian ethics to daily living with others.

The word for **upright** means "just" or "righteous" in the sense in which it is used concerning Cornelius in Acts 10:22 (cf. Rom. 5:7; 1 John 3:7). It is used in the same sense where masters are urged to deal "justly" with their servants (Col. 4:1). In another sense, as Paul would affirm, there are none who are just or upright (cf. Gal. 3:11, and see comments on 1 Tim. 1:9). But, in the sense used here, Paul even said of himself that he behaved in a manner that was "holy, righteous and blameless" (1 Thess. 2:10).

The word for **holy** (*hosios*) means devout and pious. Paul combines "just" and "holy" in Ephesians 4:24. Here it pertains to the service of God in one's daily life, as in 1 Thessalonians 2:10-12 (cf. Luke 1:75). See the comments on the "holy hands" of the men who lead the church in public worship in 1 Timothy 2:8.

The word for **self-controlled** (*egkratēs*) is the word Paul used in 1 Corinthians 7:9 and 9:25, as well as in Galatians 5:23. It signifies continence and temperance.

Their Duties, 1:9-16

[9] A bishop must cling devotedly to or **hold firm to the truth**. This is the word Jesus used in Matthew 6:24 concerning a servant being "devoted" to one master and despising another. He must be devoted to **the sure word as taught**, or to the faithful word which accords with the doctrine. The elder's ministry is a ministry of the word (see the discussion of 1 Tim. 3:2). He, like other ministers of the word, must "follow the pattern of sound words" which Paul taught (2 Tim. 1:13), which "agree with the sound words of our Lord Jesus Christ and the teaching which accords with godliness" (1 Tim. 6:3).

Through such devotion to the faithful word a bishop will be **able to give instruction in sound doctrine.** The word

[10] **For there are many insubordinate men, empty talkers and deceivers, especially the circumcision party;**

---

for **give instruction** (*parakaleō*) means to exhort (1 Tim. 5:1) and to preach (1 Tim. 4:13; 2 Tim. 4:2). It is also translated "to urge" (2:6; cf. 1 Tim. 1:3; 2:1). For the emphasis on **sound doctrine** see 2:1, 8 (cf. also 1 Tim. 6:2-3; 2 Tim. 1:13; 4:3). Special reference should be made to the qualification of a bishop as "an apt teacher" (1 Tim. 3:2).

An elder must not only be skilled in exhorting the brethren concerning the sound doctrine, but he must also be prepared **to confute those who contradict it.** The word for **confute** means to convict, and signifies "reproof" (2 Tim. 3:6) and "rebuke" (1 Tim. 5:20; 2 Tim. 4:2). The word for **contradict** (*antilegō*) means to speak against (cf. Acts 28:22). Paul used this word in quoting Isaiah about people who were "contrary" and disobedient (Rom. 10:21).

[10] Such contrary men are also described as **insubordinate,** which means undisciplined, rebellious, and lawless. See the comments on 1:6 (cf. 1 Tim. 1:9). The word for **empty talkers** is also translated "vain discussion" (see the comments on 1 Tim. 1:6). The word for **deceivers** is found only here in the New Testament; but it is a cognate form of the word meaning "to deceive" which is found only in Paul where he speaks of one who deceives himself by thinking that he is something (Gal. 6:3).

The **circumcision party** (literally "they of the circumcision") was especially guilty of insubordination, vain discussion and deception. Titus himself was uncircumcised and his ministry had been plagued by the opposition of those of the circumcision (cf. Gal. 2:3-5, 12). Paul had been "entrusted with the gospel to the uncircumcised" (Gal. 2:7-9). From the very beginning and throughout his ministry to the Gentiles he had been compelled to convict and rebuke the gainsayers who made this rite a test of fellowship (cf. Gal. 2:4-6, 11-16). As time passed, circumcision became the chief symbol of the false doctrine of justification by the works of the law of Moses (cf. Gal. 2:16; Rom. 2:25-29; 4:9-12). For more on Paul's teaching on the value of circumcision see Colossians 2:11 and 1 Corinthians 7:19.

[11] **they must be silenced, since they are upsetting whole families by teaching for base gain what they have no right to teach.** [12] **One of themselves, a prophet of their own, said, "Cretans are always liars, evil beasts, lazy gluttons."** [13] **This testimony is true. Therefore rebuke them sharply, that they may be sound in the faith,**

---

[11] The task of the elders, as well as Titus, was to silence such men. Literally, Paul says that "their mouths must be stopped," or **silenced.** Paul believed in an "open mouth" for the truth (2 Cor. 6:11), but in the "stopped mouth" for wicked men who boasted justification by the law (Rom. 3:9-20). The only way to silence such people was through the ability and devotion of the men of God who had the courage to speak the truth in love.

These lawless men, who boasted in the law and in their circumcision, were **upsetting whole families.** The word for **upsetting** means to overthrow and destroy. It is used figuratively here and in 2 Timothy 2:18. These empty talkers were **teaching for base gain.** The word for **base** means shameful and dishonest. The word for **gain** signifies material riches. The two words are combined into one word in 1:7 above, as well as in 1 Timothy 3:8, where it is translated "greedy for gain." Elders, as teachers of the truth in opposition to false teachers, must be free of such base desire for monetary reward. See the comments on the sin of using religion as a means of dishonest gain, in 1 Timothy 6:5, 6. Not only were these men teaching for dishonest gain, but they were also teaching **what they have no right to teach,** or, literally, what they "must not" or ought not to teach.

[12] Epimenides, a Cretan poet of the 6th century B.C., was a good one to call to witness, in view of Plato's appraisal of him as a divinely inspired man, and Plutarch's description of him as a man dear to the gods. Paul's recognition of him would not imply that he himself held such reverence for the man. He writes **a prophet of their own** to turn their estimate of the poet against themselves. Paul chose a revered Cretan as his witness to the fact that Cretans had long been notorious as **liars, evil beasts, and lazy gluttons.** This defect made them easy prey to false teachers.

[13] Paul's experience with Cretans, even among Chris-

[14] instead of giving heed to Jewish myths or to commands of men who reject the truth. [15] To the pure all things are pure, but to the corrupt and unbelieving nothing is pure; their very minds and consciences are corrupted. [16] They profess to know God, but they deny him by their deeds; they are detestable, disobedient, unfit for any good deed.

---

tians, confirmed this basic weakness. He urges Titus to **rebuke them sharply.** The word for **rebuke** is the same as in verse 9 above. The word **sharply** (*apotomōs*) means "severely." Paul did not enjoy being severe in the use of the authority which the Lord had given him for building up the church, but he could be if all else failed (cf. 2 Cor. 13:10).

For the meaning of **sound,** see the discussion of 1 Timothy 1:10 and 2 Timothy 4:3; and for a discussion of **the faith,** see 1 Timothy 3:9.

[14] The hope for curing this defect in the character of the Cretan Christians was in the proper use of sound, healthful teaching. This would make them less susceptible to the myths of the Jewish teachers and stronger in their ability to resist the **commands** of such men. A knowledge of the truth would enable them to discern between truth and error. The word **myth** is discussed in connection with 1 Timothy 1:4. See also 1 Timothy 1:6, 7 for comments on the false knowledge of these Jewish teachers.

[15, 16] The statement that **all things are pure** to those who are pure does not seem to refer to food laws, as in 1 Timothy 4:3-4, since Paul goes on to say that **nothing is pure** to those who are corrupt and unbelieving. There is another phrase here which associates Paul's meaning here with what he said in 2 Timothy 2:21, 22. Here he says that these **detestable, disobedient** teachers of error are corrupt in mind and conscience. As a result they are **unfit** (*adokimos*) or useless for **any good work** (*pan ergon agathon*). The same vocabulary is used to Timothy concerning vessels of honor who purify themselves from the people and things that are ignoble and are ready and useful for "any good deed" (*pan ergon agathon*). In 2 Tim. 3:8, Paul went on to describe those who withstand the truth as men with corrupt minds and counterfeit faith, or men who are "worthless" (*adokimos*) as far as the faith is concerned.

[1] But as for you, teach what befits sound doctrine. [2] Bid the older men be temperate, serious, sensible, sound in faith, in love, and in steadfastness.

The word for **minds** means understanding or way of thinking (cf. 1 Cor. 14:19; Rom. 12:2). Using the same word Paul speaks of base minds or depraved thoughts (Rom. 1:28), depraved and corrupt minds (1 Tim. 6:5; 2 Tim. 3:8). The word for **conscience** is the same as in 1 Timothy 1:5 and 1:19. Here, as elsewhere, Paul stresses the vital relationship between sound, healthy teaching and the good conscience (see the comments on 1 Tim. 1:5 and 1:19).

The word for **profess** is the same as in 1 Timothy 6:12 where Paul speaks of the good confession. The word for **know** (*oida*) implies that they claim that they have a positive relationship with God and are in fellowship with Him. In the same language Paul said, "I know whom I have believed" (2 Tim. 1:12). John joins Paul in a succinct indictment of those who say, "I know him," but are liars because they do not keep his commandments (1 John 2:3, 4).

Amending the Defects in Christian Behavior, 2:1—3:11

Various Groups in the Church, 2:1-10

[1] Paul follows his description of corrupt men, who teach error for base gain, by charging Titus with the words **but as for you.** This is the pattern he used with Timothy following his description of the men of depraved mind who use godliness as a means of gain (cf. 1 Tim. 6:4-11). Both Timothy and Titus were to **teach** and exhort the brethren: a ministry of instruction in sound doctrine and of urgent exhortation to Christians to pattern their lives accordingly (2:1, 6). Exhortation based on **sound doctrine** is essential in curing spiritual diseases and building up the body of Christ (1 Tim. 1:10; 2 Tim. 4:3).

Older Men and Women, 2:2-4a. [2] Here, as in 1 Timothy 5:1, Paul begins a series of instructions which Titus is to exhort the brethren to follow in their relationship to each other and to those outside the Christian fellowship.

[3] Bid the older women likewise to be reverent in behavior, not to be slanderers or slaves to drink; they are to teach what is good,

---

The word for **bid** is supplied by the translators. There are only two imperative verbs in the entire section including verses 1-10; they are "speak" (*laleō,* to declare) in 2:1, and "urge" (*parakaleō,* to exhort), 1:6. The word **bid,** meaning teach and urge, is implied by the command to declare sound doctrine, together with the verb to **be** in verse 2, followed by the command "likewise urge" in verse 6.

Just as he did in writing to Timothy, Paul divides God's family according to age and sex, with the same basic division of the **older** and the **younger** (see the comments on 1 Tim. 5:1, 2). The word for **older men** (*presbutēs*) signifies aged men in general. It does not have the specific connotation here that the word for elder (*presbuteros*) has in 1:5 and in 1 Timothy 4:14 and 5:17. Here the masculine and feminine (*presbutis*) refers generically to all older Christians.

The following instructions are given for the older men: (1) Be **temperate,** meaning sober-minded (see comments on 1 Tim. 3:2. (2) Be **serious,** meaning worthy of respect, noble and dignified (see comments on 1 Tim. 3:4, 11). (3) Be **sensible,** meaning thoughtful and self-controlled (see 1 Tim. 3:2). (4) Be **sound** in three things: **in faith,** meaning trustworthiness, reliability, and fidelity (as in 2:10), or perhaps faith in the Lord (as in 2 Tim. 3:15); **in love** (cf. 1 Cor. 8:1; 13:4-7; 16:14, and see comments on 1 Tim. 1:5); and thirdly, in **steadfastness,** meaning patience, fortitude, and perseverance (see 1 Tim. 6:11; and cf. 2 Tim. 3:10).

[3] The older women are urged to be **reverent in behavior.** The word for **reverent** means befitting or becoming one who is a holy person, one who is engaged in sacred service. For the meaning of **slanderers** (*diabolos*) see the discussion of 1 Timothy 3:11. The word for **drink** is "wine" (*oinos*) which is discussed in 1 Timothy 3:3, 8; 5:23. Being **slaves,** literally, enslaved, is used figuratively by Paul in a good sense (Rom. 6:22) and in a bad sense (Gal. 4:3). This verb matches the noun he used to describe himself as a servant or slave of God (1:1).

Older women are to **teach what is good** i.e., to teach

[4] and so train the young women to love their husbands and children, [5] to be sensible, chaste, domestic, kind, and submissive to their husbands, that the word of God may not be discredited. [6] Likewise urge the younger men to control themselves.

---

what is morally upright and honorable. The word for **good** (*kalos*) is used frequently by Paul in the letters to Timothy and Titus (2:7, 14; 3:8, 14; cf. 1 Tim. 3:7; 5:10, 25; 6:18). Paul uses it in this same sense in 1 Corinthians 8:21 where it is translated "honorable" (cf. also Gal. 6:9).

The Younger Men and Women, 2:4b-6. [4, 5] The older women are to be reverent and sober, not merely to save themselves, but in order that they may be able also to **train the young women.** The word for **train** means to school them and encourage them in matters of good sense, wise descretion, and sober conduct, especially in relationship to husband and children. They are to be "lovers of husbands" and "lovers of children."

The word for **sensible** (*sōphronas*) is the same as in verse 2 above, and is a cognate form of the word for **train** in verse 4. The word for **chaste** (*hagnos,* meaning "pure") in reference to persons is distinctively Pauline (cf. "pure bride," 2 Cor. 11:2). See the comments on "purity" in 1 Timothy 4:12. The word for **domestic** signifies a worker at home. The word for **kind** (meaning benevolent) suggests that the young women should be given to kindly deeds of benevolence and hospitality, doing good in every way. See the comments on the kind of wife and mother the honored widow must have been according to 1 Timothy 5:10. See also God's will concerning the importance of family responsibility for the younger widows (1 Tim. 5:14). The younger woman is urged to be **submissive** to her own husband, literally "her man." On woman's submissiveness, see the comments on 1 Timothy 2:11, and 14 (cf. Eph. 5:22, 23; Col. 3:18). Such domestic piety is an essential aspect of her reverence for God, and it does credit to the word of God. The word for **discredited** is the word for blasphemy and defamation (see the comments on 1 Tim. 6:1).

[6] It may seem at first glance that Paul's only requirement of young men is **self-control.** But what he says to Titus

7 Show yourself in all respects a model of good deeds, and in your teaching show integrity, gravity, 8 and sound speech that cannot be censured, so that an opponent may be put to shame, having nothing evil to say of us.

---

in verses 7 and 8 is actually addressed to all younger men. It is a charge to Titus that relates to Paul's special word for younger men. The word **likewise** suggests that the word **urge** pertains to all the exhortations given in verses 1-10.

Titus and other younger men are urged to exercise **self-control** (*sōphroneō*), meaning to be discreet and sensible. It is the same word used above in verses 2 and 5 in reference to the older men and younger women. See the comments on "self-controlled" in the comments on the qualifications of the elders in 1:8 above.

[7, 8] The word for **model** means example and pattern. It was used by Paul in urging the Philippians to "join in imitating me" (Phil. 3:17). Paul was determined to be "an example to imitate" (cf. 2 Thess. 3:9). Through Titus, as their example, younger men are also urged to do **good deeds** (cf. 2:14 on good deeds, and see also the comments on 1 Tim. 5:10; 6:18). Titus, by his teaching, must exemplify and encourage the following Christian virtues in young men: **integrity**, meaning sincerity, a rare word which has also been interpreted to mean purity and soundness; **gravity**, meaning reverence and holy dignity (see comments on 1 Tim. 2:2; 3:4).

Paul's term for **speech** (*logos*), meaning word, is usually interpreted to mean his teaching and preaching (cf. "word" in 1 Tim. 5:17; 1 Tim. 1:10; 6:3). In all his speech he is urged to use wholesome language. The word for **cannot be censured**, meaning uncondemned, is a form of the word which Paul used in Galatians 2:11 in speaking of the conduct of Peter for which he stood condemned (Gal. 2:11; cf. also 1 John 3:20). The word for **sound** may be studied in connection with 1 Timothy 6:3 (cf. also 2 Tim. 1:13).

The word for **opponent** (*enantios*) means one who is hostile and contrary. In 1 Thessalonians 2:15 Paul refers to the opposition and hostility of the Jews who killed Christ and opposed his message of truth. Paul's admonition to Titus to act in such a way as to make his opponents **ashamed**

[9] **Bid slaves to be submissive to their masters and to give satisfaction in every respect; they are not to be refractory,**
[10] **nor to pilfer, but to show entire and true fidelity, so that in everything they may adorn the doctrine of God our Savior.**

---

is essentially the same thought as that expressed to Timothy about "correcting his opponents with gentleness" in the hope that God might bring them to repentance and a knowledge of the truth (2 Tim. 2:25). The word **ashamed** may also signify to cause someone to have regard for or to respect something or someone (cf. Matt. 21:37; Heb. 12:9). See also Paul's use of "shame" in 1 Corinthians 6:5. The opponent is thus to become respectful, **having nothing evil to say of us.** The word for **evil** is used four times elsewhere in the New Testament, two of which are in Paul (Rom. 9:11; 2 Cor. 5:10; cf. John 3:20; 5:29). It signifies that which is morally bad or base.

The Slaves, 2:9-10. [9, 10] The word for **slave** is the same as in 1:1. See the comments on 1 Timothy 6:1, 2 concerning slaves and masters. The word for **submissive** is the same as in verse 5 above (cf. also 1 Tim. 2:11, 14). Here Paul urges slaves **to give satisfaction,** literally to be well-pleasing or acceptable. This word is found only in Paul's writings (including Hebrews; e.g., Rom. 12:1; 14:18; 2 Cor. 5:9; Phil. 4:8; cf. Heb. 11:5; 13:21). According to Paul in Colossians 3:22-24, Christian slaves may please their masters by serving them as they would serve Christ himself, not as men-pleasers. They are not to be **refractory** meaning to speak against. In Romans 10:21 it is translated "contrary" or obstinate.

Christian slaves are urged not to **pilfer,** meaning to misappropriate. The only other use of this word is in Acts 5:2f. concerning the sin of Ananias and Saphira. They are, rather, to show true **fidelity** (*pistis*) or loyalty and faithfulness (see the comments on "faithful" in 1:6).

The admonition to **adorn the doctrine of God** applies not only to slaves, but to all those admonished in verses 1-10, and it also provokes the following words to all Christians concerning the doctrine of salvation by grace and the

[11] For the grace of God has appeared for the salvation of all men, [12] training us to renounce irreligion and worldly passions, and to live sober, upright, and godly lives in this world,

---

kind of life and conduct which appropriately make this doctrine attractive. The word for **adorn** meaning to make something beautiful, is discussed in connection with 1 Timothy 2:9.

Salvation by Grace, 2:11-14

What Paul is saying in verses 10b-14 is the very cornerstone of the entire structure of Christian ethics, and he does here what he does consistently in all his instructions on the good life which Christians live. His words to Titus, as well as to Timothy, contain wholesome teaching on the kind of conduct by which Christians "adorn the doctrine of God our Savior," giving it drawing power by making it attractive to those whom we are striving to win to Christ through the preaching of the gospel. The lawless, immoral life is contrary to the grace of God (cf. 1 Tim. 1:8-11). Christian ethics is based on God's nature. Jesus Christ is the very image of God's character. In putting on Christ, we are being created in God's image (see Col. 1:15, 19; 3:1-14). Good works are not enjoined as a means of meriting God's favor; the Christian is created in Christ Jesus for good works (Eph. 2:8-10).

[11, 12] Paul's discussion of **the grace of God** is brief and concise, but it is beautiful and complete and serves his purpose in keeping his emphasis on good deeds in proper perspective. (For a fuller discussion of God's grace read Eph. 1:3 to 2:10; see the comments on 1 Tim. 1:14-17).

God's grace saves us by **training us.** Jesus Christ, the supreme manifestation of God's love, came preaching and teaching. The task of teaching and preaching is the divine means of grace. God's saving grace **appeared** when Jesus appeared (see the comments on "his appearing" in 2 Timothy 4:1, 8). In Christ God made it known clearly that he wants all men to be saved (cf. 1 Tim. 2:4; 4:10). The word for **training** is the word used in 2 Timothy 3:16 in reference

[13] awaiting our blessed hope, the appearing of the glory of our great God and Savior[e] Jesus Christ, [14] who gave himself for us to redeem us from all iniquity and to purify for himself a people of his own who are zealous for good deeds.

[e] Or of the great God and our Savior

---

to the value of the sacred scriptures in "training in righteousness" (see comments on 2 Tim. 2:25 where the same word is translated "correcting"). Paul's definition of saving grace does not allow any suggestion that God will save man in his lawless wickedness (cf. Rom. 6:1-2). He does say that God's grace will **train us** in two respects: (1) **to renounce irreligion and worldly passions,** and (2) **to live sober, upright, and godly lives in this world.** His grace not only instructs us but it also disciplines us (Heb. 12:5-11).

The word for **renouncing** (*arneomai*) means to repudiate or deny. The same word is used in 1:16 concerning those who "deny" God by their evil deeds. It is also used concerning those who hold a mere form of piety and "denying the power of it" (2 Tim. 3:5). The word for **irreligion** signifies a life that is ungodly. It is a form of the word which is one of the key words of 1 Timothy, *eusebeia* (see the comments on 1 Tim. 2:2; cf. 2 Tim. 2:16). The word for **worldly** suggests a love of the world which John calls the "lust of the flesh and the lust of the eyes and the pride of life" (1 John 1:15-17).

The word for **sober** is also translated "discreet" and "self-control" (see 2:5-6 above). The word for **upright** means "righteously" in the sense of being law-abiding (1 Tim. 1:9) and doing what is right (Rom. 5:7; 1 John 3:7). The word for **godly lives** is discussed in connection with 1 Timothy 2:2 (cf. also 2 Tim. 3:12). The term for **world,** meaning "age," is discussed in connection with the love of Demas for this present world (2 Tim. 4:10).

[13, 14] Here Paul speaks of the second **appearing** of God in the person of Jesus Christ (see the comments on 2 Tim. 4:1, 8). God's children live a life of earnest expectation, **awaiting** their **blessed hope.** In 1 Timothy 1:1 he describes Jesus Christ as "our hope." Paul speaks of the Christian's hope of sharing the glory of God in Romans 5:1-5,

[15] **Declare these things; exhort and reprove with all authority. Let no one disregard you.**

---

an excellent parallel reading in connection with his emphasis on grace and our hope of glory (cf. also Rom. 9:23; Col. 1:27; Phil. 4:19). Strict grammar would apply both **God** and **Savior** to **Jesus Christ,** but exceptions are sufficient to allow that two persons are meant (2 Peter 1:1 offers the same problem). God is declared Savior in 1:3; 2:10; and 3:4; Christ is so named in 1:4 and 3:6.

In view of this second advent of God's **glory,** Jesus brought God's grace for two vital reasons: (1) **to redeem us from all iniquity,** and (2) **to purify for himself a people of his own who are zealous for good deeds.** That **he gave himself for us** is central to the Gospel (1 Tim. 2:6; 2 Cor. 5:15; Gal. 1:4; 2:20). For the meaning of the word **redeem** see the comments on 1 Timothy 2:6. The word for **iniquity** signifies lawlessness (see 1 Tim. 1:9; cf. 1 John 3:4-6). The phrase quotes Psalm 130:8. The word for **purify** means to cleanse and to consecrate (cf. Ezek. 37:23 for purifying a people). Paul uses it magnificently in connection with the church and her future splendor (see Eph. 5:26-27; cf. 2 Cor. 11:2-3 and Rev. 21:9-11). The reference to the church as **a people for his own,** or a people for his own possession, finds parallels in Exodus 19:5 and Deuteronomy 7:6; 14:2; 26:18. The church has been purchased with the price of the blood of God's son (cf. Acts 20:28). Having bought her, he now seeks to sanctify her as his own. He especially wants her to be **zealous** for the **good works** (Eph. 2:10) which Paul has emphasized in his instructions to the older men and women. In Galatians 4:18, Paul says it is right to be zealous in a good thing. For **good deeds** see 2:7 and 3:14.

A Charge to Titus, 2:15

[15] Paul breaks into his discussion of adorning the doctrine of God by a life of good deeds with an urgent appeal to Titus to make these matters very clear to the churches of Crete. **These things** refer to what Paul has said and what he will go on to say. The word for **exhort** is dis-

[1] **Remind them to be submissive to rulers and authorities, to be obedient, to be ready for any honest work,**

---

cussed in the comments on 1 Timothy 4:13. For the meaning of **convict,** see 1:9. The word for **authority** signifies the command of one who is in position of authority (see 1:3, cf. 1 Tim. 1:1). Since Paul is urging Titus to speak about things that Christians must be and do, the power of command is also essential. For Paul's method of exercising authority in matters of truth see 1 Timothy 1:1. The word for **disregard** means to look down on. In similar words to Timothy, he speaks of despising (1 Tim. 4:12).

Seven Rules for Christian Behavior, 3:1, 2

[1] Paul resumes his instructions on Christian behavior that accords with and beautifies the gospel of God's saving grace. The word for **remind** is the word Paul used with special emphasis in his second letter to Timothy (see 2 Tim. 1:6; 2:14, cf. 2 Peter 1:12, 13; 3:1-2).

The exhortation here in regard to submission to the civil powers is the same as that given in Romans 13:1-10, where Paul used the same two words, **rulers** and **authorities** (cf. 1 Peter 2:13). God ordained rulers to be a terror to evil conduct, as a servant of God on behalf of the good (Rom. 13:3, 4). God did not delegate to these servants the prerogative of deciding what is good and what is evil. God himself did this. As a Roman citizen, Paul affirmed faithfully that he would not refuse to die if he were found guilty of any crime (cf. Rom. 13:4; Acts 25:11). But as an obedient citizen he did insist on his right of appeal to Caesar for a fair hearing (Acts 25:10, 11; 16:35-39). Some rulers seem to have been more just than others (cf. Acts 19: 35-39; 23:26-30). Unfortunately for Paul and many early Christians, certain others violated God's orders to them and became a terror to good conduct. But Christians are committed to good conduct, as God defines it, regardless of the character of the administrators of civil justice. Paul urged continued prayer for those in high places (cf. 1 Tim. 2:1-3), even if these prayers must be offered up behind prison walls.

[2] to speak evil of no one, to avoid quarreling, to be gentle,
and to show perfect courtesy toward all men. [3] For we our-
selves were once foolish, disobedient, led astray, slaves to
various passions and pleasures, passing our days in malice
and envy, hated by men and hating one another;

Christians are also urged **to be ready for any honest work.** The word **honest** (*agathos*) means "good" (cf. 1:16). **Ready** means to be prepared and willing (cf. Acts 21:13; 1 Peter 3:15). The equivalent verb is used in 2 Timothy 2:21 concerning the vessels of honor who are useful and "ready for any good work."

[2] Christians under Christ's control are to **speak evil of no one.** Paul said elsewhere, "Let no evil talk come out of your mouths" (Eph. 4:29; cf. Eph. 4:31-32; Col. 4:5-6). This is the kind of conduct that adorns the doctrine of grace (see 1:10, 11 above).

Christians are to **avoid quarreling.** In this connection, see the comments on 2 Timothy 2:24 (cf. also 1 Tim. 3:3). They are to avoid strife and contention and live "peaceable" lives (1 Tim. 2:2). The word for **gentle** is the same in the qualifications of elders (see 1 Tim. 3:3). Christians must **show perfect courtesy toward all men.** The word for **courtesy** (*prautēs*) signifies meekness, gentleness, and kind consideration. In Galatians 6:1 it is translated "gentleness" or "meekness" (cf. also James 3:13).

Aspects of Behavior Before Salvation, 3:3

[3] Paul now gives a sevenfold picture of their own behavior before God's grace came into that darkness to redeem and purify them for good deeds. (References to preconversion life are found in Eph. 5:8; Col. 3:7; 1 Peter 4:3).

Including himself, Paul says we ourselves (1) **were once foolish** meaning useless and without understanding. Compare "senseless and foolish desires" (1 Tim. 6:9), and his warning to the "foolish Galatians" (Gal. 3:1). He felt a personal obligation "both to the wise and the foolish" (Rom. 1:14). (2) The word for **disobedient** is the word used in reference to disobedience to parents (Rom. 1:30;

2 Tim. 3:2), and in his testimony before king Agrippa that he himself was not disobedient to the heavenly vision (Acts 26:19). (3) The word **led astray** means to be deceived (see the comments on "deceivers and deceived," 2 Tim. 3:13). (4) They had been **slaves,** not to God and the good, **but to various passions and pleasures** (see 2:3 above on "slaves to drink"). The word for **passions** means lusts. Paul used this word with a good meaning in 1 Thessalonians 2:17, in reference to his longing to see them. It is used with a bad connotation in Romans 7:8, where it is translated "covetousness" (cf. James 1:14, 15; see comments on "youthful passions" in 2 Tim. 2:22). The word for **pleasures** also signifies the indulging of one's sinful passions (cf. 2 Peter 2:13; James 4:1, 3). Jesus used it in speaking of the pleasures of life which choke the word of God so that their fruit does not mature (Luke 8:14). We were, says Paul, (5) living, or **passing our days** (*diagontes*) **in malice.** This word for "living" is used only twice elsewhere. Jesus spoke of living in luxury (Luke 7:25), and Paul spoke of living or "leading" quiet and peaceable lives (1 Tim. 2:2). The word **malice** means wickedness, but here it has the special connotation of ill-will and malignity (cf. Col. 3:8; Eph. 4:31; 1 Peter 2:1). Paul used it in urging Christians to be like children in malice (1 Cor. 14:20). (6) Another dark aspect of the life before Christ was their **envy,** meaning jealousy. This is one of the sins that crucified Jesus (Matt. 27:18). Peter, like Paul, urged Christians to put it away (1 Peter 2:1). Paul had been made to suffer by certain men who preached Christ "from envy and rivalry," hoping to afflict Paul in his imprisonment (Phil. 1:15, 16). He warned Timothy against men whose teaching stirs up envy (1 Tim. 6:4). It is one of the deadly works of the flesh (Gal. 5:21) which darkens the lives of those who refuse to acknowledge God (Rom. 1:29). (7) Finally, Paul says, before we were saved by grace, **we were hated by men and hating one another.** The word **hated** (*stugētos*) is found only here. But Paul is the one New Testament writer who used the word with the prefix *apo,* in urging Christians to hate, or to abhor, that which is evil (Rom. 12:9). The word for **hating** (*miseō*) is synonymous with darkness, just as love is synonymous with light (cf. 1 John 2:9, 11).

[4] but when the goodness and loving kindness of God our Savior appeared, [5] he saved us, not because of deeds done by us in righteousness, but in virtue of his own mercy, by the washing of regeneration and renewal in the Holy Spirit, [6] which he poured out upon us richly through Jesus Christ our Savior,

---

The Divine Plan for Saving Man, 3:4-8

[4] The **goodness and loving kindness of God appeared** when Jesus Christ appeared to give himself for the redemption of man from all iniquity (see comments on 2:11 above; cf. also 2 Tim. 4:1, 8). Here Paul reaffirms this good news, but he is also being careful to explain the value of good deeds which we do, lest we do them in an effort to earn our salvation (cf. 2:11-14 above).

Paul's word for **goodness** signifies the kindness of God, expressed in his benevolent actions toward man. It is used elsewhere by Paul in reference to the goodness of man toward man. In each instance, however, he recognizes God's goodness as the source of all true goodness in man (cf. 1 Cor. 6:6; Gal. 5:22; Col. 3:12). He speaks of "God's kindness to you, provided you continue in his kindness" (Rom. 11:22). The "immeasurable riches of his grace" was manifested "in kindness toward us in Christ Jesus" (Eph. 2:7), and is to continue in us so that through us God may reach into the lives of all men with redeeming love. Paul describes the Christian life as "putting on Christ," and this includes putting on his kindness (Col. 3:12). It is an essential virtue of the fruit of the Spirit (Gal. 5:22).

The word for **loving kindness** is found only here in the New Testament, but the adverbial form is found in Luke's description of the kindly treatment which Julius showed Paul (Acts 27:3). The word conveys the idea of love for man, and a more exact translation of this passage might be, "when God's kindness and love for man appeared."

[5, 6] The good **deeds** which this letter emphasizes are not the cause of man's salvation (2 Tim. 1:9; Eph. 2:4, 8f.). Paul gives a twofold analysis of God's great plan for purifying a people of his own who will be zealous of good works (cf. 2:14 above) as a result of God's grace.

[7] so that we might be justified by his grace and become heirs in hope of eternal life.

---

(1) **By the washing of regeneration.** The word for **regeneration** (*palingenesia*) is used elsewhere only in Matthew 19:28, where Jesus spoke to his apostles about the coming "regeneration" (in the RSV translated "a new world"). The word for **washing** (*loutron*) occurs only in Ephesians 5:26, where Paul speaks of the church as a people who have been cleansed "by the washing of water with the word" in order that God "might present the church to himself in splendor." Paul also uses a verb form for washing (*apolouō*) in making a point to the Corinthians which is essentially the same as the one he is making to the Cretans (1 Cor. 6:9-11). The same verb for washing (*apolouō*) was used in Ananias' words to Paul found in Acts 22:16. This is the initial cleansing, the washing of regeneration, which Paul described as the beginning of a new life (Col. 2:12, 13). Jesus spoke to a grown man about the absolute necessity of a man being born from heaven, born of God, a birth described as a birth of the water and the Spirit (John 3:5). Paul continues his description of God's plan for saving man by his emphasis on:

(2) **Renewal in the Holy Spirit.** The first gospel sermon following the resurrection and glorification of Christ closed with a divine mandate to all men, "Repent, and be baptized," followed immediately with a promise, "and you shall receive the gift of the Holy Spirit" (Acts 2:38, 39). In line with Peter's beginning message of God's saving grace, Paul too emphasizes that God saves man **by** (*dia*), or through, **a renewal in the Holy Spirit.** The use of the genitive here suggests that the Spirit is the agent through whom God renews man. It is the Spirit himself who was **poured out on us richly through Jesus Christ our Savior.** This agrees with Paul's words in Romans 5:5. The ethical implications of this indwelling of God's Spirit in our hearts is underscored by Paul in 1 Corinthians 6:19, 20.

[7] What God has done and is doing in saving man through the washing of rebirth and renewal in the Spirit **is so that,** words that indicate the divine purpose. This too is stated in a twofold way: (1) that **we might be justified**

8 **The saying is sure.**

I desire you to insist on these things, so that those who have believed in God may be careful to apply themselves to good deeds;[d] these are excellent and profitable to men.

[d] Or *enter honorable occupations*

---

by his grace, and (2) **become heirs in hope of eternal life.**

The word **justified** is always in the passive form in reference to man. It is God who actively justifies, or reckons man as just or righteous. Men "are justified by his grace as a gift, through the redemption which is in Christ Jesus" (Rom. 3:24). Men are justified by Christ (Gal. 2:16); they are justified by his blood (Rom. 5:9); they are justified by faith (Rom. 5:1), through faith in his blood (Rom. 3:35; see 1 John 1:7-9; Rom. 8:17). The indwelling of his Spirit is the Christian's certificate of sonship: "he has put his seal upon us and given us his Spirit in our hearts as a guarantee" (2 Cor. 1:22). The fruit of this indwelling Spirit is the harvest which Paul seeks in the lives of Cretan Christians (cf. Gal. 5:22-24).

[8] **The saying is sure** seems to point back to what Paul has just said (see the comments on 1 Tim. 1:15; 3:1; 4:9). The word **desire** expresses will (see 1 Tim. 2:8). Paul's will is that Titus **insist** on these things, meaning to affirm and to confirm strongly. False teachers were strong in their affirmations (1 Tim. 1:7), so God's servant must speak "confidently," which is one meaning of the word **insist.** So Paul confidently reaffirms what he has been saying all along, that **those who have believed in God may be careful to apply themselves to good deeds.** The word for **careful** means to be thoughtful, intent, and concerned about something. Paul used a cognate form of this word in Colossians 3:2, urging Christians to "set your minds on things that are above." They are to give constant thought to deeds that are **excellent** and **profitable** to men. The word for **excellent** (*kalon*) means good. The word for **profitable** means useful and of value. Paul used it to Timothy in reference to godliness being profitable for this life and for the life to come (1 Tim. 4:8), and the Scriptures being profitable in equipping the man of God for every good work (2 Tim. 3:16-17). Compare "unprofitable" in the next verse.

[9] But avoid stupid controversies, genealogies, dissensions, and quarrels over the law, for they are unprofitable and futile. [10] As for a man who is factious, after admonishing him once or twice, have nothing more to do with him, [11] knowing that such a person is perverted and sinful; he is self-condemned.

Evil to Be Avoided, 3:9-11

[9] Here Paul is specific about certain deeds, or activities, that are **unprofitable** (see comments on verse 8 above), and **futile.** The word for **futile** is used earlier in describing "empty" talkers (1:10), and "vain" discussion (1 Tim. 1:6). The word for **avoid** (*periïstēmi*) means to stand aloof from. It is the word used in 2 Timothy 2:16. Another word meaning "to turn away from" is used in 2 Timothy 3:5. For the meaning of **stupid controversies,** see 2 Timothy 2:23; for **genealogies** see 1 Timothy 1:4; concerning **dissension** or strife, see 1 Timothy 6:4; for **quarrels over the law** see the discussion of 2 Timothy 2:23, 24 and 1 Timothy 1:7.

[10, 11] Titus is also to reject, or **have nothing more to do with** a man who, after one or two admonitions, continues to be **factious.** The word for reject (*paraiteomai*) is also used in 2 Timothy 2:23 (cf. also 1 Tim. 4:7; 5:11). The word for **factious** (*hairetikon*), meaning heretic, refers to one who causes division, faction, and dissension by pressing his destructive opinions upon others. These factious people are **perverted,** or corrupted (*ekstrephō*), and they are **self-condemned** (*katakrisis*). This concept of "self-condemnation" is very Pauline (cf. Rom. 2:1; 1 Cor. 11:29). Titus would need wisdom in deciding that a man really was not a truth seeker, and that further admonition would not be in the best interest of the truth nor his own stewardship as a preacher who must make the best use of his time and energy. Such continued involvement with the man would also expose the church to the man's sickness (cf. 1 Tim. 6:4, 5). For Paul's own actions in his relations with such men, see 1 Timothy 1:20. For other instances of discipline see Matthew 18:15-17; 2 John 10; 2 Thessalonians 3:14f.

[12] When I send Artemas or Tychicus to you, do your best to come to me at Nicopolis, for I have decided to spend the winter there. [13] Do your best to speed Zenas the lawyer and Apollos on their way; see that they lack nothing. [14] And let our people learn to apply themselves to good deeds,[d] so as to help cases of urgent need, and not to be unfruitful.

[15] All those who are with me send greetings to you. Greet those who love us in the faith.

Grace be with you all.

[d] Or *enter honorable occupations*

Conclusion, 3:12-15

Two Final Instructions, 3:12-14

[12-14] Titus is given two final instructions in each of which Paul says **do your best** (cf. 2 Tim. 2:15; 4:9).

(1) **Do your best to come to me at Nicopolis.** In order for Titus to do this, Paul is sending either **Artemas or Tychicus** to carry on the vital work in Crete. It may be that he finally sent Artemas, with Tychicus being sent to Ephesus (cf. 2 Tim. 4:12). Of this we cannot be sure, since we are not certain just how much time elapsed before Paul wrote 2 Timothy from Roman imprisonment. The reference to **Artemas** here is the only information given about him. We are better informed about **Tychicus.** He was from Asia Minor (Acts 20:4). References to him are in Ephesians 6:21; Colossians 4:7; 2 Timothy 4:12.

(2) **Do your best to speed Zenas and Apollos on their way.** This meant to help them with whatever material assistance they needed for their journey. Paul did not hesitate to insist on the duty of Christians in speeding a man of God on his journey (Rom. 15:24; 1 Cor. 16:6, 11; 2 Cor. 1:16; 1 Cor. 9:9, 14). **Apollos** was a very faithful gospel preacher (Acts 18:24; 1 Cor. 3:5f.; 16:12). **Zenas** was a lawyer, which could mean he was a Roman jurist.

Final Greeting and Benediction, 3:15

[15] Paul does not follow any particular pattern in regard to naming those who are joining him in sending

greetings. His letters vary from a long list of names (Rom. 16) to no names at all (Phil. 4:21), and sometimes no final word from anyone. Here he sends a greeting to **those who love us in the faith.** His word for **love** here is *phileō* (see comments on 1 Tim. 1:5 concerning the meaning of this kind of love). It is the same word that he used in the final words of 1 Corinthians, "If any one has no love (*ou philē*) for the Lord, let him be accursed" (16:22).

It seems especially appropriate that a letter with such emphasis on the grace of God should conclude with **Grace be with you all.** In these last words Paul moves from the singular to the plural **you** in order to include Titus' associates.